D1090612

KALMBACH PUBLISHING CO.
DAVID P. MORGAN MEMORIAL LIBRARY
P.O. BOX 1612
WAUKESHA, WI 53187-1612

US GUIDED MISSILES

US GUIDED MISSILES
The definitive reference guide

Bill Yenne

www.crecy.co.uk

Crécy Publishing Ltd

www.crecy.co.uk

Published in 2012 by Crécy Publishing Limited

Copyright © 2012 Bill Yenne

All rights reserved. No part of this book may be reproduced or transmitted in any form or by any means electronic or mechanical, including photocopying, recording or by any information storage without permission from the Publisher in writing. All enquiries should be directed to the Publisher.

A CIP record for this book is available from the British Library

ISBN 9 780859 791625

Title Page: *US Air Force Lieutenant Colonel Brian "Slurpy" Sivertson fires an AIM-7 Sparrow missile from an F-16A during the Combat Archer Air-to-Air Weapons System Evaluation Program in October 2003.* (US Air Force photo by Master Sergeant Michael Ammons)

Front Cover Main Picture: *A PGM-17 (then SM-75) Thor is prepared for a dawn launch in the early summer of 1962.* (Author's collection)

Front Cover Insert Picture: *A classic ground launch image of a BQM-34 Firebee target drone.* (Northrop Grumman)

Inside Front Flap Top: *Designated as AQM-91A, Teledyne Ryan's Model 154 Firefly reconnaissance drone was a waypoint on the technological evolution from the Model 147/AQM-34 Firebee family and the larger YQM-98 Compass Cope aircraft.* (Author's collection)

Inside Front Flap Bottom: *Aviation ordnancemen inspect an AIM-54C Phoenix missile on the flight deck of the carrier USS Saratoga during Operation Desert Shield in December 1990.* (US Navy photo by CW02 Bailey)

Back Cover Main Picture: *A RIM-161B Standard Missile-3 (SM-3) Block 1A is launched from the Japan Maritime Self-Defense Force destroyer JS Myoko in a joint missile defense intercept test with the US Missile Defense Agency in the Pacific Ocean in October 2009.* (DoD)

Back Cover Top: *The Gargoyle was America's answer to German weapons such as the Henschel Hs.293 and the legendary Fritz X weapon which got everyone's attention when it was used to sink the British cruiser HMS Spartan and several other vessels off Salerno in 1943.* (Author's collection)

Back Cover Bottom: *An F-4G "Wild Weasel" Phantom II armed with an AGM-78A Standard ARM, an air-launched variation on the ship-launched RIM-66A fitted with a radiation seeker.* (Author's collection)

Printed in India
and print managed by Jellyfish Print Solutions

Crécy Publishing Limited
1a Ringway Trading Estate, Shadowmoss Road,
Manchester M22 5LH

www.crecy.co.uk

© 2012 Bill Yenne
(415) 285-8799
PO Box 460313
San Francisco, CA 94146
www.BillYenne.com

Table of Contents

Introduction

T HIS BOOK IS DESIGNED to fill a gap in the literature of military hardware. Not until now has there been a book which provides a comprehensive, number by number, consecutive encyclopedia of all the widely varied United States guided missile systems that have been designated with the "M" prefix.

Such a number by number encyclopedic work for bombers designated with a "B for Bomber" was developed by Lloyd Jones in the 1960s, while Jay Miller has done it for American experimental aircraft with his excellent and frequently updated *X-Planes* books. The present work does this for the diverse vehicles, mainly missiles, which are designated within the "M for Missile" series.

The term "missiles" embraces a broad spectrum of weapons systems. To fit the definition, they can be fired

from air, land, sea or underwater — and they can be aimed at targets in any of those environments. They can even be used as reconnaissance, rather than strike, weapons. They can be launched vertically, fired as projectiles, or fly through the air supported by wings. They can have a range of a few hundred yards, or they can hit targets at distances equal to most of the circumference of the earth.

Above: Intercontinental ballistic missiles are positioned in a static display the main gate of Francis E. Warren AFB. They include, from foreground: the LGM-118A Peacekeeper, LGM-30G Minuteman III and LGM-30F Minuteman II. (US Air Force photo by Staff Sergeant Mike Doncell)

Left: Standing inside the fuselage of a Convair Atlas ICBM at the Convair manufacturing facility in Kearny Mesa, north of San Diego. (Author's collection)

This exhibit at the National Museum of the United States Air Force includes this display of (left to right) the Chrysler SM-78/PGM-19A Jupiter MRBM, the Douglas SM-75/PGM-17A Thor ballistic missile, the Martin Marietta SM-68B/LGM-25C Titan II and the Martin Marietta SM-68A/HGM-25A Titan I intercontinental ballistic missiles. (US Air Force photo by Tech Sergeant Tracy DeMarco)

World War II

The use of unguided rockets as weapons of war can be traced back centuries. The Chinese are known to have used operational war rockets in the thirteenth century. During World War II, unguided rockets were fired against ground targets from attack aircraft, and they were ground launched against ground targets. The widely used Soviet Katusha rocket system was an example of the latter. It is still being used, especially in the Middle East conflicts.

While the history of unguided war rockets is long, the use of *guided* missiles in wartime came of age during World War II as ballistics engineers tackled the intertwined problems of aiming and guidance — and to develop guided missiles that could eclipse the capability of the best artillery.

Left: *An F-16 Fighting Falcon from the 157th Fighter Squadron, armed with AGM-88 HARM, AIM-9 Sidewinder and AIM-120 AMRAAM missiles.* (US Air Force photo by Lans Stout)

Though other countries developed guided missiles, Germany became the world leader in guided missiles through World War II, and the German missile mastermind was a visionary engineer named Wernher von Braun. His signature weapon was the precursor to both American an Soviet postwar Intermediate Range Ballistic Missiles, was the weapon his team designated as A4, but which Adolf Hitler dubbed *Vergeltungswaffe* ("Vengeance Weapon") 2, or V-2. First deployed operationally in September 1944, the V-2 was by far the most sophisticated ballistic missile system in the world at the time, and so advanced that it literally defined the direction of large missile development in the United States and the Soviet Union for decades.

Germany also led the world in what we know today as cruise missiles, long-range winged vehicles that fly like pilotless airplanes. The remarkable Fieseler Fi.103, which Hitler named V-1, brought together a radically new aerodynamic shape and the emerging technology of pulsejet engines.

First launched in July 1950, the "Bumper WAC" was an ambitious two-stage rocket program that topped a German V-2 missile with a WAC Corporal rocket. The upper stage was able to reach then-record altitudes of almost 250 miles. (NASA)

The Genesis of the American Missile Program

Even before the war ended, many V-1s and V-2s were captured by the Allies, and some were later used as the basis for further developments. Under the high priority Operation Paperclip, the US Army also scooped up Wernher von Braun and much of his team. Von Braun was anxious to be "captured" by the Americans. He saw the United States as being the place in the world where it was most likely that he could resume his dreams of space travel. He would not be disappointed. The German scientists were taken to the Redstone Arsenal in Alabama, which became the center of early postwar ballistic missile development. In the 1960s, Von Braun and his team spearheaded the successful American effort to put human beings on the surface of the Moon.

The first V-2 launch in the Western Hemisphere occurred at the US Army's White Sands Proving Ground in New Mexico in April 1946. In October 1947, the Soviet Union conducted its first test launch of a captured V-2 at Kapustin Yar near Stalingrad. In May 1948, the United States first successfully tested its "Bumper WAC," a two-stage rocket that used a WAC Corporal sounding rocket atop a V-2 for higher altitude flights. On February 24, 1949, a Bumper WAC achieved an altitude of 250 miles, the highest altitude ever reached by an object made by human hands, and the first flight into space by such an object.

Meanwhile, the United States had been tinkering with cruise missiles even before the details of the German V-1 were known. The Northrop JB-1 originated in late 1943 under the highly secret USAAF Project MX-543. John Knudsen "Jack" Northrop, president of Northrop Aircraft proposed a jet-propelled flying wing to be powered by a General Electric B-1 turbojet engine.

The aircraft was delivered under the USAAF designation JB-1, for "Jet-propelled Bomb, First." The first one, designated simply as JB-1, was an unpowered vehicle intended for aerodynamic glide tests. Powered JB-1As would also be built, and Northrop converted some on the assembly line to pulsejet power under the designation JB-10. During flight testing, which began in April 1945, the JB-10 demonstrated a range of 200 miles and a cruising speed of 400 mph.

The second missile designated under the USAAF "Jet-propelled Bomb" series was the Republic JB-2, later named "Loon.", which would be manufactured by the auto maker, Willys-Overland (best known for the ubiquitous "Jeep" vehicle. Unlike the JB-1, however, it was not an American original, but a reverse-engineered copy of the V-1.

The US Navy also got into the act, ordering its own version of the Loon under the designation KGW-1 (Missile, Ground Attack, Willys, First). At the same time, the Navy drafted plans for launching them from aboard landing ships, escort carriers and even PB4Y patrol bombers. In February 1947, a KGW-1 (now redesignated as LTV-N-2 for Launch Test Vehicle-Navy-Second) was the first missile launched from a US Navy submarine – albeit from the surface.

During World War II, the Germans had also led the world in air-to-surface missiles with their Hs.293 and the Bv.143, but there were several interesting and little known American projects. One of the most promising, however, was the McDonnell Gargoyle anti-ship missile, which was first flown in March 1944 with a small rocket engine attached.

As McDonnell was developing the Gargoyle as an offensive weapon, the company also produced the Katydid, a pulsejet-powered target drone. The US Navy initiated the project in 1942, assigning the designation TD2D-1 (Target Drone, Second Douglas Type, First in the series). The Katydid was redesignated as the KDH-1 (missile, Target Drone, McDonnell, First) in 1946.

A direct descendant of the Gargoyle and Katydid was the Kingfisher family of anti-ship missiles, developed by the US Navy Bureau of Ordnance, and built by various manufacturers, such as McDonnell and Fairchild. Like the previous missiles, they had the distinctive "V" tail, and were visually very similar to the Katydid. Both the Katydids and Kingfishers were powered by jet engines while the Gargoyle was rocket-propelled. As with the Gargoyle, the Kingfisher carried a 1,000-pound warhead.

As was the case with McDonnell, with whom it would merge in 1967, the Douglas Aircraft Company began building guided missiles during World War II. Such work had begun as early as 1940 under secret Project MX-601 and resulted in the radar guided Roc I, named for the large bird of Arabian mythology and acquired by the US Army Air Forces under the Vertical Bomb designation VB-9.

The VB-10 Roc II, which appeared in 1943, was similar, but used a television guidance system. It was one of the first weapons to successfully exploit the emerging technology of television for guidance systems.

The USS Cusk *fires a KGW-1 Loon, a cruise missile derived from a German V-1, in a 1951 test.* (US Navy)

The Gargoyle was America's answer to German weapons such as the Henschel Hs.293 and the legendary Fritz X weapon which got everyone's attention when it was used to sink the British cruiser HMS Spartan *and several other vessels off Salerno in 1943.* (Author's collection)

The airframe of the Katydid pulse-jet-powered missile clearly has a lot in common with that of the Gargoyle. Both missiles were produced by the McDonnell Aircraft Company. (Author's collection)

An XAUM-6 Kingfisher is seen here at the McDonnell factory in St. Louis, mounted on the underwing pylon of a Douglas JD-1. The JD-1 was a variation on the US Army Air Forces A-26 Invader that was used by the US Navy for testing missiles and target drones. (Author's collection)

A technician checks the unique tail surfaces of the Douglas VB-10 Roc II. The program that had begun in 1940 as the supersecret Project MX-601 culminated in the 1943 roll-out of the Roc II. This television-guided weapon would later be complemented by the infrared-guided VB-11 Roc III and the visually guided VB-13 Roc IV. (Courtesy Harry Gann)

Toward a Ballistic Missile

As these tactical missiles were taking shape, work was continuing on developing the German V-2 into a new American strategic ballistic missile. Indeed, both the US Army and the newly-formed US Air Force (independent of the Army after 1947) were involved in parallel V-2-derived projects.

The Army had achieved the first suborbital flight into space by combining a WAC Corporal with a V-2 functioning as a first stage. This set the Army on the course that would lead to the Jupiter and Redstone ballistic missiles.

Meanwhile, in 1946, the US Air Force commissioned Consolidated-Vultee Aircraft (Convair) to build an improved V-2 variant under a project designated as MX-774. The idea was to build a missile with a 5,000-mile range, a better than ten-fold increase over the range of the German missile. Though the emphasis was on range, the "Research Test Vehicle" missile, designated as RTV-A-2, was called Hiroc, for "High-Altitude Rocket." The project was canceled in July 1947, but Convair continued the project on its own dime, conducting the first Hiroc launch a year later in July 1948.

The first several Hiroc test flights failed after successful launches, but Convair gained the experience which led it directly into its development of the later Project MX-1593, and the experimental X-11 and X-12 missiles (which were designated as "X-Planes.") These steps, in turn, opened the door that led to the B-65 Atlas, the world's first successful Intercontinental Ballistic Missile (ICBM).

Parenthetically, it is worth pointing out that several other 1950s X-Planes were actually scaled-down precursors to later missiles that were used experimentally to evaluate various design parameters and hardware. The X-7 preceded to AQM-60, the X-9 preceded the B-63 Rascal, and the X-10 preceded the B-64 Navaho.

Categorizing Ballistic Missiles

During the Cold War, the United States Defense Department developed a classification system of ballistic missiles capable of carrying nuclear weapons, based on their range. These definitions were subsequently used in various arms control treaties. The ultimate such vehicle was the Intercontinental Ballistic Missile (ICBM), which could carry a nuclear payload from the United States to the Soviet Union and vice versa. Specifically, it had a range greater than 3,500 miles (5,500 kilometers).

Next came the Intermediate-Range Ballistic Missile (IRBM) with a range of 1,900 to 3,500 miles (3,000 to 5,500 kilometers). Below that was the Medium-Range Ballistic Missile (MRBM), with a range between 620 miles/1,000 kilometers and that of the IRBM. Some missiles have been described alternately as either an IRBM or as an MRBM. Below the 1,000 kilometer-range were Short-Range Ballistic Missiles (SRBM). Today, categories short of ICBM range are referred to as Theater Ballistic Missiles.

The History of Missile Designation Systems

To best understand the grouping of guided missiles and "M-designated" hardware which are cataloged in this book, it is useful to take a look at the history of missile designating in the United States armed forces since World War II.

The "M" designator in its present incarnation came about in 1963 as part of the effort by the Defense Department to merge various disparate designation systems for aerospace vehicles. Most, though not all, missiles from all services which had been in service since the creation of the US Air Force in 1947, were redesignated within the lineage contained within this book. In turn, subsequent missile systems were included, and they continue to be added to the numeric list to this day.

Meanwhile, one year earlier in 1962, the Defense Department had merged the US Navy nomenclature system with that of the Army and Air Force for fixed wing aircraft and helicopters. This was done by adopting the Air Force Mission Design Series (MDS) system ("B for Bomber," "F for Fighter," "C for Cargo," etc.), and restarting all groups at "1." US Air Force aircraft still in service, such as B-52 bombers and F-105 fighters, etc., retained their old designations, while US Navy aircraft still in service were all redesignated.

For the record, the official details of the MDS system are described in Department of Defense Publication 4120, *Model Designation of Military Aerospace Vehicles*, which continues to be published roughly every three to five years with a complete and updated list of all current aerospace systems, their designators and explanations of these designators.

Like the pre-1962 aircraft nomenclature, pre-1963 missile nomenclature systems were a reflection of the conceptual self-image of each of the armed services. During World War II, the US Navy and the USAAF had separate nomenclature for their missiles, just as they had for aircraft since the two services had bought their first airplanes.

Starting in World War II, the USAAF lumped its missiles among its guided bombs, using the prefix "JB" to describe jet-propelled missiles, and "BQ" to describe powered drones used as bombs. During World War II, the US Navy used "LB" meaning "Bomb Carrying Glider" for its missiles, but in 1946 adopted such prefixes as "KA" for anti-aircraft, "KG" for ground attack, and "KS" for anti-ship missiles. The "K" in this nomenclature system stood for "missile" or "pilotless

Initiated in 1946, the Consolidated-Vultee MX-774 (later RTV-A-2) High-Altitude Rocket (HIROC) was the first American intercontinental ballistic missile (ICBM) program. Its roots in the German V-2 program are obvious by its overall appearance and configuration. The MX-774 evolved into the SM-65/PGM-16 Atlas. (National Archives)

aerial vehicle". As the service did when designating airplanes, the manufacturer's letter was added at the end. Hence, the McDonnell LBD-1 anti-ship missile became the KSD-1 ("D" was McDonnell's letter).

In 1947, with the creation of the Defense Department, and the new US Air Force spun off as a third equal service, there was a short-lived effort at a joint system for designating missiles until the services went their separate ways for 12 years in 1951-1963. (See Appendix 1)

Rivalry Breeds Separate Missile Acquisition

Interservice rivalry and conceptual self image played an important part ion determining what weapons systems were developed. In the immediate postwar years, a turf war ensued as each service attempted to define itself within the parameters of the Defense Department. There was a great deal of duplication, especially in aircraft and missile systems.

The US Air Force came into existence with a mandate to control American air power. Many within the new service theorized that with long-range airpower, it would now assume the role of projecting American military power around the world that had traditionally been held by the US Navy. The Navy naturally took exception, and this squabble reached its crescendo in 1949 in the so called "Admirals' Revolt", the furious reaction to the decision by Secretary of Defense Louis Johnson to cancel the Navy's 'United States' Class of supercarriers, while authorizing the purchase of B-36 bombers by the Air Force.

As a result, the Navy accelerated the acquisition of aircraft, such as long-range carrier-based bombers, which competed both literally and conceptually with Air Force capabilities. With regard to missiles, both services developed long-range cruise missiles for strategic strike missions. These programs included the Navy's Regulus and the Air Force's Snark.

The US Army, meanwhile, had surrendered its aircraft to the Air Force, but retained a robust ballistic missile development program. The theory was that surface-to-surface ballistic missiles, regardless of range, were a natural extension of *artillery*. The Air Force, of course, saw long-range missiles as *bombers*. When it came to surface-to-air missiles, the Army saw them as a natural extension of antiaircraft guns, while the Air Force saw these missiles as interceptors.

The US Army continued making ballistic "artillery" missiles bigger and with longer range until 1956, when Secretary of Defense Charles Wilson gave the US Air Force exclusive responsibility for missiles over 200 miles range. At the time, the Army and Air Force were developing their respective Jupiter and Thor IRBMs, direct competitors with ranges in excess of 1,500 miles. Under the Wilson decree, the Jupiter was transferred to Air Force control.

Rivalry Breeds Separate Missile Designations

In 1951, the Army and Air Force withdrew from the joint designation system and went their separate way, while the Navy continued to use the 1947 system until it was superseded by the present joint system in 1963.

The Air Force defaulted to the familiar in 1951 (see Appendix 2). In retrospect, it was probably predictable that the service would designate missiles as bombers and fighters. The SAM-A-1 Matador became the B-61 "bomber," and the SAM-A-3 Snark became the B-62 "bomber," while the Bomarc interceptor missile was designated as the F-99 "fighter."

Just four years later, these designations were superseded by a new system (see Appendix 2). Under the 1955 system, tactical "B for Bomber" missiles were redesignated with "TM" prefixes, while strategic "B for Bomber" missiles were given "SM" prefixes. The B-61 Matador became the TM-61 "tactical missile," and the B-62 Snark became the SM-62 "strategic missile." The F-99 Bomarc became the IM-99 "interceptor missile."

New designations were introduced in 1955, including "GAM" for "Guided Air-launched Missile," and "GAR," for "Guided Air-launched Rocket."

Meanwhile, between 1955 and 1963, the US Army used the system that it had long used for other hardware, in which numerals were preceded with an "M," an "ordnance designator" that stood, not for "Missile," but "Model," just like they designated everything from rifles to tanks to trucks. The Army SAM-G-7 Nike-Ajax became the M1 Guided Missile, the SAM-G-14 Redstone became the M8, and so on (see Appendix 3).

As noted in the appendix, the US Army also designated unguided rockets, such as the Honest John, under this same series. The Honest John was designated as M31.

In 1963, when the joint, tri-service "M for Missile" nomenclature came in, unguided rockets were split out and given a separate "R for Rocket" designation system (see Addendum 2). The Honest John, to use it as an example again, went from M31 to first on the new "Rocket" list as MGR-1.

Still Making Changes

While the unified MDS system of 1963 brought order to the chaos of the earlier designation systems, it has been modified by some conceptual changes along the way. The most significant later change came in 1997. From 1963 until that date, unmanned drones had been included within the "M" lineage because most in service during that time had been used as aerial targets. Being "projectiles" they fit in the broad definition of "missiles." For example, in 1963, ten existing drones were redesignated with consecutive "M for Missile" numbers from MQM-33 through MQM-42. Still others followed over the next 34 years.

Back in 1942, the USAAF began using the designation "OQ" to denote "pilotless radio controlled models" used as aerial targets, later called "target drones." After World War II, the US Air Force abbreviated this primary designation for drones to "Q."

Between 1963 and 1997, the "Q" was relegated to use as a secondary mission indicator rather than as a primary designator. There were a number of others designated with BQM and MQM prefixes. For example, the BQM-34 Firebee and BQM-155 Hunter were numbered in the "M for Missile" series, and qualified as drones (Q) that could be launched from multiple platforms (B).

In 1997, as unmanned aircraft came to be regarded as important for other missions, the Defense Department readopted the "Q" as a primary "vehicle type" MDS prefix.

After 1997, the Hunter was redesignated as RQ-5, numbered in the new "Q for drone" lineage, with "Q" as its primary designator, and modified with an "R" to indicate that its basic mission was reconnaissance.

New unmanned aerial vehicles that were introduced or designated after 1997 started out with the "Q" MDS prefix. However, this applies only to reconnaissance and multi-mission UAVs. New unmanned target drones, such as the post-1997 GQM-163 and BQM-167, continued to be designated as "missiles."

The Missiles in This Book

This book is a numerical order compendium of all the American guided missiles to be designated under the "M for Missile" designator system. Though the nomenclature was introduced in 1963, it was imposed retroactively on key missile systems going to the immediate aftermath of World War II.

The systems within the series are widely varied, including cruise missiles, air intercept missiles, Intercontinental Ballistic Missiles, and even piston-engined drones. Some of the systems in this consecutive list are long-forgotten, and others were never produced. Still others were produced in the tens of thousands over many decades and have become household words.

The great variety in size, shape, performance and mission makes this list an interesting cross section of American weapons technology, as well as an important study in evolving strategy and tactics.

Making Sense of Three-Letter Missile Designation Prefixes

Assigned to nearly all operational guided missiles (and several non-operational missiles) since 1963, the basic designations contained herein consist of *three letters preceding the consecutive numbers*. Occasionally, an "X" or "Y" precedes the three letters. As in aircraft, these stand for "experimental" or "service test." For many years during the Cold War era, a "Z" prefix was occasionally seen in designating conceptual projects at an early stage of development before an experimental missile had actually been built.

Among the three basic letters, the third is always "M for Missile," even in pre-1997 hardware when UAVs were included among this lineage. The other two letters are keyed out as follows:

First letter: Launch or Deployment Environment:
   A: Air launched
   B: Multiple launch environments
   C: Container or "Coffin" stored
   F: Launched by an individual person
   G: Runway (ground) launched
   H: Silo stored
   L: Silo stored and launched
   M: Mobile (ground) launched
   P: Soft Pad (ground) launched
   R: Surface Ship launched
   U: Underwater launched

Middle Letter: Mission Type:
   D: Decoy
   E: Electronics
   G: Surface (Ground) Attack
   I: Intercept
   Q: Target Drone (also UAV until 1997)
   T: Training*
   U: Underwater Attack

* Many of the missiles contained in this book had training variants in which the "T" was inserted as a middle letter and all other digits remained the same. For example, the ATM-88A was the dummy training version of the AGM-88A.

Note: For details of pre-1963 designation systems, see the appendices.

The Missiles:
MGM-1 through MQM-175

Air Force crews prepare an MGM-1 (then QYB-61) Matador for flight, circa early 1950s. (National Archives)

MGM-1 Matador

The first missile to have received an "M for Missile" designator, the Matador originated just after World War II as US Air Force project MX-771. A winged, surface-to-surface cruise missile like the German V-1, it was the first such Air Force missile in the second technological generation beyond the V-1.

Originally designated as XSSM-A-1, the Matador was first flown at the White Sands Missile Range on January 20, 1949. One of the weapons systems considered for elimination in the constricted postwar military budgets, the Matador got a new lease on life after the Korean War caused a rethinking of budgetary priorities. However, the Matador was not deployed until after the end of the Korean War.

In 1951, as the US Air Force redesignated surface-to-surface missiles as bombers, experimental Matadors became XB-61, and service test missiles were designated as YB-61. Tests of production series B-61A missiles took place at Eglin AFB in Florida in the fall of 1953.

The first operational B-61As were deployed overseas to West Germany in 1954, where they were assigned to the 1st and 2nd Pilotless Bomber Squadrons of the 38th Tactical Missile Wing, located at Bitburg AB and Hahn AB, respectively. Here they were deployed on mobile launchers for operational flexibility, and to make their positions harder to track.

The Cold War mission was to use the Matador, armed with a nuclear warhead, against invading Soviet armies. The Matador could also carry a one-ton high explosive payload, but the nuclear payload was the primary weapon on deployed missiles. Other operational US Air Force Matadors were deployed to units in Taiwan and South Korea. Some were also deployed with *Flugkorpergruppe* 11 of the German *Bundeswehr*.

Top right: *A photo of a 1952 launch of a Martin Matador, which is identified in accompanying Air Force paperwork (probably incorrectly) as an "operational" B-61.* (National Archives)

Bottom right: *A forward view of a 1953 test launch of a Martin QYB-61 (later MGM-1) Matador missile.* (Author's collection)

A Martin MGM-1 (then B-61A) Matador missile posed with its launch equipment and support vehicles in 1954. (Martin)

The Matador was redesignated as a "Tactical Missile," TM-61A in 1955, by which time, Martin was working on a much improved TM-61B. The TM-61B later evolved into the TM-67 (MGM-16) Mace. In the meantime, Martin delivered a slightly improved TM-61C Matador, which was first deployed in 1957, as a stop-gap measure.

Around 1,200 Matadors, mostly "A" models, were built. They were withdrawn from service by the US Air Force in 1962.

Manufacturer: Glenn L. Martin Company

Length: 39 feet 7 inches (12.1 meters) (with booster) feet inches (meters)

Diameter: 4 feet 6 inches (1.2 meters)

Wingspan: 27 feet 10 inches (8.5 meters)

Weight: 12,000 pounds (5,400 kilograms)

Range: 620 miles (1,000 kilometers)

Speed: Mach 0.9

Ceiling: 35,000 feet (10,500 meters)

Guidance system: Radar directed, radio controlled

Propulsion system: Allison J33 turbojet, with Aerojet solid-fuel rocket booster

Warhead: nuclear

First tested: 1949

First deployed: 1954

(Specifications for MGM-1C)

An RIM-2 Terrier surface-to-air missile is fired from the guided-missile destroyer USS Farragut *in June 1979.* (US Navy photo by PHAN J. Rickards)

RIM-2 Terrier

The US Navy's interest in a fast, ship-launched anti-aircraft missile stemmed from their experience fending off Japanese kamikazes during World War II. The idea was to have a middle layer of defense for ships between interceptor aircraft and anti-aircraft guns aboard ships. Under the Navy's postwar Project Bumblebee, a number of surface-to-air (SAM) systems were studied, with the radar-guided Terrier being the first deployed. Originally designated as SAM-N-7, earlier Terrier variants were also designated with the suffixes "BT" and "BW" depending upon whether they were flown with beam-riding guidance with tail or wing control.

First tested in 1951, the Terrier went on to shipboard tests aboard the converted battleship USS *Mississippi*. After lengthy evaluations the missile was finally deployed at sea in 1956 aboard the cruisers USS *Boston* and USS *Canberra*. Terriers were launched from a twin-arm launcher, and cruisers were typically equipped with a 40-missile magazine. Such ships did carry as many as 80 to 120, though.

In 1963, wing-control missiles were dredesignated as RIM-2A and RIM-2B, while tail-control missiles were redesignated as RIM-2C and RIM-2D. Most operational missiles carried a conventional high explosive warhead, although the RIM-2D was equipped with a nuclear weapon. Earlier Terriers were all guided through beam riding, but later RIM-2E and RIM-2F had semi-active radar homing capability. The RIM-2F, with an improved engine, had its range extended from a dozen miles in the RIM-2B, to nearly 50, its speed from Mach 1.8 to Mach 3, and its ceiling from 40,000 feet to 80,000 feet.

Around 8,000 Terriers were manufactured before production ended in 1966. Despite the US Navy having deployed successor missiles, such as the RIM-8 Talos, Terriers remained in service until the 1980s.

Manufacturer: Convair Division of General Dynamics

Length: 27 feet 1 inch (8.25 meters)

Diameter: 13.5 inches (0.34 meters)

Span (fins): 40.3 inches (1.03 meters)

Weight, less booster: 1,060 pounds (480 kilograms)

Range: 11.5 miles (18.6 kilometers)

Speed: Mach 1.8

Ceiling: 40,000 feet (12,200 meters)

Guidance system: Beam riding

Propulsion system: Solid-fuel rocket

Warhead: 218 pounds (100 kilograms) blast fragmentation

First tested: 1951

First deployed: 1956

(Specifications for RIM-2B)

An aft view of RIM-2 surface-to-air missiles on their Mk.10 twin-arm launchers aboard a US Navy guided missile cruiser, circa the mid-1950s. (Author's collection)

A MIM-3 Nike Ajax on its launcher, probably at the White Sands Missile Range in New Mexico. (US Army)

MIM-3 Nike Ajax

The US Army began considering missiles as anti-aircraft weapons in 1944. With the advent of jet aircraft, it was apparent that their speed and altitude were beyond the intercept capability of conventional anti-aircraft guns.

After World War II, as the US Air Force became independent of the US Army, the anti-aircraft missile program separated onto two tracks. The Army pursued the Nike program under its mandate to maintain an anti-aircraft artillery capability, while the Air Force carried on with Project Thumper, which was considered an evolution of interceptor aircraft, and which led to the MIM-10 Bomarc.

The Nike program, including guidance and tracking, was developed by Bell Laboratories, the technological development side of the Bell Telephone Company. The radar and computing equipment was built by Western Electric, a Bell subsidiary. The missile was built by Douglas Aircraft as a subcontractor to Western Electric. The radar system included target acquisition, target tracking and missile tracking. The missile was a two-stage vehicle for extended range.

As the Terrier was the first US Navy surface-to-air missile, the Nike was the first for the US Army. The latter moved on a faster track, in part because the urgent problem of protecting American cities from Soviet bomber attacks. The Nike Ajax was designed specifically for this mission.

The Nike missile was first tested under the designation XSAM-G-7 in 1946 with eight small rocket motors, but these were replaced by a single large solid rocket booster, and a liquid-fuel rocket on the upper stage. In its first successful live-fire test in November 1951, a Nike downed an unmanned QB-17 Flying Fortress.

Designated as guided missile M1, the Nike Ajax was initially known simply as "Nike." It became known as "Nike Ajax" in 1956 to distinguish it from the successor Nike Hercules. The Nike Ajax was first operationally deployed to a launch site at Fort Meade, Maryland in December 1953. From here, around 1,000 missiles were deployed to nearly 250 fixed launch sites organized into Defense Areas surrounding major American population centers and key military bases. During the next several years, the US Army phased out all of its anti-aircraft guns deployed to protect fixed locations within the United States.

Each encompassing several acres, the Nike sites consisted of an integrated launch control center and several missile batteries. Here, up to three missiles were kept underground until being raised for launching either one at a time or all at once, depending on the site. The sites were manned continuously, with at least one battery on alert to be fired within 15 minutes. The payload consisted of three warheads totaling about 300 pounds of high explosives that were located at various places within the missile and detonated remotely when the missile crossed paths with the target aircraft.

Meanwhile, Western Electric and Douglas were already developing the next generation Nike. Initially known as Nike B and designated as SAM-G-25, the successor missile was deployed as the M6 Nike Hercules. In 1963, as the Nike Ajax became the MIM-3 and the Nike Hercules became the MIM-14, the latter was well on its way to replacing the original Nike at all of the fixed sites across the United States.

Manufacturer: Western Electric/ Douglas Aircraft

Length: 21 feet (6.4 meters) (with booster) 34 feet 10 inches (10.6 meters)

Diameter: 12 inches (0.3 meters)

Span (fins): 4 feet 6 inches (1.4 meters)

Weight: 2,460 pounds (1,110 kilograms) (with booster)

Range: 30 miles (48 kilometers)

Speed: Mach 2.3

Ceiling: 70,000 feet (21,000 meters)

Guidance system: ground control supported by tracking radar

Propulsion system: Bell liquid-fuel rocket, Allegheny solid rocket booster

Warhead: 300 pounds of high explosives

First tested: 1951

First deployed: 1953

(Specifications form MIM-3A)

A MIM-3 Nike Ajax site on Angel Island in San Francisco Bay. (US Army)

A US Air Force weapons load team assigned to the 119th Fighter Wing "Happy Hooligans," North Dakota Air National Guard, handle an inert AIM-4C Falcon air-to-air missile during a William Tell Weapons Competition at Tyndall AFB in October 1972. Pictured from left to right are Doreen Thomas, Patricia McMerty, Jacqueline Sanders, and Ellen Rising. (US Air Force Photo)

AIM-4 Falcon

The first operational guided air-to-air missile was the X4, developed for the German Luftwaffe during World War II. The Falcon, destined to be the first American guided air-to-air missile, originated in 1946 as the USAAF's Project MX-798. This morphed into Project 904, which called for the missile to be supersonic.

The missile was first tested in 1949 under the designation XAAM-A-2, and redesignated as the XF-98 unmanned fighter in 1951. A Falcon variant designed to be launched from supersonic manned fighters was briefly known as XF-104, but it was redesignated, first as XF-98A, and in 1955 as Guided Aerial Rocket GAR-1. All Falcons were powered by various Thiokol solid rocket motors and all were armed with high explosive warheads, but there was some variance in guidance system and specific engine.

The first production Falcon was delivered in 1954, and they began equipping US Air Force F-89 and F-102 interceptors by 1956. The definitive GAR-1 was the GAR-1D, of which about 12,000 were built.

Subsequent variants were designated as GAR-2 through GAR-4. While the GAR-1 used semi-active radar homing, the GAR-2, also operational in 1956, was

infrared guided. Typically, interceptors were armed with both types. There were more than 26,000 GAR-2s built. In 1959, the GAR-1 and GAR-2 were superseded by the GAR-3 and GAR-4, of which around 3,400 and 2,700 were made. These used the respective guidance types of the previous Falcons, albeit upgraded versions, of the earlier Falcons, and had improved dual-thrust engines to extend the range of the missiles.

In 1963, the AIM-4 Air Intercept designation was adopted for all Falcons. The GAR-1D became AIM-4A, and the GAR-2 became the AIM-4B, while the GAR-3A became the AIM-4F, and the GAR-4A became the AIM-4G. It was the AIM-4D (formerly GAR-2B), of which 4,000 were built, that was most widely used in the Vietnam War. Because Falcons were designed for long-range intercepts of bombers, however, they were not as useful for aerial combat as were AIM-7 Sparrows and AIM-9 Sidewinders.

While AIM-4Ds were phased out by 1973, AIM-4F and AIM-4G Falcons continued to arm F-106 interceptors until these aircraft were retired in the 1980s.

Further developments of the Falcon family, designated as AIM-26, AIM-47 and AIM-76, are covered later in this book.

Convair F-102 pilot Robert Laurence and a friend pose with a Hughes GAR-2 (later AIM-4) Falcon missile at Edwards AFB in December 1956. She holds a Zuni five-inch unguided and undesignated Folding-Fin Aircraft Rocket (FFAR). (Author's collection)

Manufacturer: Hughes Aircraft

Length: 7 feet 1.8 inches (2.2 meters)

Diameter: 6.6 inches (0.17 meters)

Span (fins): 24 inches (0.61 meters)

Weight: 150 pounds (68 kilograms)

Range: 7 miles (11.3 kilometers)

Speed: Mach 4

Guidance system: (see text for overview)

Propulsion system: Thiokol M46 solid-fuel rocket

Warhead: high explosive

First tested: 1949

First deployed: 1956

(Specifications for AIM-4F)

MGM-5 Corporal

The Corporal program was one of several long-range surface-to-surface missile projects that were begun by the US Army during 1944-1945 after the German V-2 became known. A parallel project was the Hermes program, which envisioned a more complex missile. Both projects evolved after World War II as Army and contractor engineers were able to benefit from examining V-2s and pick the brains of German V-2 program scientists. There were several Hermes variants, with the A1 model (CTV-G-5) based closely on the German *Wasserfall* (waterfall) surface-to-air missile, and later iterations based more closely on the V-2.

A spin-off of the Corporal was the smaller "WAC Corporal" (later designated as RTV-G-1) sounding rocket, which was first launched in September 1945. Later, this vehicle was combined with a V-2 as an upper stage, and tested in 1948-1950 as the "Bumper WAC," the first man-made vehicle in outer space (see Introduction). The prototype for the full-size SSM-A-17 Corporal tactical nuclear missile was first flown in 1947. The production series Corporal was first tested in August 1952.

Operational missiles, designated as Guided Missile M2, reached the US Army for training purposes two years later. While the Jet Propulsion Laboratory (JPL) at Caltech developed the Corporal program in conjunction with the US Army, early vehicles were built by Douglas Aircraft. The production tactical missiles were manufactured by Firestone.

Systems reliability issues, including problems with transmission of guidance data, led to a series of reworked Corporals, culminating with the Corporal IIb M2A1 (MGM-5B after 1963), which entered production in 1958. More than 1,100 Corporal tactical variants of all designation were built. They were operationally deployed with the US Army, as well as being tested by Britain's Royal Artillery. Corporals were phased out in 1964 in favor of the larger MGM-29 Sergeant.

A test launch of an SSM-A-17 (later MGM-5) Corporal missile. (US Army)

Manufacturer: Firestone Tire & Rubber

Height: 45 feet 4 inches (13.8 meters)

Diameter: 30 inches (0.76 meters)

Span (fins): 7 feet (2.1 meters)

Weight: 11,000 pounds (5,000 kilograms)

Range: 80 miles (130 kilometers)

Speed: 2,200 mph (3,500 km/h)

Ceiling: 25 miles (40 meters)

Guidance system: radar data transmitted from ground

Propulsion system: JPL liquid-fuel rocket

Warhead: W7 nuclear

First tested: 1945 (WAC Corporal), 1952 (M2 Corporal)

First deployed: 1954

(Specifications for MGM-5B)

A Corporal missile on its mobile launcher. (US Army)

A June 1957 test launch of a US Navy RGM-6 (then SSM-N-8) Regulus from aboard the cruiser USS Helena *in the Philippine Sea.* (National Archives)

RGM-6 Regulus I

The Regulus was the first US Navy long-range strategic nuclear missile. It was the first operational submarine-launched missile, although it was launched when the sub was surfaced.

The Navy had previously experimented with launching KUW-1 Loons (adapted from German V-1s) from submarines, and had also commissioned a new generation of sub-launched test missiles. These included the 47-foot SSM-N-6 Grumman Rigel, a supersonic missile that was tested in 1951 and 1952 and the 45-foot SSM-N-2 Triton, which was tested between 1951 and 1955. Developed by the Applied Physics Laboratory (APL) at Johns Hopkins University, Triton was faster than the Rigel and one of the first missiles developed for the US Navy that was capable of carrying a nuclear warhead. Neither the Rigel nor Triton entered operational service.

The 33-foot Vought SSM-N-8 Regulus was a small turbojet powered cruise missile capable of delivering a 3,000-pound nuclear payload up to 600 miles. Flight testing began in March 1951, and it became operational in 1954. The US Navy deployed the Regulus missiles aboard surface ships, especially cruisers, as well as aboard submarines.

The first successful shipboard launch came in November 1952, with the first submarine launch from the deck of the USS *Tunny* following in July 1953. The first shipboard deployment was on the cruiser USS *Los Angeles* in 1955. Submarine deployments began the following year. In 1960, the USS *Halibut*, specifically built for the Regulus, became the first nuclear submarine to successfully launch a guided missile.

Though innovative and forward looking when it was conceived in the 1950s, the Regulus program was soon overtaken by the Polaris program, with its underwater launch capability. The last operational Regulus deployment was aboard the *Halibut* in 1964.

In parallel with the deployment of the subsonic Regulus, Vought was also commissioned develop a supersonic Regulus II under the designation SSM-N-9. In 1963, the two winged cruise missiles were designated as RGM-6 and RGM-15 respectively. Shortly thereafter, the RGM-6, now called "Regulus I," was withdrawn.

Manufacturer: Vought

Length: 33 feet 4 inches (10 meters)

Diameter: 56 inches (1.4 meters)

Span (wings): 21 feet (6.4 meters)

Weight: 10,300 pounds (4,670 kilograms)

Range: 600 miles (960 kilometers)

Speed: 600 mph (960 km/h)

Ceiling: 40,000 feet (12,200 meters)

Guidance system: radio ground control

Propulsion system: Allison J33 turbojet with Aerojet solid-fuel rocket boosters

Warhead: nuclear (later thermonuclear)

First tested: 1951

First deployed: 1954

(Specifications for RGM-6B)

A 1958 photo of AIM-7 (then AAM-N-2) Sparrow I missiles arming a Douglas F3D Skyknight. (Author's collection)

AIM-7 Sparrow and RIM-7 Sea Sparrow

The lowest number missile in the "M for Missile" series to be in service into the twenty-first century, the Sparrow family originated as a US Navy air-to-air missile program in 1947. The idea was to create a beam-riding guidance system for the High Velocity Aerial Rocket (HVAR), but the program evolved into a larger weapon. The Sparrow I first successfully intercepted an aerial target in 1952 and entered service as AAM-N-2 in 1958. It armed a variety of naval interceptors until being superseded by the AAM-N-6 Sparrow III. The Sparrow III and all later Sparrows were guided by semi-active radar homing.

The program was redesignated in 1963, with the AAM-N-6 becoming the AIM-7C. The standard production missile was the AIM-7E, of which around 25,000 were built. This missile traded the earlier Aerojet solid-fuel rocket engine for a new family of Rocketdyne engines which greatly improved the speed from Mach 2.5 to Mach 4, and which increased the range from around four miles to nearly 20.

The Sparrow armed both US Navy and US Air Force F-4 Phantom II aircraft throughout the Vietnam War, with the first aerial victory attributed to an AIM-7 occurring against a pair of MiG-17s on June 7, 1965.

Nevertheless, disappointing results early in the war led to the more maneuverable "dogfight model" AIM-7E-2, introduced in 1969. During the war, Air Force Phantoms alone downed 50 enemy aircraft with Sparrows, compared to 31 with AIM-9 Sidewinders.

Meanwhile, the Sparrow was adapted as a ship-based surface-to-air "Sea Sparrow" missile under the RIM-7 designation. The first, the RIM-7E, was deployed in 1967 with performance equivalent to the AIM-7E.

A semi-active radar homing version of the AIM-7E was also license-produced by British Aerospace under the name Skyflash. These were delivered to the Royal Air Force and to the Swedish air force, Royal Saudi Air Force and Italian Air Force.

Gradual improvements in solid state and digital electronics led to much more capable Sparrows, including the AIM-7F, AIM-7M and AIM-7P, which entered production in 1975, 1982 and 1987 respectively. Some AIM-7Ps were built new, but many AIM-7Ms were upgraded to that standard and redesignated. At the same time, the US Navy was taking delivery of shipboard equivalent RIM-7M and RIM-7P Sea Sparrows. These missiles are compatible with the Mk.41 Vertical Launch System (VLS).

A US Air Force F-15 Eagle from the 199th Fighter Squadron, Hawaii Air National Guard, fires an AIM-7 Sparrow at an ADM-141 tactical air-launched decoy in July 2006. (DoD photo by Tech Sergeant Shane Cuomo, US Air Force)

Men from Marine Fighter Attack Squadron 235 (VMFA-235) load an AIM-7 Sparrow III missile aboard an F-4 Phantom II aircraft in February 1982. (USMC photo by Sergeant C. Taylor)

A RIM-7 M Sea Sparrow missile is fired from the aft launcher aboard the US Navy Amphibious Assault Ship USS Essex *in June 2006.* (US Navy photo by PHAN Marvin Thompson)

US Air Force Staff Sergeants Arthur Hamabata and Gabriel Coronado install the wings and fins on an AIM-7 Sparrow missile at Hickam AFB, Hawaii in July 2006. (US Air Force photo by Tech Sergeant Shane Cuomo)

During Operation Desert Storm in 1991, the AIM-7M and AIM-7P variants accounted for 26 Iraqi aircraft downed, achieving a kill ratio of 37 percent, nearly four times better than was achieved with older Sparrows in Vietnam.

A dual-mode infrared and radar guidance system was developed during the 1990s for the Sparrow, but the plan to upgrade existing missiles under the Missile Homing Improvement Program (MHIP) to the newer AIM-7R standard was terminated for cost reasons.

More than 60,000 Sparrows and 9,000 Sea Sparrows had been produced when production wound down early in the twenty-first century. The AIM-7 Sparrow will gradually be replaced by the AIM-120 AMRAAM, with the Sea Sparrow is superseded by the RIM-162 Evolved Sea Sparrow Missile (ESSM).

Manufacturer: Raytheon

Length: 12 feet (3.66 meters)

Diameter: 8 inches (0.23 meters)

Span (fins): 40 inches (1.02 meters)

Weight: 510 pounds (231 kilograms)

Range: 45 miles (70 kilometers)

Speed: Mach 4

Guidance system: semi-active radar homing

Propulsion system: Hercules Mk.58 solid-fuel rocket

Warhead: high explosive blast fragmentation

First tested: 1952 (Sparrow I)

First deployed: 1956 (Sparrow I), 1967 (Sea Sparrow)

(Specifications for AIM-7P. Dimensions unchanged since AIM-7E)

Top left: *A RIM-7 Sea Sparrow missile is launched after locking onto its target during a March 2001 live fire missile exercise aboard the USS* Bataan. (US Navy photo by PHAN John Taucher)

Bottom left: RIM-7 Sea Sparrow missiles fill a Mk.29 launcher aboard the USS Ronald Reagan *as Fire Controlman 1st Class Darrel Cook shouts orders down the launching chamber.* (US Navy photo by Mass Communication Specialist 3rd Class Benjamin Brossard)

A Talos at the US Navy's "USS Desert Ship*" at the White Sands Missile Range in June 1957.* (Author's collection)

RIM-8 Talos

Having been responsible for downing three MiGs during the Vietnam War, the Talos can be described as the US Navy's most effective Cold War-era surface-to-air missile. Like the RIM-2 Tartar, the Talos came out of the Navy's Project Bumblebee effort to develop a defense system for fending off air attacks against the fleet.

The Talos first flew as the RTV-N-6 test vehicle in 1951, and as the SAM-N-6 surface-to-air missile prototype in 1952. Modifications and upgrades delayed operational deployment to 1959, and in 1963, the Talos was redesignated as RIM-8.

The Talos was first deployed aboard the converted light cruisers USS *Galveston*, USS *Little Rock*, and USS *Oklahoma City*, and later aboard converted heavy cruisers USS *Albany*, USS *Chicago*, and USS *Columbus*, as well as the nuclear-powered cruiser USS *Long Beach*. Meanwhile, the US Air Force briefly entertained thoughts of a land-based Talos, and even reserved the IM-70 interceptor designation for the project.

A dual shipboard launcher with a pair of Talos surface-to-air missiles, circa 1961. (Author's collection)

A Talos surface-to-air missile is fired from the guided missile cruiser USS Oklahoma City *in October 1979.* (US Navy photo by PH1 David MacLean)

The RIM-8A had a range of nearly 60 miles, while the RIM-8C had twice that range. Talos missiles were deployed with conventional high explosive warheads, but provisions were made for equivalent RIM-8B and RIM-8D missiles to carry nuclear warheads.

RIM-8G and RIM-9J missiles, with improved guidance systems were deployed in 1966 and 1968 respectively. The RGM-8H was a surface-to-surface missile that was designed in 1965 for shipboard attacks against land-based radar systems. The USS *Oklahoma City*, USS *Chicago*, and USS *Long Beach* deployed to the Gulf of Tonkin with the RGM-8H to conduct strikes against North Vietnamese radar installations.

In 1974, the US Navy began to phase out the Talos, replacing them with the RIM-67 Standard Missile using a smaller launcher. The last shipboard Talos missiles were retired in 1979. From then through the early twenty-first century, existing Taloses were used as supersonic targets known as MQM-8G Vandals.

Manufacturer: Bendix

Length with booster: 21 feet (6.4 meters)

Diameter: 28 inches (0.7 meters)

Span (fins): 81 inches (2.06 meters)

Weight with booster: 7,800 pounds (3,530 kilograms)

Range: 115 miles (185 kilometers)

Speed: Mach 2.5

Ceiling: 80,000 feet (24,400 meters)

Guidance system: semi-active radar homing

Propulsion system: Bendix ramjet with solid-fuel rocket booster

Warhead: 300 pounds of high explosive or W30 nuclear

First tested: 1951

First deployed: 1959

(Specifications for RIM-8G)

*F-104 Starfighters armed with AIM-9B Sidewinders over San Francisco Bay in 1957. (*Lockheed)

AIM-9 Sidewinder

Among America's most widely produced guided missiles, the Sidewinder has passed the half century mark in service, with more than 150,000 units having been built and put into service by more than two dozen countries. This is not to mention 15,000 built in Germany by Bodenseewerk GmbH, and a very large (but unknown) number of reverse-engineered copies that were manufactured in China and the Soviet bloc during the Cold War.

The project began in 1950 as a US Navy effort toward developing a simple heat-seeking air intercept missile. It was developed by the Naval Ordnance Test Station (later Naval Weapons Center) at China Lake, and originally manufactured by both General Electric and Philco (Philco-Ford after 1961, Ford Aerospace after 1976, Loral after 1990). Raytheon produces the twenty-first century AIM-9X variant.

The first tests were conducted in 1951, with the first successful anti-aircraft hit being achieved in September 1952. The AAM-N-7 (later AIM-9A) Sidewinder

*An F-104 from the 69th Tactical Fighter Training Squadron carrying AIM-9J Sidewinder missiles in August 1979. (*US Air Force photo by Ken Hackman)

Two AIM-9P Sidewinder missiles mounted on the wing pylon of an F-4C Phantom II of the 154th Composite Group, Hawaii Air National Guard, March 1980. (US Air Force photo by Staff Sergeant Bert Mau)

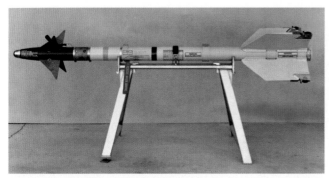

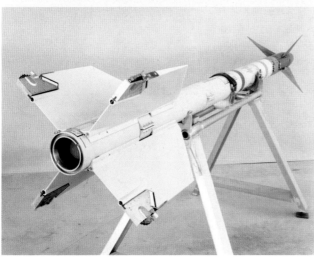

Above left: *A side view of an AIM-9L/M Sidewinder on a display stand at the Naval Weapons Center in 1982. (US Navy)*

Above: *A front view of an AIM-9L/M Sidewinder on a display stand at the Naval Weapons Center in 1982. (US Navy)*

Left: *An aft view of an AIM-9L/M Sidewinder on a display stand at the Naval Weapons Center in 1982. (US Navy)*

became operational with the US Navy in May 1956. The US Air Force tested the Sidewinder in 1955, ordered it under the designation GAR-8 (later AIM-9B), and acquired 80,000 units through 1962. The later AIM-9E was like the AIM-9B, but with a much improved guidance system.

An AAM-N-7 (later AIM-9C) was developed with semi-active radar homing instead of heat-seeking guidance for all weather applications but only a few were built.

The Sidewinder's combat career began in September 1958, when Taiwanese F-86Fs downed Communist Chinese MiG-15s with AIM-9Bs in the first ever successful use of air-to-air guided missiles in a dogfight. During the Vietnam War, where both the US Navy and US Air Force used Sidewinders, they achieved more than 80 kills with them. Most of these were by US Navy F-4 Phantoms.

Deployed during the air campaigns of 1972, were the much-improved Navy AIM-9H and Air Force AIM-9J. During the 1970s, advances in engine technology and solid state electronics led to further upgrades. During this time, many AIM-9Bs and AIM-9Es were retrofitted to AIM-9J standard.

A major step forward was the infrared guided AIM-9L (aka "Lima"), which was capable of hitting a target from

Above: *Performing preflight maintenance on an AIM-9L Sidewinder mounted on an F-16 Fighting Falcon aircraft at Kunsan AB in Korea during Exercise Team Spirit in 1982.* (US Air Force photo by Staff Sergeant James Pearson)

Below: *Ordnancemen prepare to mount AIM-9L/M Sidewinder missiles on a Fighter Squadron 102 (VF-102) F-14A Tomcat aircraft aboard the carrier USS* Theodore Roosevelt *in 1987.* (US Navy)

US Air Force Senior Airman John Farley, Staff Sergeant Calyn Coffee, and Senior Airman Curtis Stuart of the 12th Aircraft Maintenance Unit upload an AIM-9X Sidewinder onto the LAU-129 rail of an F-15C at Elmendorf AFB, Alaska in November 2003. (US Air Force photo by SRA Joe Laws)

any point on the compass, including a head-on. The "all-aspect" AIM-9L was combat proven during 1982 by the British in the Falklands, and by Israel over Lebanon. In Vietnam, the United States achieved a kill ratio in combat of around 15 percent. With the AIM-9L, this jumped to 80 percent. The AIM-9M (aka "Mike"), which was like the AIM-9L, but with improved guidance and an ability to outfox infrared countermeasures, was introduced in 1982.

The complexity of the periodic upgrades to the Lima and Mike model Sidewinders, which proceeded through the 1990s pointed out a need for a simplification. This led Raytheon to develop the AIM-9X model, for which upgrades are a matter of reprogramming software. This is an easier step, which can be carried out at the field, rather than depot, level.

The first AIM-9X Sidewinders were operationally deployed in November 2003, with an imaging infrared focal plane array seeker and thrust-vectoring control as part of the package. The new Joint Helmet Mounted Cueing System allows a pilot to lock on to a target by looking at it. In the ensuing five years, Raytheon delivered 3,000 units to the US Navy and Air Force.

Manufacturer: currently Raytheon (see text)

Length: 9 feet 4.2 inches (2.85 meters)

Diameter: 5 inches (0.13 meters)

Span (fins): 24.8 inches (0.63 meters)

Weight: 191 pounds (86 kilograms)

Range: 12 miles (18 kilometers)

Speed: Mach 2.5

Guidance system: infrared heat seeking

Propulsion system: Hercules solid-fuel rocket

Warhead: blast fragmentation

First tested: 1951

First deployed: 1956

(Specifications for AIM-9L and AIM-9M)

CIM-10 Bomarc

The Bomarc was an interceptor missile developed jointly by Boeing and the Michigan Aerospace Research Center (MARC), with this consortium providing the acronym by which the missile is known. Under USAAF Project MX-606, Boeing began studies of surface-to-air guided missiles in 1946, and later conducted over 100 flight tests of its XSAM-A-1 Ground-to-Air Pilotless Aircraft (GAPA). In 1949, the Air Force contracted with Boeing under Project MX-1599 to develop an operational, ramjet-powered, nuclear-armed surface-to-air missile. This program led to the Bomarc, originally designated as the "pilotless fighter" F-99.

As noted in the MIM-3 section above, the Air Force maintained ownership of the Bomarc under the theory that an interceptor missile was a natural extension of manned interceptors. The Army retained the parallel Nike program, with its identical mission, under the theory that the Nike was a natural extension of the Army's anti-aircraft artillery mandate.

Testing of the XF-99 Bomarc got underway in September 1952. Three years later, while testing was still underway, the Bomarc was redesignated as interceptor missile XIM-99A. In 1957, after successful tests, the IM-99A Bomarc entered production. The missile and its Semi-Automatic Ground Environment (SAGE) radar and control infrastructure became operational in September 1959.

The ramjet-powered IM-99A was boosted by a liquid fuel rocket, which was seen as having an especially slow reaction time, so a Thiokol solid-fuel rocket booster was developed and fielded on the IM-99B, first tested in May 1959, but it did not achieve a successful flight until July 1960. The IM-99B became operational with the US Air Force in June 1961, and later with the Royal Canadian Air Force.

In addition to 30 pre-production Bomarcs, Boeing delivered 269 IM-99As and 301 IM-99Bs through 1965. Some Bomarc As were upgraded to Bomarc B standard. Meanwhile, in 1963, the Bomarcs were redesignated under the "M for Missile" system as CIM-10A and CIM-10B, with the "C" indicating that they were based in blast-proof concrete "coffins," then raised hydraulically for launch.

The last Bomarc interceptor sites were deactivated by 1972, but surviving missiles were used as CQM-10A and CQM-10B aerial target drones.

A Boeing Bomarc interceptor missile is launched. Originally designated as F-99, the Bomarc was later IM-99, and finally MIM-10. (Author's collection)

Above: *White-jacketed technicians in the Bomarc final assembly area. The "IM" for "Interceptor Missile" prefix identifies each numbered airframe.* (Author's collection)

Below: *A 1977 Bomarc launch at Vandenberg. AFB* (US Air Force)

Manufacturer: Boeing

Length: 45 feet 1 inch (13.7 meters) (with booster)

Diameter: 35 inches (0.89 meters)

Wingspan: 18 feet 2 inches (5.54 meters)

Weight: 16,000 pounds (7,250 kilograms)

Range: 440 miles (710 kilometers)

Speed: Mach 3

Ceiling: 100,000 feet (30,000 meters)

Guidance system: radio remote control with radar terminal homing

Propulsion system: Marquardt RJ43 ramjets with Aerojet liquid (CIM-10A) or Thiokol solid (CIM-10B) rocket boosters

Warhead: W47 nuclear (alternately, high explosive)

First tested: 1952

First deployed: 1959

(Specifications for CIM-10B)

PGM-11 Redstone

Taking its name from the US Army's Redstone Arsenal in Alabama, where it was developed, this surface-to-surface missile was part of the family tree of US Army vertically-launched ballistic missiles created with input from Wernher von Braun and the German scientists who were responsible for the V-2.

As noted in the MGM-5 section, the Corporal missile developed in parallel with the Hermes program, based on the wartime German *Wasserfall* missile. The Redstone was a fruit of the Hermes branch of the family tree. Like the wartime V-2, both Hermes and Redstone were liquid fuel rockets. As a platform for launching tactical nuclear weapons, the Redstone program received a high priority after the start of the Korean War in 1950, and the first missile made its debut flight in 1953.

In 1958, the Redstone was introduced into active front-line US Army units in West Germany as guided artillery missile M8 (later PGM-11A). It was the first operational American Medium Range Ballistic Missile (MRBM) to be deployed. With a range of about 250 miles, it was competitive with the missiles being developed by the US Air Force, which sought an exclusive mandate for missiles with a range greater than 200 miles.

More than 1,000 Redstones were built by Chrysler through 1960, but they were withdrawn from service as offensive weapons shortly thereafter. PGM-11As were later adapted for use as space launch vehicles for NASA. America's first two Project Mercury astronauts went into space in 1961 atop Redstones.

Manufacturer: Chrysler

Height: 69 feet 4 inches (21.13 meters)

Diameter: 70 inches (1.78 meters)

Span (fins): 12 feet (3.66 meters)

Weight: 61,000 pounds (27,500 kilograms)

Range: 175 miles (325 kilometers)

Speed: Mach 5.5

Ceiling: 300,000 feet (92,000 meters)

Guidance system: inertial guidance

Propulsion system: Rocketdyne liquid-fuel rocket

Warhead: thermonuclear

First tested: 1953

First deployed: 1958

(Specifications for PGM-11A)

Left: *First tested in 1946 at White Sands Proving Ground, the Hermes was a modified V-2 German rocket, utilizing the German aerodynamic configuration. Information that was gathered in the process contributed directly to the development of the US Army Redstone missile. Note the tail fins, which are like those of both V-2 and Redstone. (NASA)*

Opposite: *A Redstone missile on the launch pad at Cape Canaveral, Florida in May 1958. This was the first Block I Tactical System missile and the first Redstone launched by the US Army, specifically by the 217th Field Artillery Missile Battalion, 40th Artillery Group. (NASA Marshall Space Flight Center)*

Test firing a Martin AGM-12 Bullpup from an A-4 Skyhawk. (Martin)

AGM-12 Bullpup

As missiles such as the Sparrow grew out of an effort to wed a guidance system with unguided air-to-air rockets, the Bullpup was a pioneering effort to produce a guided air-to-ground weapon that would improve the accuracy of unguided bombs and rockets against small, critical targets. Though such weapons had been built in Germany and the United States during World War II, the Bullpup was the first successful one to reach operational American service.

The US Navy initiated the project in 1953 at the end of the Korean War, selected a proposal from Martin and ordered the missile produced under the designation ASM-N-7. Initially, it was powered by a solid-fuel rocket, but the program later shifted to a series of Thiokol/Reaction Motors liquid-fuel engines. The XASM-N-7 was first successfully tested in 1955, and the Bullpup reached squadron service in 1959. In the meantime, the US Air Force ordered a variant of the Bullpup under the designation GAM-79, with the name White Lance. Eventually, the Air Force procured the weapon as the GAM-83, using the Bullpup name. In 1963, Bullpups for both services were redesignated as AGM-12.

Because guidance was radio-controlled from the launching aircraft, the pilot had to maintain visual contact throughout the flight profile, which made the missile hard to use. Despite this, Bullpups were widely used during the Vietnam War against targets such as bridges. The results left much to be desired, although the missile was preferable to bombs against highly defended targets.

By the time that Martin ended production in 1969, more than 22,000 Bullpups had been built.

Manufacturer: Glenn L. Martin Company

Length: 10 feet 6 inches (3.2 meters)

Diameter: 12 inches (0.31 meters)

Span (fins): 37 inches (0.94 meters)

Weight: 570 pounds (260 kilograms)

Range: 7 miles (11 kilometers)

Speed: Mach 1.8

Guidance system: line of sight radio control

Propulsion system: Thiokol LR58 liquid-fuel rocket

Warhead: blast fragmentation
(W45 nuclear was optional)

First tested: 1955

First deployed: 1959

(Specifications for AGM-12B)

A Martin MGM-13 (Then TM-76A) Mace missile, seen here on its transport vehicle in 1959. (Martin)

MGM-13 Mace

The Mace was the successor to Martin's Matador cruise missile. Indeed, it originated as the TM-61B Matador B, and was flight- tested as such in 1956. Changes introduced included a longer fuselage with increased volume, meaning more fuel and greater range. Improvements included the autonomous Automatic Terrain Recognition And Navigation (ATRAN) guidance system, a precursor to Terrain Contour Matching (TERCOM) systems. However, ATRAN was limited by the need to compile radar maps of potential targets.

Redesignated as TM-76A and renamed Mace, the missile entered US Air Force squadron service in West Germany in 1959, gradually replacing the Matador. The TM-76A was itself superseded operationally in 1961 by the TM-76B Mace B, which traded ATRAN for inertial guidance. While the earlier Mace was launched from mobile launchers like the Matador, the Mace B was based in fixed launch bunkers, or "coffins." In 1963, the TM-76A and TM-76B were redesignated as MGM-13B and CGM-13C.

Between 1966 and 1971, the Mace was replaced by the US Army

MGM-31A Pershing missile because of the latter's faster reaction time. Many existing Maces were converted for use as target drones.

Manufacturer: Glenn L. Martin Company

Length: 44 feet 9 inches (13.64 meters)

Diameter: 4 feet 6 inches (1.37 meters)

Wingspan: 22 feet 11 inches (6.99 meters)

Weight: 18,750 pounds (8,500 kilograms)

Range: 800 miles (1,300 kilometers)

Speed: 650 mph (1,040 km/h)

Ceiling: 40,000 feet (12,200 meters)

Guidance system: see text

Propulsion system: Allison J33 turbojet with Thiokol solid-fuel rocket booster

Warhead: thermonuclear

First tested: 1956

First deployed: 1959

(Specifications for MGM-13B)

A 1960 test of a container-launched Martin CGM-13 (Then TM-76A) Mace missile. (Martin)

An April 1959 photo of a battery of operational MIM-14 Nike Hercules surface-to-air missiles at a site in southern California. (Author's collection)

MIM-14 Nike Hercules

The successor to the MIM-3 Nike Ajax as the principal anti-aircraft missile defending the United States, the Nike Hercules was deployed into existing Ajax launch complexes in the late 1950s. Meanwhile, radar systems at the ground facilities were also upgraded.

Originally called Nike B and designated as SAM-N-25, the Hercules was a part of the natural evolution of the earlier missile technology. Bell Labs and Western Electric designed the system with improved guidance and radar, and Douglas redesigned the airframe. Among the noticeable latter changes were a slightly longer fuselage and four tail fins rather than three.

While many Hercules would be armed with blast fragmentation warheads, greater range meant interceptions farther from the launch site, paving the way for safely arming the Hercules with a nuclear warhead. The idea was that a nuke exploded anywhere within a Soviet bomber formation would take down most or all of the bombers.

In 1960, a Nike Hercules successfully intercepted a Corporal missile demonstrating a potential for missile defense that predated the modern Ground-Based Midcourse Defense system that was deployed nearly a half century later.

The Nike Hercules entered service in 1958 as Guided Missile M6, and was redesignated as MIM-14 in 1963. Of the roughly 25,000 Nike Hercules that were built, most were of the improved MIM-14B (formerly M6A1) variant.

In addition to their being based in the United States, many Nike Hercules missiles were deployed to Europe by the US Army, as well as being under the control of the armed forces of Belgium, Greece, Italy, the Netherlands and Turkey. Japan also acquired the Nike Hercules for its air defense, and was a leader in retrofitting the missile with solid state electronics.

By the late 1960s, with the threat of a Soviet bomber attack supplanted by that of an ICBM attack, the US Army gradually began the deactivation of its Nike sites across the United States. This was completed by 1974, although the Hercules remained operational with the US Army in Europe until 1984, when it was superseded by the MIM-104 Patriot.

Remnants of many stateside Nike sites still remain. Site SF-88L near San Francisco is almost completely intact and open to the public. It is operated by the National Park Service as a historic site, complete with a complement of inert MIM-14s.

This subterranean bunker containing a MIM-14 Nike Hercules is at the US Army's Nike Site SF-88L in Fort Barry, across the Golden Gate from San Francisco. (Bill Yenne photo)

A MIM-14 Nike Hercules emerges from its bunker at the US Army's Nike Site SF-88L in Fort Barry, across the Golden Gate from San Francisco. (Bill Yenne photo)

Manufacturer: Western Electric/ Douglas Aircraft

Length: 26 feet 10 inches (8.18 meters)
(with booster: 41 feet 1 inch; 12.52 meters)

Diameter: 21 inches (0.53 meters)

Span (fins): 6 feet 2 inches (1.88 meters)

Weight (with booster): 10,710 pounds (4,850 kilograms)

Range: 88 miles (140 kilometers)

Speed: Mach 3.165

Ceiling: 150,000 feet (46,000 meters)

Guidance system: ground control supported by tracking radar

Propulsion system: Thiokol M30 with Hercules M42 booster (both solid-fuel rockets)

Warhead: W37 nuclear or blast fragmentation

First tested: 1955

First deployed: 1958

(Specifications for MIM-14B)

Raised nearly to the vertical, this MIM-14 Nike Hercules is about to be in a typical launch configuration. (Bill Yenne photo)

A Vought RGM-15 (in GQM-15 configuration) Regulus II at a desert airfield in California. (National Archives)

RGM-15 Regulus II

The Regulus II was conceived in 1953 as the higher altitude, supersonic follow-on to the Vought SSM-N-8 (RGM-6) Regulus ship-launched cruise missile. Vought delivered the XRSSM-N-9 prototype missile to the US Navy in 1956 for a year and a half of flight testing with a Wright J65 turbojet engine. Early test missiles were equipped with landing gear so that they could be recovered like pilotless airplanes. The plan was to delete this feature on operational missiles.

Testing with the General Electric J79 intended for operational Regulus IIs began in 1958, with the first successful submarine launch coming on in September. However, with the Polaris Submarine-Launched Ballistic Missile (SLBM) then under development, the US Navy decided to terminate the winged Regulus II at the end of 1958 after around 50 had been built. Five years later, the long-cancelled missile was formally designated as RGM-15A. As with other early winged cruise missiles, some of the surviving Regulus IIs were later used as target drones.

Manufacturer: Vought

Length: 57 feet 6 inches (17.52 meters) (without nose probe)

Diameter: 50 inches (1.27 meters)

Wingspan: 20 feet 1 inch (6.12 meters)

Weight: 23,000 pounds (10,400 kilograms)

Range: 340 miles (550 kilometers)

Speed: Mach 2

Ceiling: 59,000 feet (18,000 meters)

Guidance system: inertial guidance

Propulsion system: General Electric J79 turbojet with Rocketdyne solid-fuel rocket booster

Warhead: W27 thermonuclear

First tested: 1956

First deployed: never

(Specifications for RGM-15A)

*A Convair SM-65A Atlas ICBM on the pad at Point Loma, California. (*Author's collection)

Floodlights cast a ghostly glow on a Convair SM-65A Atlas ICBM at Point Loma, California. (Author's collection)

CGM-16/HGM-16 Atlas

The first American Intercontinental Ballistic Missile (ICBM), the Atlas had its roots in Project MX-774, which evolved though the Hiroc program discussed in the Introduction. The US Air Force terminated these activities in 1947 but Convair continued its studies of a large intercontinental vehicle. In 1951, Air Force interest was renewed and the concept officially revived as Project MX-1593. The first vehicles initially received "X-plane" designations, with X-11 being a single engine test vehicle and X-12 having three engines. Operational Atlas missiles were designated as the B-65 "bomber," and later changed as SM-65 "Strategic Missiles."

The first Atlas to fly was the XSM-65A "Atlas A" in 1957, and the first production variant was the SM-65D, which entered service in 1959.

To minimize vehicle weight, Convair adopted the unique design of using the liquid fuel inside to make the structure rigid. The Atlas was limp, like an enormous Mylar balloon until it was "inflated" by fuel inside.

The launch of a Convair SM-65A Atlas ICBM from Point Loma, California. (Author's collection)

Atlas ICBMs on the factory floor at Convair's Kearny Mesa facility near San Diego. (Author's collection)

In 1955, as President Eisenhower placed the highest national defense priority on the development of the ICBM, and in 1957 Convair created Convair-Astronautics as a separate operating division for production of the Atlas. This was housed at a 250-acre facility constructed on Kearny Mesa in San Diego County.

After the first successful Atlas launch in September 1957, the missile reached its intended range of 700 miles in a test in December.

In 1958, the Air Force's Strategic Air Command (SAC) activated the first Atlas unit, the 4320th (later 706th) Strategic Missile Wing at Francis E. Warren AFB in Wyoming. By August 1959, there were four active Atlas D units in SAC, and three Atlas E units were activated in 1960. By the end of 1962, six Atlas F squadrons had also been added. By this time, Convair had delivered 30 Atlas Ds, 32 Atlas Es and 80 Atlas Fs to 13 active SAC squadrons. The later Atlas variants were distinguished by a higher gross weight and a range of 11,500 miles.

The original basing mode for the Atlas was in a hardened "coffin," with missiles raised from horizontal to vertical. The Atlas F, however was configured for launch from underground silos. In 1963, the coffin-based Atlases were designated as CGM-16, and the silo-based Atlas F became HGM-16F.

An Atlas ICBM is raised into the Static Tower by Convair crews during development tests of the mechanism that would elevate and lower operational missiles. When deployed, early Atlases were stored horizontally in "coffins" and erected into vertical firing position thusly. (Author's collection).

A Convair SM-65E (later CGM-16E) Atlas ICBM on the pad at Point Loma, California. (Author's collection)

The launch of a Convair SM-65E (later CGM-16E) Atlas ICBM at Point Loma, California. (Author's collection)

The Atlas era was short-lived. In 1964, SAC began to implement the 1961 Defense Department plan to replace the Atlas and Titan ICBMs with the newer Minuteman. They were replaced because the cost of maintaining a liquid-fuel rocket in a constant state of readiness was greater than for the solid-fuel Minuteman.

By June 1965, all of the Atlas ICBM fleet had been retired, but the Atlas continued to evolve as a launch vehicle for boosting spacecraft into orbit. This use of the Atlas had paralleled that of the ICBM variant. Among many other space applications, the Atlas was also used for all of the orbital flights of NASA's Mercury manned spaceflight program, beginning with John Glenn's February 1962 mission in *Friendship 7*.

In the 1980s, General Dynamics developed a solid-fuel launch vehicle that it called Atlas II, but which had little in common with the original Atlas. This program was sold to Martin Marietta (now Lockheed Martin) in 1993, who developed later Atlas vehicles, such as Atlas V, which are still widely used to launch payloads into orbit.

Manufacturer: Convair Division of General Dynamics

Height: 82 feet 6 inches (25.15 meters) (with re-entry vehicle for payload)

Diameter: 10 feet (3.05 meters)

Weight: 260,000 pounds (118,000 kilograms)

Range: 11,500 miles (18,500 kilometers)

Speed: 15,500 mph (25,000 km/h)

Ceiling: 500 miles (800 kilometers) (outside the Earth's atmosphere)

Guidance system: inertial guidance

Propulsion system: 2 Rocketdyne LR89 liquid-fuel boosters, with Rocketdyne LR105 vernier liquid-fuel rockets

Warhead: W38 thermonuclear

First tested: 1957

First deployed: 1959

(Specifications for CGM-16E and HGM-16F)

Top left: *The aluminum skin of an SM-65E (later CGM-16E) gleams in the spotlights as it rests on the pad.* (Author's collection)

Left: *The captive firing of a liquid-fueled Rocketdyne engines on an SM-65E (later CGM-16E) as Convair's Sycamore Canyon facility.* (Author's collection)

Opposite: *A CGM-16F Atlas missile is launched from Vandenberg AFB.* (DoD)

A 1959 helicopter view of a PGM-17 (then SM-75) Thor launch facility. (Author's collection)

PGM-17 Thor

The Thor program was initiated in 1954 during the lengthy development of the Atlas ICBM as an urgent measure aimed at getting a less complex ballistic missile deployed sooner. The necessary compromise was a shorter range Intermediate Range Ballistic Missile (IRBM).

The urgency was fueled by current ballistic missile developments in the Soviet Union, but there was also a bit of interservice rivalry. Like Atlas, Thor was a US Air Force program, undertaken at a time when the US Army was still competing with the "blue-suiters" with its own robust and ambitious ballistic missile program, specifically, its Jupiter IRBM. Both missiles are also referred to in some sources as Medium-Range Ballistic Missiles (MRBM).

Indeed, the Thor program adopted the same Rocketdyne liquid-fuel rocket engine already in development for the Jupiter. Thor also borrowed the inertial guidance system in development for the Atlas program, another step which accelerated the Thor program.

Designated as strategic missile XSM-75, the first Thor was delivered for testing in October 1956, though the first successful launch came in September 1957. Douglas built more than 35 XSM-75s and more than 75 SM-75s, which became PGM-17As in 1963.

A PGM-17 (then SM-75) Thor is prepared for a dawn launch in the early summer of 1962. (Author's collection)

Because of their range, the missiles could not reach the Soviet Union from the United States, so they were forward-deployed to the United Kingdom, where they became operational with the Royal Air Force Bomber Command in 1959. By the end of 1961, there were 20 three-missile squadrons on alert between Yorkshire and Suffolk. They remained in service for only four years.

Though Thor was soon replaced by ICBMs, it went on to be adapted by NASA for use as a space launch vehicle. Using the Able upper stage, Thor was used to launch many important spacecraft projects during the 1960s. Douglas (McDonnell Douglas after 1967) eventually developed the Thor into the extremely successful Delta series of space launch vehicles. A Boeing product since 1997, the program is still going strong in the twenty-first century.

A Thor Intermediate Range Ballistic Missile (IRBM) in Royal Air Force markings, circa 1959. (Author's collection)

A PGM-17 (then SM-75) Thor on the launch pad, ready for launch. (US Air Force)

Manufacturer: Douglas Aircraft

Height: 65 feet (19.8 meters)

Diameter: 8 feet (2.4 meters)

Weight: 11,000 pounds (16,100 kilograms)

Range: 1,500 miles (2,400 kilometers)

Speed: 10,000 mph (16,000 km/h)

Ceiling: 300 miles (480 kilometers)

Guidance system: inertial guidance

Propulsion system: Rocketdyne LR79 liquid-fuel booster, with Rocketdyne LR101 vernier liquid-fuel rockets

Warhead: W39 thermonuclear

First tested: 1957

First deployed: 1959

(Specifications for PGM-17A)

A 1958 view of an MGM-18 (then designated as M4) LaCrosse on its mobile launcher. (US Army)

MGM-18 Lacrosse

The Lacrosse program originated in 1947 as a short-range artillery missile for the US Marine Corps which could carry either conventional or nuclear munitions. As with many early missile systems, the project and its guidance system were developed within the halls of academia, specifically Cornell University and the Applied Physics Laboratory (APL) at Johns Hopkins University, where the US Navy's Regulus was born. Indeed, the original Lacrosse designation, SAM-N-9 was later transferred to the Regulus. The airframe was built by Martin.

Because the Defense Department wished to concentrate short-range, land-based nuke programs within one service, the Lacrosse program was transferred in 1950 to the US Army, and designated as SSM-G-12 (later SSM-A-12). It was understood that Marine units would eventually have access to operational Lacrosses, but the Marines never availed themselves of this.

The first flight of an XSSM-A-12 came in 1954, but a flight of a production ready Lacrosse did not come until 1957. The Lacrosse was finally deployed to operational US Army units in 1960 under the guided artillery missile

designation M4. Necessity for the operator to have a line-of-sight view of the target limited the potential utility of the Lacrosse in battle, so they were pulled out of service shortly after being redesignated as MGM-18A in 1963.

Manufacturer: Glenn L. Martin Company
Length: 19 feet 2 inches (5.84 meters)
Diameter: 20.5 inches (0.52 meters)
Span (fins): 4 feet 8 inches (1.42 meters)
Weight: 2,300 pounds (1,040 kilograms)
Range: 12 miles (19 kilometers)
Speed: Mach 0.8
Guidance system: radio controlled line-of-sight
Propulsion system: Thiokol solid-fuel rocket
Warhead: high explosive or W40 nuclear
First tested: 1954
First deployed: 1960
(Specifications for MGM-18A)

PGM-19 Jupiter

The Jupiter program originated in 1954 at Wernher von Braun's workshop within the US Army's Redstone Arsenal, and was essentially an evolution of the Redstone program. Like the Redstone and von Braun's wartime V-2, it was liquid fueled. As with the Redstone, the prime contractor for Jupiter would be Chrysler.

When Secretary of Defense Charles Wilson decreed in 1956 that the US Air Force should control all ballistic missiles with a range greater than 200 miles, Jupiter was transferred to that service under the "B for bomber" designation B-78 (later SM-78). It preceded Thor chronologically but received its designation later, hence the higher number. In 1963, the Jupiter was redesignated as PGM-19A.

Like the Douglas Thor, the Jupiter was an Intermediate Range Ballistic Missile (IRBM), although it was slightly smaller than the Thor. Flight testing of pre-production vehicles began in 1955, and the first flight test of a fully configured Jupiter IRBM occurred in May 1957.

The Jupiters were deployed overseas to put them within range of targets in the Soviet Union. Detachments were placed in Italy and Turkey, where they were on station beginning in 1960. As part of the secret understanding between President John Kennedy and Soviet Premier Nikita Khrushchev that ended the Cuban Missile Crisis in 1962, the Jupiters and their launch infrastructure were withdrawn from Turkey. By 1965, all of the Jupiters everywhere had been withdrawn from active duty. Advances in ICBM technology had rendered them obsolete.

After the Jupiter IRBM was transferred to the Air Force, the Army and von Braun's team continued the parallel development of a Jupiter family of space launch vehicles, which culminated in the Jupiter C. On January 31, 1958, a Jupiter C was used to launch Explorer 1, the first American satellite in orbit.

Above left: *A PGM-19A (then SM-78A) Jupiter A on the pad in Air Force markings. April 1959.* (US Army)

Above: *The May 14, 1959 launch of an SM-78A (PGM-19A) Jupiter A.* (US Army)

Manufacturer: Chrysler

Height: 60 feet 4 inches (18. 40 meters)

Diameter: 8 feet 9 inches (2.67 meters)

Weight: 110,000 pounds (50,000 kilograms)

Range: 1,850 miles (2,980 kilometers)

Speed: 10,000 mph (16,100 km/h)

Ceiling: 380 miles (610 kilometers)

Guidance system: inertial guidance

Propulsion system: Rocketdyne LR79 liquid-fuel rocket

Warhead: W49 thermonuclear

First tested: 1955

First deployed: 1960

(Specifications for PGM-19A)

A McDonnell GAM-72 (later ADM-20) Quail air-launched decoy missile. (Author's collection)

ADM-20 Quail

Resembling in size and shape a winged refrigerator, the clumsy-looking Quail actually had the same radar signature as a B-52 bomber. The idea was for a decoy which would like exactly like a bomber on radarscope, thereby misdirecting enemy air defenses away from actual bombers.

Beginning in the early 1950s, the US Air Force looked into developing self-propelled decoys that could be carried aboard bombers such as the B-36 and B-47,

which were tasked potentially with flying missions into Soviet air space. In turn, the service commissioned a series of decoy vehicles that were numbered sequentially from 71 through 74. These were the Convair GAM-71 Buck Duck, the McDonnell GAM-72 Green Quail (later Quail), the Fairchild SM-73 Bull Goose, and the unnamed Convair Project MX-2223, which was designated as SM-74. Of these, only the Quail and Bull Goose were ever flown. The Quail alone reached operational status and remained in service long enough to receive an "M for Missile" designation.

A GAM-72 (later ADM-20) Quail in Strategic Air Command markings. The technician working on the missile provides an idea of scale. On radar, though, the Quail appeared vastly larger. (Author's collection)

The first test flight of a powered Quail occurred in August 1958 after glide tests beginning late in 1957. Operational Quails entered service with SAC units in early 1961, being flown aboard B-52s exclusively. Their wings could be folded down so that eight Quails could be carried in a B-52 bomb bay, though operationally the bombers carried fewer.

The Quail's autopilot could be preprogrammed for a flight path simulating that of a bomber, and an infrared device aboard mimicked the heat signature of a bomber's engines.

Redesignated as ADM-20 in 1963, more than 500 Quails were delivered. They remained in service until 1978, by which time radar technology had improved to the point where the Soviets could distinguish bombers from Quails.

Manufacturer: McDonnell Aircraft
Length: 12 feet 11 inches (3.94 meters)
Height: 3 feet 4 inches (1.02 meters)
Wingspan: 5 feet 5 inches (1.65 meters)
Weight: 1,200 pounds (540 kilograms)
Range: 400 miles (650 kilometers)
Speed: Mach 0.95
Ceiling: 50,000 feet (15,200 meters)
Guidance system: preprogrammed autopilot with terrain matching capability
Propulsion system: General Electric J85 turbojet
First tested: 1957
First deployed: 1961
(Specifications for ADM-20B)

An Aérospatiale (Nord) SS.10 (later AGM-21) wire-guided anti-tank weapon, at Redstone Arsenal in March 1961. (US Army)

MGM-21

The use of tube-launched rockets against tanks was a mainstay of American infantry operations during World War II. Most units were equipped with the famous M1 Bazooka, firing M6 aimed, but unguided, rockets. After the war, numerous such weapons proliferated in armies around the world. The US Army's M72 Light Anti-tank Weapon (LAW) and the widely used Rocket-Propelled Grenade (RPG) launcher are among such weapons.

An obvious step taken after the war was toward small *guided* anti-tank missiles for infantry use. Germany had already taken that step during World War II. Dr. Max Kramer of Germany's Air Transport Research Institute, the *Deutsche Versuchsanstalt fur Luftfahrt* (DVL) developed both the X-4 air-to-air missile, and the X-7 anti-tank missile. Both were wire-guided weapons in which the missiles trailed a wire through which the operator controlled them.

Kramer's X-7 *Rotkappchen* (Little Red Riding Hood) was born out of a crash program initiated at the start of 1944 and aimed at developing a means of stopping masses of Soviet tanks. Several hundred X-7s reached front line troops for "evaluation" purposes, and some were probably "evaluated" against Soviet tanks.

After World War II, the idea of using wire to guide anti-tank missiles languished for some time. Neither the Soviet Union nor the United States took up Kramer's idea until the 1950s, and no such weapon was used again in combat until the 1960s. France was the first nation to create a postwar wire-guided anti-tank weapon. The

Arsenal de l'Aeronautique dusted off Kramer's notebook in 1948 and created an all-new X-7-sized missile that went into production as the Nord Aviation 5200 series (SS-10). This program, in turn led to the *Nord Engin Téléguidé Anti-Char* (ENTAC), or Remotely Guided Anti-Tank weapon.

The US Army evaluated the SS-10 in 1954, later using it as the basis for its first wire-guided missile, the larger SAM-A-23 Dart. In 1959, after the Dart was cancelled, they briefly acquired the SS-10, but soon replaced it with the ENTAC. In 1963, the phased-out SS-10 was redesignated as MGM-21A, and the ENTAC was designated as MGM-32A.

Manufacturer: Nord Aviation

Length: 34 inches (0.86 meters)

Diameter: 6.5 inches (0.17 meters)

Span (fins): 29.5 inches (0.75 meters)

Weight: 33 pounds (15 kilograms)

Range: 1 mile (1,600 meters)

Speed: 180 mph (290 km/h)

Guidance system: wire-guided line-of-sight

Propulsion system: solid-fuel rocket

Warhead: armor-piercing high explosive

First tested: 1954

First deployed: 1959

(Specifications for MGM-21A)

The Aérospatiale (Nord) SS.11 (later AGM-22) anti-armor missile aboard a UH-1 test helicopter at the Redstone Arsenal. (US Army)

AGM-22

This weapon evolved as an air-launched variation on the Nord SS-10 that was developed for the French army and deployed in 1956 as the SS-11. First evaluated by the US Army in 1959, it was acquired for use aboard UH-1 helicopters, and produced in the United States under license by General Electric. Nearly 200,000 were built in France and the United States.

Designated as AGM-22, the missile saw limited use throughout the Vietnam War. Despite the fact that hitting a target from the air with a wire-guided missile under combat conditions proved impractical, AGM-22s remained with units in Southeast Asia until 1972, and in the US Army inventory until 1978.

A proposed air-launch configuration of the Aérospatiale (Nord) SS.11 (later AGM-22) wire-guided anti-armor missiles. (US Army)

Manufacturer: Nord (Aérospatiale after 1970) and General Electric

Length: 47 inches (1.2 meters)

Diameter: 6.5 inches (0.17 meters)

Weight: 66 pounds (30 kilograms)

Range: 9,800 feet (3,100 meters)

Speed: 425 mph (685 km/h)

Guidance system: wire-guided line-of-sight

Propulsion system: solid-fuel rocket

Warhead: armor-piercing high explosive

First tested: 1959

First deployed: 1961

(Specifications for AGM-22B)

MIM-23 Hawk surface-to-air missiles are attached to the launcher at Spruce Cape on Alaska's Kodiak Island during Exercise Brim Frost in February 1985 (US Army photo by Sergeant Zachs)

MIM-23 Hawk

A mobile surface-to-air missile, the Hawk served for more than four decades with US forces without downing a single enemy aircraft. However, Israel used the Hawk to destroy around three- dozen enemy aircraft in 1969-1973, and Iran shot down at least that many Iraqi aircraft with Hawks during the 1980s. The French army also shot down a Libyan Tu-22 bomber over Chad in 1987 with an MIM-23B Hawk.

Hawk batteries were seen deployed around Washington, DC following the September 11, 2001 attack on the Pentagon.

The Hawk anti-aircraft missile project originated in 1952 with the US Army, who sought a medium-range, radar-guided surface-to-air missile to protect its troops in the field from air attack. The Hawk was first test flown in 1954 under the designation XSAM-A-18, and redesignated as guided missile M3 a year later. Hawks were first deployed on their signature mobile launchers in 1959 by the Army, and in 1960 by the Marines.

Initially deployed to American forces in Europe, Hawks soon stood guard in the southern United States during the 1962 Cuban Missile Crisis. In 1965, the Marines first sent MIM-23A Hawks to Vietnam to guard their base at Danang.

Also in 1965, Israel became one of an eventual two-dozen foreign operators of the Hawk. During the 1970s,

Iran acquired American military hardware, and was a major Hawk user. Between them, Israel and Iran accounted for the majority of aircraft downed by Hawks in combat, although the exact number is unconfirmed. Kuwait claimed more than a dozen Iraqi aircraft shot down during the 1990 invasion, of which two are confirmed.

Other export customers included Singapore, Saudi Arabia, South Korea and most European NATO members.

Through the years, a number of upgrades to both the Hawks and their radar control systems were introduced. The first major upgrade was the Improved Hawk, or "I-Hawk" program of the late 1960s and early 1970s, which resulted in the MIM-23B, a missile with more precise guidance, a more powerful motor and a larger warhead. This was followed by a three-stage Product Improvement Plan (PIP), which unfolded into the 1980s, improving the guidance systems and progressively upgrading the electronics.

To counter potential electronic jamming threats expected in a Central Europe war, electronic counter-countermeasures (ECCM) upgrades in the early 1980s resulted in the MIM-23C and MIM-23D. Further improvements resulted in the MIM-23E and MIM-23F, introduced in 1990, and in variants up to MIM-23L and MIM-23M by 1995. By this time, around 40,000 missiles had been built over four decades.

Though the Hawk was phased out by the United States early in the twenty-first century, it continued in service in more than a dozen countries.

Top: *A right side view of a US Army M727 self-propelled launch vehicle for MIM-23 Hawk surface-to-air missiles in Germany's Black Forest in 1973.* (US Army)

Above: *US Army personnel from the 11th Air Defense Artillery Brigade deploy an MIM-23B Hawk surface-to-air missile system during Operation Desert Shield.* (US Army photo by Specialist Henry)

Manufacturer: Raytheon

Length: 16 feet 6 inches (5.03 meters)

Diameter: 14.5 inches (0.374 meters)

Span (fins): 3 feet 11 inches (1.93 meters)

Weight: 1,400 pounds (635 kilograms)

Range: 25 miles (40 kilometers)

Speed: Mach 2.5

Ceiling: 58,000 feet (17,700 meters)

Guidance system: semi-active radar homing

Propulsion system: Aerojet M112 solid-fuel rocket

Warhead: blast fragmentation

First tested: 1954

First deployed: 1959

(Specifications for MIM-23B)

A close-up view of a Mk.13 guided missile launcher armed with an RIM-24 Tartar surface-to-air missile on the deck of the guided missile frigate USS Gary during the commissioning ceremony at Long Beach in November 1984. (US Navy photo by PH2 Jesus Diaz)

A bow view of the Australian guided missile frigate HMAS Darwin launching an RIM-24 Tartar missile during Exercise RIMPAC (Pacific Rim) '86. (US Navy photo by PH1 Javner)

RIM-24 Tartar

Technically, the Tartar was a variation on Convair's Terrier ship-launched surface-to-air missile for the US Navy. It was smaller, lacking the booster stage of the Terrier, and was conceived specifically as a weapon to counter low-flying enemy aircraft. Rather than a beam-riding guidance system as the Terrier, the Tartar used semi-active radar homing.

The RIM-24A variant first deployed in 1962 was quickly superseded by the RIM-24B Improved Tartar, with all-around improvements to guidance, propulsion and performance. Later in the decade, the Tartar Reliability Improvement Program (TRIP) resulted in the RIM-24C, which had solid state electronics, better countermeasures and multiple-target tracking capability.

The Tartar's career was short-lived, however, as it was replaced by the Raytheon RIM-66, which was first deployed in 1967.

Manufacturer: General Dynamics, Convair Division

Length: 15 feet 6 inches (4.7 meters)

Diameter: 13.5 inches (0.34 meters)

Span (fins): 42 inches (1.07 meters)

Weight: 1,310 pounds (600 kilograms)

Range: 19 miles (30 kilometers)

Speed: Mach 1.8

Ceiling: 65,000 feet (20,000 meters)

Guidance system: semi-active radar homing

Propulsion system: Aerojet Mk.27 solid-fuel rocket

Warhead: high explosive

First tested: 1958

First deployed: 1962

(Specifications for RIM-24B)

An LGM-25 Titan II of the Strategic Air Command 381st Strategic Missile Wing in its silo at McConnell AFB in 1963. (US Air Force)

HGM-25/LGM-25 Titan

The largest of the Strategic Air Command arsenal of ICBMs was the aptly named Titan. The Titan I stood 98 feet tall, and the Titan II was 103 feet. Their respective launch weights were 110 and 165 tons. They were much heavier than the contemporary Atlas because of their size and the use of a rigid structure, unlike the "inflatable" Atlas.

Titan was the first United States ICBM project that began after President Eisenhower made ICBM technology the top defense priority in 1955. Originally conceived under the same Weapons System 107 program as Atlas, the Titan ICBM would be developed and built by Martin under the

Rising from an underground silo at Vandenberg AFB, an LGM-25 Titan II begins a test flight. (Air Force Space Division)

Left: *Airman 1st Class Jane Hoapili, a Titan ballistic missile analyst technician with the 532nd Strategic Missile Squadron, at work at McConnell AFB in March 1981.* (US Air Force)

"B for Bomber" designation B-68. Later designated as Strategic Missile SM-68A, the Titan I would be a two-stage, liquid-fueled ICBM utilizing both radio and all-inertial guidance, with a range of more than 6,000 miles. Whereas the Atlas ICBMs were designed to be surface launched, the Titan was always a silo launched weapon.

The first successful Titan I launch occurred in February 1959, and SAC made 31 successful long-range test firings on the Pacific Missile Range in 1961. The following year, two squadrons of SAC's 703rd Strategic Missile Wing became operational with the Titan I, now designated HGM-25A. By 1965, the Titan Is were phased out in favor of the larger LGM-25C Titan II, which had a range of 9,300 miles. The "H" prefix identified the "A" model as silo-stored, but taken out for launch. The "L" identified the "C" model as silo-launched. The "B" models were a handful of Titan Is used for inertial guidance tests and not deployed operationally.

First tested in November 1961, the Titan II became operational in June 1963 with the 570th Strategic Missile Squadron. By year's end, SAC had six squadrons active with nine missile sites each. Eventually, 135 Titan IIs would be produced. The nine-megaton W53 thermonuclear warheads were the largest deployed on a United States ICBM during the Cold War, and they represented more than a quarter of SAC megatonnage, even though Titans were outnumbered ten to one by Minutemen. At the peak of Titan deployment in 1965, SAC had 56 LGM-25As and 59 CGM-25Cs. After the Titan I retirement, the peak number of Titan IIs was 63 in 1967.

In 1981, because of maintenance issues, the Department of Defense initiated Operation Rivet Cap, an immediate deactivation of the 56 remaining liquid-fueled Titan IIs. The last Titan II was retired from Little Rock AFB, Arkansas in August 1987, leaving the solid-fuel Minutemen as the principal American ICBM.

Like the Atlas — but unlike the Minuteman — the Titan would go on to be adapted for a long life as a space launch vehicle that continued past the turn of the century.

Manufacturer: Glenn L. Martin Company

Height: 103 feet (31.40 meters)

Diameter: 10 feet (3.05 meters)

Weight: 330,000 pounds (150,000 kilograms)

Range: 9,300 miles (15,000 kilometers)

Speed: 15,000 mph (24,000 km/h)

Ceiling: 600 miles (960 meters)

Guidance system: inertial guidance (later Universal Space Guidance System)

Propulsion system: 2 Aerojet LR87 (first stage), 1 Aerojet LR91 (second stage, both liquid-fuel rockets

Warhead: W53 thermonuclear

First tested: 1958

First deployed: 1962

(Specifications for LGM-25C)

AIM-26 Nuclear Falcon

As the name suggests, the AIM-26 was a larger, nuclear armed variation on the AIM-4 Falcon family of air-to-air missiles. The project originated in 1956, aimed at developing a missile that could be fired into a bomber formation, where it could potentially destroy a mass of enemy aircraft in a single detonation. It could also be used to destroy a missile or aircraft that was moving too fast for a conventional guidance system to allow a direct hit.

The first round of Nuclear Falcons were designated as XGAR-5 and XGAR-6, the former with semi-active radar guidance, the latter with infrared guidance. Neither was built, but the project was revived in 1959 with the radar-guided XGAR-11 project. This missile was tested in 1961, and became operational as the GAR-11 with the US Air Force Air Defense Command interceptors a year later.

The nuclear GAR-11s were complemented by GAR-11As, which were armed with conventional warheads. Most of the latter were exported to Sweden, and later manufactured there. In 1963, the two missiles were redesignated as AIM-26A and AIM-26B.

The conventional AIM-26B had a career in Sweden that lasted until the 1990s, but the US Air Force phased out their AIM-26As in 1971, by which time the Soviet bomber threat had faded, and guidance technology made it possible for conventional missiles to achieve hits against fast-moving targets.

Manufacturer: Hughes

Length: 84 inches (2.14 meters)

Diameter: 11 inches (0.28meters)

Span (fins): 24 inches (0.62 meters)

Weight: 200 pounds (92 kilograms)

Range: 10 miles (16 kilometers)

Speed: Mach 2

Guidance system: radar homing

Propulsion system: Thiokol M60 solid-fuel rocket

Warhead: W54 nuclear

First tested: 1960

First deployed: 1961

(Specifications for AIM-26A)

A UGM-27 Polaris A3 fleet ballistic missile lifts off from the nuclear-powered strategic missile submarine USS Robert E. Lee *on November 20, 1978.* (US Navy)

Lockheed UGM-27 Polaris

Beginning in the late 1940s, the US Navy evaluated submarine based, surface-launched cruise missiles, and later deployed such weapons in the RGM-6 Regulus I. The obvious next step for a service keen on developing a strategic nuclear strike capability (independent of the rival US Air Force) was a ballistic missile that could be launched against the Soviet heartland from a *submerged* submarine.

Having toyed with the idea of adapting a variant of the US Army's Jupiter Intermediate Range Ballistic Missile (IRBM), the US Navy turned to Lockheed for an all-new Fleet Ballistic Missile (FBM), or Submarine-Launched Ballistic Missile (SLBM). The Navy initiated the Polaris program in 1956, the same year that the Soviet navy conducted the first submerged launch of the R-21 ballistic missile. Polaris would be a crash program aimed at creating the first ballistic missile capable of *both* intercontinental range and of being launched underwater.

The test launch of a British Royal Navy Polaris missile from Cape Canaveral on May 19, 1980. (DoD)

Lockheed was charged with this enormous engineering challenge, and program moved relatively quickly. The first generation Polaris A1 (later UGM-27A) would achieve its first launch from a submerged submarine in July 1960, and the first Polaris equipped submarine was on patrol four months after that.

The two-stage Polaris A1 had its first submerged launch in July 1960 from the USS *George Washington* off Cape Canaveral, Florida. It was followed by a second launch three hours later.

In 1959, Lockheed had already begun work on the Polaris A2 (UGM-27B), which was first tested in November 1960, with a first submerged launch in October 1961 from the USS *Ethan Allen*, the first submarine designed from the keel up as a nuclear-powered, ballistic missile submarine. The A2 had the same 54-inch diameter as the A1, so that it could fit the same launch tubes as the A1. The A2 became operational in June 1962 aboard the *Ethan Allen*.

The longer range Polaris A3 (UGM-27C) SLBM was within two inches of the same size as the A2, thus fitting the same tubes as either of its predecessors. Like the US Air Force land-based Minuteman family, the Polaris family was now making the transition from a single nuclear warhead to multiple reentry vehicles.

The first A3 test launch occurred at Cape Canaveral in August 1962, and the first submerged launch was from the USS *Andrew Jackson* in October 1963. The Polaris A3 was first used to equip an operational submarine on patrol with the Atlantic Fleet when the USS *Daniel Webster* put to sea with 16 A3s in September 1964. Three months later the USS *Daniel Boone* became the first A3-equipped

submarine on patrol in the Pacific. Eventually, the A3/UGM-27C variant replaced all previous Polaris types in operational US Navy submarines.

In 1963, the British Royal Navy also undertook to acquire the Polaris for its Resolution Class ballistic missile submarines. Italy seriously considered the Polaris for deployment aboard surface ships. The project was later terminated, but only after one cruiser was modified with Polaris firing tubes.

Beginning in 1962, Lockheed and the US Navy undertook studies of an SLBM that would have a great capacity to evade the missile defense system that the Soviet Union was known to be constructing. This led to the Polaris B3 concept, which involved increasing the missile's gross weight and expanding the diameter to 74 inches. New systems included the warm gas reaction attitude control system code named Mailman.

Both single and multiple warheads configurations were considered for the B3. At the same time, the US Air Force and General Electric were developing the Mk.12 multiple-target reentry vehicle for the Minuteman, and it was decided to incorporate these into the next generation Polaris. There was considerable discussion over whether to use only the Mk.12, or to also include additional, smaller warheads. The latter configuration was nicknamed "Flexible Flyer" after the popular sled that many of the engineers had used as children.

By 1964, the design for the US Navy's new SLBM had evolved so far that it was decided to create a new family name to distinguish it from the earlier Polaris family. The Polaris B3 was abandoned in favor of a new missile, the UGM-73 Poseidon C3.

Manufacturer: Lockheed Missiles & Space Company

Height: 32 feet 4 inches (9.86 meters)

Diameter: 4 feet 6 inches (1.4 meters)

Weight: 35,700 pounds (16,200 kilograms)

Range: 2,900 miles (4,600 kilometers)

Speed: 8,000 mph (13,000 km/h)

Ceiling: 500 miles (800 meters)

Guidance system: inertial guidance

Propulsion system: Aerojet (first stage) and Hercules (second stage) solid-fueled rockets

Warhead: three W58 thermonuclear

First tested: 1960 (first submerged launch)

First deployed: 1960

(Specifications for UGM-27C Polaris A3)

A low level test flight of a GAM-77 (later AGM-28) Hound Dog cruise missile over the desert Southwest. (Author's collection)

AGM-28 Hound Dog

The Hound Dog was conceived and deployed as an air-launched cruise missile, or stand-off attack missile, to extend the reach of US Air Force Strategic Air Command

A large number of GAM-77 (later AGM-28) Hound Dog cruise missiles on the factory floor at the North American Space and Information Systems Division in Downey, California. (Author's collection)

An artist conception of an AGM-28 Hound Dog, marked with the Strategic Air Command shield, headed for its target. A B-52 is banking away in the distance. (Author's collection)

bombers by allowing them to strike heavily defended targets without endangering aircrews. As such, it was a harbinger of a genre of missiles that are still a standard part of Air Force strategic doctrine. Indeed, the missile was originally designated as the B-77 bomber, though it was deployed as GAM-77. The Hound Dog's predecessor, the B-63 (later GAM-63) Rascal, was technically the first Air Force stand-off missile, but it was not operationally deployed.

Amazingly, there is to definitive answer to the popular assumption that the name Hound Dog is a reference to the Jerry Lieber-Mike Stoller song of the same name that was made immensely popular by Elvis Presley in 1956. No other probable source for the name has been brought to light.

The Air Force initiated the project in 1959, and contracted with North American to develop the missile as Weapon System 131. The company relied heavily on its experience with the technologically advanced X-10 and SM-64 Navaho ballistic missile projects which had been ongoing for several years. The Hound Dog inertial guidance system was adapted from that of the Navaho.

The first test firing of the XGAM-77 prototype came in April 1959, with the first guided, air-launched flight four months later. The first Hound Dog was in service with SAC by the end of the year.

Operationally, two missiles were carried by a single B-52 on underwing pylons. They could then be launched nearly 800 miles from the target, allowing the B-52 to

turn for home before they struck the target. Hound Dogs, now designated as AGM-28A, were deployed quickly, reaching a peak inventory of 593 in service with SAC by 1963. Eventually, nearly 500 missiles were modified to have a smaller radar cross section and redesignated as AGM-28B.

The Air Force intended to supersede the Hound Dog with the larger AGM-48 Skybolt missile, but when this was cancelled, the Hound Dog remained operational until 1978, with more than 300 deployed as late as 1975.

Manufacturer: North American Aviation

Length: 42 feet 6 inches (13 meters)

Diameter: 28 inches (0.7 meters)

Wingspan: 12 feet (3.7 meters)

Weight: 10,000 pounds (4,500 kilograms)

Range: 700 miles (1,100 kilometers)

Speed: Mach 2.1

Ceiling: 55,000 feet (16,800 meters)

Guidance system: inertial guidance

Propulsion system: Pratt & Whitney J52 turbojet

Warhead: W28 thermonuclear

First tested: 1959

First deployed: 1959

(Specifications for AGM-28B)

A US Army master sergeant eyes a JPL/Sperry MGM-29 Sergeant. (US Army)

The launch of a JPL/Sperry MGM-29 Sergeant. (US Army)

MGM-29 Sergeant

Just as sergeant is the next highest US Army rank from corporal, the US Army's Sergeant tactical surface-to-surface missile superseded the Corporal missile. The Sergeant evolved from the Hermes program which ran in parallel to the original Corporal program.

Briefly designated as SSM-A-27, the Sergeant was developed by the Redstone Arsenal as the XM15 artillery missile, and about 500 production M15 Sergeants were built by Sperry. The first test launch came in 1956, with the first operational deployment in 1962. Like the Corporal, the Sergeant was launched from a mobile launcher. Unlike the liquid-fueled Corporal, the Sergeant's solid-fuel engine made it easier to maintain and prepare for launch. The launch sequence took about an hour, compared for nine with the Corporal, which had to be fueled before launch.

Redesignated as MGM-29A in 1963, the Sergeant remained in service with the US Army until 1977, and with the German Bundeswehr until 1979. In the 1960s, the Sergeant was also adapted as the second stage of the Scout space launch vehicle.

Manufacturer: Sperry

Height: 34 feet 6 inches (10.5 meters)

Diameter: 31 inches (0.8 meters)

Weight: 10,000 pounds (4,570 kilograms)

Range: 90 miles (140 kilometers)

Speed: Mach 1 plus

Guidance system: inertial guidance

Propulsion system: Thiokol solid-fuel rocket

Warhead: W52 thermonuclear

First tested: 1956

First deployed: 1962

(Specifications for MGM-29A)

A Minuteman I missile is fired from Vandenberg AFB's Launch Facility 03 in June 1978. (US Air Force)

LGM-30 Minuteman

The Minuteman is America's longest serving Intercontinental Ballistic Missile (ICBM), and probably the most important offensive missile system in the history of the United States arsenal. It was also the world's first solid-fuel ICBM. As such, it offered virtually instantaneous reaction time, compared to the hours that it took to fuel and prepare the liquid-fuel Atlases and Titans. As such, the Minuteman outlived its early contemporaries to remain as a key fixture of the American nuclear deterrent force from the 1960s to beyond the turn of the century.

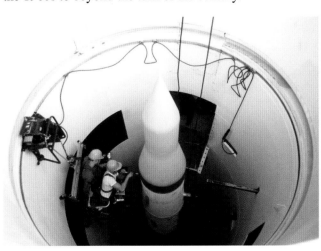

The Minuteman development program began in 1958 under the designation SM-80, and became LGM-30 in 1963. The first generation Minuteman I had its debut launch in February 1961. The first LGM-30A and LGM-30B Minuteman II missiles were deployed in 1963, with the first operational unit being SAC's 10th Strategic Missile Squadron at Malmstrom AFB in Montana. By year's end, six squadrons were active with the first 372 of an eventual 650 Minuteman I missiles.

The next operational variant was the longer range LGM-30F Minuteman II, first tested in 1964, and first operational with the 321st Strategic Missile Wing at Grand Forks AFB, North Dakota in 1965. By the spring of 1967, 500 LGM-30Fs were in their silos.

The LGM-30G Minuteman III incorporated a Multiple Independently-targetable Reentry Vehicle (MIRV) capability. Each of a Minuteman III's three 175 to 340-kiloton warheads could be directed to a different target. Work on this ultimate Minuteman began in 1965, and the first test launch occurred in August 1968.

Senior Airmen David Wade and Eugene Clark, and Staff Sergeant Kevin Gorney perform an electrical check on an LGM-30F Minuteman III ICBM (ICBM) in its silo at Whiteman AFB in 1980. (US Air Force photo by Tech Sergeant Bob Wickley)

A member of the 321st Strategic Missile Wing works at a control panel inside a Minuteman III ICBM silo at Grand Forks AFB in June 1983. (US Air Force photo by Staff Sergeant Louis Comeger)

By 1974, all of SAC's Minuteman I missiles had been replaced by either the Minuteman II or Minuteman III, and the total in service had reached 999. The Minuteman III would remain in production until 1977, bringing the total number produced — of all variants — to over 2,400.

SAC reached its peak Minuteman deployment in 1978, with 1,180. These were grouped into nine Minuteman II squadrons and 11 Minuteman III squadrons. The Minutemen were all operationally based in hardened silos, although SAC had studied various mobile basing scenarios, especially railroad basing, through the years. In 1960, under Operation Big Star, a modified test train was sent throughout the western and Midwestern United States so that factors from communications to road-bed vibration could be evaluated. The study proved the feasibility of such basing, but in 1961, the Department of Defense decided not to proceed with mobile basing for the Minuteman.

Technicians work on the multiple warheads of an LGM-30G Minuteman III ICBM at Malmstrom AFB in 1985. (US Air Force)

A Minuteman transporter-erector is raised to the 45 degree angle position in preparation for unloading the missile into a silo at Vandenberg AFB. (US Air Force)

For nearly three decades, Minuteman crews across the United States stood ready, 24 hours a day to immediately initiate their launch sequences, but in 1991, with the Cold War over, President George H.W. Bush officially took the Minuteman force off high alert.

In 1992 and 1993, the United States removed and destroyed all the Minuteman IIs. Meanwhile, under the START II agreement, the Air Force "de-MIRVed" the Minuteman III fleet, retrofitting them with single warheads. After the turn of the century, the Minuteman force consisted of 450 LGM-30Cs. These were based in vast fields controlled by and surrounding Francis E. Warren AFB, Malmstrom AFB, and Minot AFB.

Ironically, the LGM-30G Minuteman III was earmarked for retention by the US Air Force after the retirement of the LGM-118A Peacekeeper, which had originally been conceived as a Minuteman replacement.

Manufacturer: Boeing

Height: 59 feet 10 inches (18.2 meters)

Diameter: 5 feet 6 inches (1.7 meters)

Weight: 78,000 pounds (35,000 kilograms)

Range: 8,100 miles (13,000 kilometers)

Speed: 15,000 mph (24,100 km/h)

Ceiling: 700 miles (1,100 kilometers)

Guidance system: inertial guidance

Propulsion system: Thiokol M55 (first stage), Aerojet SR19 (second stage), Aerojet-Thiokol SR73 (third stage) solid-fuel rockets

Warhead: three W62 or W78 thermonuclear (when MIRVed), or one W87 thermonuclear

First tested: 1961

First deployed: 1963

(Specifications for LGM-30G)

Sergeant Stephen Kravitsky, a missile systems analyst with the 321st Organizational Missile Maintenance Squadron, inspects an LGM-30G Minuteman III missile inside a silo about 60 miles from Grand Forks AFB. (US Air Force photo by Staff Sergeant Alan Wycheck)

MGM-31 Pershing

The Pershing was the US Army's longest-serving and only solid-fuel tactical nuclear Medium-Range Ballistic Missile (MRBM). It is also credited with being one of the key weapons that helped to checkmate the Soviet Union and end the Cold War in Europe.

The Army began evaluating the concept of a solid-fuel MRBM in 1956, and started testing the missile under the XM14 guided artillery missile designation in 1960. In January 1962, the Pershing was first test fired from a mobile launcher, and by the end of the year it was being deployed to operational units, replacing the Redstone MRBM.

Right: *An MGM-31 Pershing II battlefield support missile is fired from an erector/launcher vehicle on the McGregor Range at White Sands Missile Range in 1982.* (US Army photo by SP5 Ted Gomes)

Below: *The fourth test flight in the MGM-31 Pershing II engineering and development program occurred at Cape Canaveral on February 9, 1983.* (US Army)

Redesignated as MGM-31 in 1963, the original Pershing I missile was superseded by 1970 with the Pershing IA, which had improved electronics and a faster reaction launch system. With production extending through the 1970s, a total of 754 Pershing I and IA were built, most of which were deployed to Europe along with 180 mobile launchers. Most Pershing IAs were operated by the US Army, but some were deployed with the West German Bundeswehr.

A parallel development was the Pershing II, which was produced as a counter to the Soviet RSD-10 (SS-20) IRBM. First tested in 1977, the Pershing II had a longer range and a smaller-yield nuclear payload. The latter made it more versatile in the context of the potentially crowded and confused Central European battlefield. There were 380 Pershing IIs built, and most were deployed to West Germany, beginning in 1984. Because of the SALT II Treaty of 1974, a new class of launcher could not be built, so 108 Pershing IA launchers were retrofitted and assigned to three Pershing battalions under the US Army 56th Field Artillery Command.

Under the Intermediate-Range Nuclear Forces Treaty of 1988, all of the Pershing IIs and Soviet RSD-10s were withdrawn from service and destroyed by 1991, except those designated as museum pieces.

Several MGM-31 Pershing II missiles are prepared for launching at the McGregor Range at White Sands Missile Range in 1987. (US Army photo by Frank Trevino)

Manufacturer: Martin Marietta

Height: 34 feet 10 inches (10.6 meters)

Diameter: 40 inches (1 meter)

Weight: 16,500 pounds (7,500 kilograms)

Range: 1,100 miles (kilometers)

Speed: Mach 8 plus

Guidance system: inertial guidance

Propulsion system: Hercules two-stage solid rocket

Warhead: W85 thermonuclear

First tested: 1962

First deployed: 1962

(Specifications for Pershing II)

An Aérospatiale (Nord) MGM-32 ENTAC in its box at the Redstone Arsenal in March 1961. (US Army)

Manufacturer: Nord Aviation (Aérospatiale after 1970)
Length: 32 inches (0.8 meters)
Diameter: 6 inches (0.15 meters)
Span (fins): 15 inches (0.38meters)
Weight: 27 pounds (12 kilograms)
Range: 6,600 feet (2,000 meters)
Speed: 190 mph (300 km/h)
Guidance system: wire-guided line-of-sight
Propulsion system: 2-stage solid-fuel rocket
Warhead: armor piercing high explosive
First tested: 1959 (US Army)
First deployed: 1963 (US Army)
(Specifications for MGM-32A)

MGM-32 ENTAC

In 1959, the US Army began acquiring the French SS-10 wire-guided anti-tank missile. Built by Nord Aviation, it was based on the German X-7 Rotkappchen (Little Red Riding Hood) of World War II. In the meantime, Nord had begun delivering the more advanced Engin Téléguidé Anti-Char (ENTAC or Remotely Guided Anti-Tank) weapon to the French Army. The US Army took a look, tested the ENTAC, and decided to switch. In 1963, the phased-out SS-10 was redesignated as MGM-21A, and the ENTAC was designated as MGM-32A.

The MGM-32A itself was phased out by 1968, replaced by the Hughes BGM-71 TOW missile.

Though plans to produce the ENTAC in the United States never materialized, around 140,000 ENTACs were built in France and elsewhere through 1974.

The Radioplane/Northrop MQM-33C (formerly OQ-19B) target drone stored in a hangar. (Bill Yenne photo)

MQM-33

The MQM-33 was the first target drone designated in the Defense Department's 1963 "M for Missile" nomenclature, but it was one of the last of a long series of military target drones that had been built by Reginald Denny's Radioplane Company since 1942. In that year, the US Army Air Forces first began using the letter "Q" to designate all unmanned aircraft — or "drones" — that were radio-controlled or remote controlled. Most of the thousands of these aircraft that were delivered during World War II were small, simple targets designated as "OQ" for "radio controlled model," but there were a small number of "BQ" radio controlled flying bombs.

In 1952, Radioplane was acquired by the Northrop Corporation as its Radioplane Division (later the Ventura Division). The Radioplane OQ-19, which became the Northrop MQM-33, dated back to 1945. Deliveries of OQ-19s to the US Army and US Air Force continued through 1960, and they were to be used by national guard units well into the 1980s. The US Navy, meanwhile, had developed an OQ-19 variant under the designation KD2R.

In 1963, the little radio-controlled aircraft were redesignated, receiving their "M for Missile" designations, bringing all pilotless flying machines under

the same nomenclature umbrella. Existing OQ-19Bs and OQ-19Ds became MQM-33A and MQM-33B, while the Navy's KD2R-5 became the MQM-36A. The variants for all services were later known collectively as Basic Training Targets (BTT). Including all types, more that 73,000 were built.

Manufacturer: Radioplane/Northrop

Length: 12 feet 3 inches (3.7 meters)

Height: 2 feet 7 inches (0.8 meters)

Wingspan: 11 feet 5 inches (3.5 meters)

Weight: 320 pounds (145 kilograms)

Range: 200 miles (320 kilometers)

Speed: 230 mph (370 km/h)

Ceiling: 25,000 feet (7,600 meters)

Guidance system: radio command remote control

Propulsion system: McCulloch piston engine

First tested: 1945

First deployed: 1946

(Specifications for MQM-33D)

A classic ground launch image of a BQM-34 Firebee target drone. (Northrop Grumman)

BQM-34 Firebee

The Firebee was the most widely produced and widely used American pilotless, winged jet in the twentieth century. More than 7,000 were built in a series of production runs that began in 1951 and continued intermittently into the twenty-first century. Firebee remotely piloted vehicles (RPV) were used for a wide variety of missions, especially as target drones, but also as unmanned reconnaissance aircraft in Vietnam, and as decoy drones during Operation Iraqi Freedom in 2003.

In 1948, the company started by Claude Ryan, the man who built Charles Lindbergh's *Spirit of St. Louis* and numerous other manned aircraft, received a US Air Force contract for the XQ-2, a jet-propelled target drone for gunnery training. This aircraft, called Firebee first flew in 1951, and entered production as the Q-2A for the Air Force and as the KDA-1 for the US Navy. The larger Q-2C Firebee made its debut in December 1958, and was BQM-34A in 1963, while the US Navy's KDA-1 and KDA-2 Firebees became BQM-34B and BQM-34C. The "B" indicates multiple launch platforms, as the Firebees

In 2003, during the opening stages of Operation Iraqi Freedom, BQM-34 Firebees served as decoys. (DoD)

were launched from land, air and ships. Those Firebees used by the US Army were all ground-launched as MQM-34D. Numerous other designations have been assigned through the decades, including AQM prefixes for air-launched reconnaissance platforms and BGM prefixes for offensive operations. Many of those that flew recon missions in Vietnam were designated only by the Ryan model number 147 and called Lightning Bugs.

The supersonic Ryan Model 166 was ordered by the US Navy in 1965 under the designation BQM-34E. Known officially as the Firebee II, it made its first flight in January 1968 and became operational in 1972. The US Air Force ordered the Firebee II in 1969 under the designation BQM-34F.

The earlier aircraft remained in production until 1982. Four years later, under the Reagan administration, production was restarted, with additional aircraft being produced as BGM-34S. Firebee production continued into 2002.

Manufacturer: Ryan Aeronautical (1951-1969), Teledyne Ryan (1969-1999), Northrop Grumman (1999-2002)

Length: 22 feet 11 inches (7 meters)

Height: 6 feet 8 inches (2 meters)

Wingspan: 12 feet 11 inches (4 meters)

Weight: 2,500 pounds (1,100 kilograms)

Range: 800 miles (1,300 kilometers)

Speed: Mach 0.9

Ceiling: 60,000 feet (18,000 meters)

Guidance system: radio command remote control

Propulsion system: Continental J68 turbojet

First tested: 1951

First deployed: 1951

(Specifications for BQM-34A and BQM-34S)

AQM-35

In 1954, even as the Radioplane Division of Northrop was building the small, piston-engine target drones discussed previously, the company received a US Air Force contract for a supersonic, jet-propelled drone to be built under the Q-4 designation.

With a mission similar to that envisioned for the Ryan BQM-34E Firebee II ordered by the US Navy a decade later, the Q-4 was designed to be air-launched by a larger aircraft. The first air launch came in 1956, but only a handful were built. It has been said that they were too fast for the air-to-air missiles against which they were tested.

Manufacturer: Northrop
Length: 35 feet 4 inches (10.8 meters)
Height: 6 feet 2 inches (1.9 meters)
Wingspan: 12 feet 8 inches (3.9 meters)
Weight: 3,400 pounds (1,540 kilograms)
Speed: Mach 2
Ceiling: 70,000 feet (21,000 meters)
Guidance system: radio command remote control
Propulsion system: General Electric J85 turbojet
First tested: 1956
First deployed: never fully operational
(Specifications for AQM-35B)

The Radioplane MQM-36 Shelduck Basic Training Target (BTT), seen here on display at the Bournemouth Aviation Museum in England, was a close cousin to the MQM-33 and the MQM-57. (Photo by Nimbus227, released into the public domain worldwide through Wikimedia Commons)

MQM-36 Shelduck

Originally designated as KD2R-5, the Shelduck was part of a series of radio-controlled Basic Training Target (BTT) drones that were ordered by the US Navy in the 1950s. The earlier KD2R-1 through KD2R-4 drones, all named "Quail," were the equivalent of the USAAF/US Air Force OQ-19 series, which were redesignated as MQM-33A in 1963. The KD2R-5, which became the MQM-36A, was more sophisticated than any of the other variants. Still in production into the late 1980s, it featured advanced radio guidance and radar reflector pods on its wingtips.

Manufacturer: Radioplane/Northrop
Length: 12 feet 8 inches (3.85 meters)
Height: 2 feet 6 inches (0.8 meters)
Wingspan: 11 feet 6 inches (3.5 meters)
Weight: 400 pounds (180 kilograms)
Range: 210 miles (340 kilometers)
Speed: 230 mph (370 km/h)
Ceiling: 27,000 feet (8,300 meters)
Guidance system: radio command remote control
Propulsion system: McCulloch piston engine
First tested: 1950s
First deployed: 1950s
(Specifications for MQM-36A)

A view of an AQM-37A target after it was uploaded onto the wing of an A-6E Intruder aircraft at the Pacific Missile Test Center in September 1981. (US Navy photo by PH3 Colleen White)

AQM-37 Jayhawk

Like the AQM-35 and Firebee II, the AQM-37 was developed to address a need for a supersonic drone to be used as a target for air-to-air missiles. Unlike the other, single-service drones, it began in 1959 as a joint project for both the US Navy and Air Force. It made its first flight in 1961 under the Navy designation XKD2B-1, and entered service as the AQM-37A in 1963. The Jayhawk delivered impressive performance, being tested at speeds up to Mach 4.7 and altitudes up to 112,000 feet.

The Air Force lost interest after evaluating the AGM-37A, but the US Army did acquire some. Jayhawks were exported to several countries, including Israel, France and the United Kingdom. Meteor in Italy manufactured the Jayhawk under license.

More than 5,000 were built, with a few later AQM-37Cs and AQM-37Ds being delivered in the twenty-first century.

Manufacturer: Beechcraft
(part of Raytheon, 1980-2007)

Length: 14 feet (4.3 meters)

Height: 2 feet 2 inches (0.7 meters)

Wingspan: 3 feet 4 inches (1 meter)

Weight: 620 pounds (280 kilograms)

Range: 113 miles (180 kilometers)

Speed: Mach 4.7

Ceiling: over 100,000 feet (30,000 meters)

Guidance system: radio command remote control

Propulsion system: Rocketdyne LR64 liquid-fuel rocket

First tested: 1961

First deployed: 1963

(Specifications for AQM-37C)

The Radioplane Model RP-76 recoverable target drone was designated as AQM-38A by the US Navy in 1963. (Author's collection)

AQM-38

The AQM-38 was developed by Northrop's Radioplane Division as the Model RP-76, a recoverable, jet-propelled drone to be used as a target by surface-to-air missiles such as the US Army's Nike Hercules. It entered service with the Army (launched by US Air Force aircraft) in 1959, and was redesignated as AQM-38A in 1963. The US Navy evaluated the similar Model RP-78 as the AQM-38B. A couple thousand were built before production ended in the 1970s.

Manufacturer: Northrop
Length: 9 feet 8 inches (2.95 meters)
Height: 1 foot 6 inches (0.46 meters)
Wingspan: 5 feet (1.52 meters)
Weight: 300 pounds (136 kilograms)
Speed: Mach 0.9 (the AQM-38B was supersonic)
Ceiling: 60,000 feet (18,300 meters)
Guidance system: preprogrammed or radio command remote control
Propulsion system: Aerojet solid-fuel rocket
First tested: 1950s
First deployed: 1959
(Specifications for AQM-38A)

MQM-39 Cardinal

Developed for the US Navy as a slow, recoverable target drone, the V-tailed Beechcraft Model 1001 Cardinal first flew in 1957 under the designation XKDB-1. It entered service two years later as KDB-1, but was redesignated as MQM-39A in 1963. Deliveries of around a thousand units continued into the 1970s. The US Army acquired the similar Model 1025 as the MQM-61A.

Manufacturer: Beechcraft
(part of Raytheon, 1980-2007)
Length: 15 feet 1 inch (4.60 meters)
Height: 3 feet 4 inches (1.0 meters)
Wingspan: 13 feet (3.964 meters)
Weight: 660 pounds (300 kilograms)
Range: 300 miles (500 kilometers)
Speed: 350 mph (560 km/h)
Guidance system: radio command remote control
Propulsion system: McCulloch piston engine
First tested: 1957
First deployed: 1959
(Specifications for MQM-39A)

MQM-40 Firefly

Immediately after World War II, the short-lived Globe Aircraft of Fort Worth, Texas built a series of inexpensive target drones for the US Navy, including the KDG and KD3G Snipe, the pulsejet KD2G Firefly and the KD4G Quail. The last Globe drone was the KD6G-1 Firefly, a piston-powered variation on the KD2G. The few KD6G-1s that were still around in 1963 were redesignated as MQM-40A.

Manufacturer: Globe Aircraft
Length: 11 feet 6 inches (3.5 meters)
Height: 1 foot 7 inches (0.48 meters)
Wingspan: 11 feet 6 inches (3.51 meters)
Guidance system: radio command remote control
Speed: 265 mph (425 km/h)
Propulsion system: McCulloch piston engine
First tested: 1951
First deployed: 1951
(Specifications for MQM-40A)

AQM-41 Petrel

The Petrel originated as the AUM-N-2 Kingfisher C, and was first tested in 1951. It was a target drone that evolved from the US Navy Bureau of Ordnance Kingfisher family of anti-ship/anti-submarine missiles whose development began during World War II. Low-rate production was turned over to Fairchild in 1954, and the Petrels were operational as anti-ship weapons from 1956 to 1959. Thereafter, they were converted to target drones and redesignated as AQM-41A in 1963.

Manufacturer: Fairchild

Length: 24 feet (7.32 meters)

Wingspan: 13 feet 2 inches (4.01 meters)

Weight: 3,800 pounds (1,700 kilograms)

Range: 20 miles (32 kilometers)

Speed: 375 mph (600 km/h)

Guidance system: semi active radar homing (AUM-N-2), later radio remote control

Propulsion system: Fairchild J44 turbojet

First tested: 1951

First deployed: 1956

(Specifications for AQM-41A)

A test launch of an MQM-42 Redhead/Roadrunner at White Sands Missile Range, circa 1961. (Author's collection)

MQM-42 Redhead and Roadrunner

The North American Model NA-273 was developed for the US Army as a recoverable, supersonic drone to be used as a target by MIM-23 Hawk surface-to-air missile batteries. First tested in 1961, it entered service as the MQM-42A, and remained in use into the 1970s. Those used in low-level intercept scenarios were called Roadrunners, and for high altitude operations, they were called Redheads.

Manufacturer: North American Aviation

Length: 24 feet 10 inches (7.57 meters)

Diameter: 12 inches (0.31 meters)

Wingspan: 6 feet 3 inches (1.91 meters)

Weight: 900 pounds (400 kilograms)

Range: 250 miles (400 kilometers)

Speed: Mach 2

Ceiling: 60,000 feet (18,000 meters)

Guidance system: radio command remote control

Propulsion system: Rocketdyne, solid-fuel rocket and Marquardt MA-74 Ramjet

First tested: 1961

First deployed: circa 1963

(Specifications for AQM-42A)

FIM-43 Redeye

During World War II, standard air defense for US Army ground forces centered mainly on .50 caliber machine guns. After the war, the service sought a weapon that might be more effective against jets. In retrospect, the obvious answer would be a supersonic rocket that could be fired from a bazooka-sized launcher. Nevertheless, it required more than a decade of studies to reach this conclusion, and in 1958, the Army contracted with the Convair Division of General Dynamics to develop the weapon.

Originally designated XM41 (later XMIM-43A), the Redeye was first tested in 1960, and first fired from its tube launcher a year later. Technical problems sent the Block I system back to the drawing boards for a series of redesigns. The Redeye was finally deployed in 1966, with its M171 launch tube, in the Block III configuration as the FIM-43C.

Through 1969, about 85,000 Redeyes were produced, including some exports to Denmark and Sweden. The US Army began the phase-out of the Redeye in 1982, but it remained in the inventory until 1995. Plans for an improved Redeye II weapon were superseded in about 1972 by development of the much superior FIM-92 Stinger man-portable anti-aircraft missile.

During the 1980s, a few Redeyes – and many Stingers – were delivered to Afghan guerrillas, who used both effectively against Soviet aircraft.

A Redeye missile just after launch, but before the sustainer motor ignites, circa 1963. (US Army)

Manufacturer: Convair Division of General Dynamics

Length: 4 feet (1.22 meters)

Diameter: 2.75 inches (0.07 meters)

Span (fins): 5.5 inches (0.14 meters)

Weight: 18.3 pounds (8.3 kilograms)

Range: 2.8 miles (4,500 kilometers)

Speed: Mach 1.7

Ceiling: 9,000 feet (2,740 meters)

Guidance system: infrared homing

Propulsion system: Atlantic Research M115 solid-fuel rocket

Warhead: blast fragmentation

First tested: 1960

First deployed: 1966

(Specifications for FIM-43C)

Newspaper reporters gather around a FIM-43 Redeye missile for a personal 1982 briefing from General Joseph Hopkins of the 2nd Marine Division. (USMC photo by Sergeant Stout)

A 1980s era test launch of a UUM-44 SUBROC. (US Navy)

UUM-44 SUBROC

The SUBmarine ROCket (SUBROC) program was submarine-launched complement to the US Navy's ship-launched Anti-Submarine ROCket (ASROC). Both weapons carried a nuclear warhead compatible with short-range operations. The projects originated in the mid-1950s, with ASROC becoming operational in 1961 and SUBROC in 1965, after the technical issues related to underwater launches were resolved.

While SUBROC was designated in the "M for Missile" lineage, ASROC was designated RUR-5 as a "Rocket" because it was an unguided weapon. Operationally, ASROC would have functioned as a long-range depth charge, with its warhead being rocketed to a target about 14 miles away, theoretically leaving the host ship outside the blast radius of the explosion. The range of the SUBROC was about 30 miles.

SUBROC was designed to be launched from an attack submarine torpedo tube. After this, its rocket engine would fire, it would surface, and travel through the air to the target vicinity. It would then drop into the water, sink to the target depth and explode. It was a last ditch weapon to be used only against targets that could not be killed by any conventional method.

Both ASROC and SUBROC were finally retired in 1989, with the former being superseded by the guided RUM-139 Vertical Launch (VL) ASROC. The intended SUBROC successor, the UUM-125 Sea Lance, suffered from numerous developmental delays during the 1980s, and was cancelled in 1990.

Manufacturer: Goodyear Aerospace

Length: 21 feet (6.40 meters)

Diameter: 21 inches (0.53 meters)

Weight: 4,000 pounds (1,800 kilograms)

Range: 35 miles (55 kilometers)

Speed: Mach 1 plus

Guidance system: inertial guidance

Propulsion system: Thiokol TE260 solid-fuel rocket

Warhead: W55 nuclear

First tested: 1959

First deployed: 1965

(Specifications for UUM-44A)

A 1978 view of an Attack Squadron 12 (VA-12) A-7E Corsair II aircraft armed with an AGM-45 Shrike and an AIM-9 Sidewinder. (US Navy)

AGM-45 Shrike

The Shrike was a pioneering Anti-Radiation (or Anti-Radar) Missile (ARM) developed by the US Navy as a means of neutralizing enemy air defenses by homing on defensive radar installations. The project began at the Naval Weapons Center in the late 1950s, and led to the mating of an AIM-7 Sparrow air-to-air missile with a radar homing system.

The AGM-45A entered service with the US Navy in 1965, and was adopted by the US Air Force in 1966. Both services began using it immediately and

A blue AGM 45A Shrike training missile mounted on the wing pylon of an F-4 Phantom II aircraft at Eglin AFB in 1979. (US Air Force)

extensively in Suppression of Enemy Air Defenses (SEAD) operations over North Vietnam. Aircraft equipped with Shrikes, such as Navy A-4s and Air Force F-105s, typically preceded strike aircraft into a target area, attacking enemy Fan Song radar installations. The Air Force referred to its aircraft flying such missions as "Wild Weasels," a term that is still in use.

The Shrike's disappointing one-in-four success rate led to development of longer range ARMs, such as the AGM-78 and AGM-88. Nevertheless, the Shrike continued to be used, and remained in the American inventory until 1992. The only true export customer for the Shrike was Israel, but the United Kingdom acquired a few specifically for use by Vulcan bombers to attack Argentine radar during the Falklands War in 1982.

Manufacturer: Texas Instruments

Length: 10 feet (3.1 meters)

Diameter: 8 inches (0.20 meters)

Span (fins): 36 inches (0.9 meters)

Weight: 390 pounds (177 kilograms)

Range: 25 miles (40 kilometers)

Speed: Mach 2

Guidance system: passive radar homing

Propulsion system: Aerojet Mk.78 solid-fuel rocket

Warhead: blast fragmentation

First tested: 1963

First deployed: 1965

(Specifications for AGM-45B)

Manufacturer: General Dynamics (Convair Pomona Division)

Length: 6 feet (1.83 meters)

Diameter: 5 inches (0.13 meters)

Span (fins): 13 inches (0.33 meters)

Weight: 120 pounds (55 kilograms)

Range: 5 miles (8 kilometers)

Speed: 2,250 mph (3,300 km/h)

Ceiling: 20,000 feet (6,000 meters)

Guidance system: semi-active radar homing

Propulsion system: Lockheed solid-fuel rocket

Warhead: blast fragmentation

First tested: 1960

First deployed: never

(Specifications for XMIM-46)

The XMIM-46A Mauler was launched from an XM546 Tracked Fire Unit, based on an M113 chassis. Each XM546 carried nine missiles in launch canisters stacked three by three. (US Army)

MIM-46 Mauler

The Mauler originated in the 1950s to address a US Army requirement for a vehicle-based anti-aircraft missile system to replace various types of vehicles equipped with anti-aircraft guns. Aimed guns were considered inadequate to defend against high- speed attack jets, so a guided missile was needed.

Under the Forward Area Air Defense (FAAD) program, the Army studied several options and settled in 1959 on the Convair proposal. Named "Mauler" in 1960, this system consisted of a battery of nine launch tubes mounted on an M113 armored personnel carrier.

Developmental issues led to the cancellation of the MIM-46 in 1965, and to the Army having to scramble for other options such as the MIM-72 Chaparral.

The AIM-47A (formerly XGAR-9) Falcon (foreground) was created as the air-to-air armament for the YF-12A, the interceptor variant of the SR-71 Blackbird, seen here in the background. (US Air Force)

AIM-47 Falcon

Originally designated as GAR-9, the AIM-47 was a high performance, Mach 4 variation on the AIM-4 Falcon air-to-air missile that could be armed either with a nuclear or high explosive warhead. It was developed in the late 1950s to equip the North American F-108 Rapier Mach 3 interceptor, which the US Air Force intended to deploy during the 1960s. When the Rapier program was cancelled in 1959, the GAR-9 program continued. Ground tests began in 1961, with the first air launches coming in May 1962 from a B-58 Hustler.

Redesignated as AIM-47A in 1963, the Falcon was now considered as the weapon to arm the Lockheed YF-12A, the Mach 3 interceptor variant of the A-12/SR-71 Blackbird family of reconnaissance aircraft. Test launches from a YF-12A showed great promise, but when the F-12B production series was cancelled, so too was the AIM-47. The later AIM-54 Phoenix was a direct descendant of the AIM-47A program.

Manufacturer: Hughes

Length: 12 feet 6.5 inches (3.85 meters)

Diameter: 13.5 feet inches (0.34 meters

Span (fins): 33 inches (0.84 meters)

Weight: 818 pounds (370 kilograms)

Range: 100 miles (160 kilometers) plus

Speed: Mach 4

Guidance system: active radar terminal seeker

Propulsion system: Lockheed XSR13 solid-fuel rocket

Warhead: high explosive, or potentially, nuclear

First tested: 1961

First deployed: never

(Specifications for XAIM-47A)

An August 1961 view of a Douglas XGAM-87A (later AGM-48) Skybolt on its hydraulic loading trailer, parked next to a B-52 bomber. (Author's collection)

AGM-48 Skybolt

Few missile systems grabbed headlines of newspapers on both sides of the Atlantic like the Skybolt. The political crisis that would surround the cancellation of this American weapon nearly brought down a British government and damaged Anglo-American relations for years.

The idea of the Skybolt was to hang a solid-fuel ballistic missile with double the range of the jet-propelled Hound Dog on a B-52. The missile itself evolved under the GAM-87 designation in the late 1950s at a time when ICBMs – liquid-fueled, cumbersome to launch and not yet fully reliable – were in their infancy. The best way to deliver a nuclear strike against the Soviet Union was still with a bomber, yet Soviet air defenses – like Western air defenses – were on the verge of rendering manned bombers obsolete for such missions.

It should be mentioned that the Skybolt as an air-launched ballistic missile was among several such concepts, including those developed under the Air Force Weapon System 199 program. The WS-199 systems included several prototype solid-fuel rockets with especially colorful names, such as the McDonnell Alpha Draco, the Martin Bold Orion and Lockheed's High Virgo. All three were test fired in the 1958-1959 time-frame, but none reached the point of consideration as operational weapons. Parenthetically, both Bold Orion and High Virgo were later tested as anti-satellite (ASAT) weapons (see ASM-135). The Air Force requirements for the Skybolt were based in part on the experiences of WS-199 testing.

As Skybolt was being developed for the US Air Force, it also attracted the attention of the British. Seeking to maintain their own independent, state-of-the-art nuclear strike capability, the British agreed in May 1960 to adopt the Skybolt and hang it on their Vulcan

bombers. It so doing, they abandoned a plan to improve their own Avro Blue Steel standoff missile.

Against the backdrop of unsuccessful test launches and the promise of the upcoming Minuteman solid-fuel ICBM, Defense Secretary Robert McNamara grew cool on the Skybolt idea. Now designated as XAGM-48A, it was first successfully air launched on December 19, 1962, the same day that McNamara chose to cancel the program. The night before, at a meeting in the Bahamas, President John F. Kennedy had told British Prime Minister Harold MacMillan that the axe was about to fall. As a consolation, Kennedy allowed MacMillan to acquire the Polaris SLBM for the Royal Navy, arguably a better operational choice for the British.

Manufacturer: Douglas Aircraft

Length: 38 feet 3 inches (11.66 meters)

Diameter: 35 inches (0.9 meters)

Span (fins): 5 feet 6 inches (1.68 meters)

Weight: 11,000 pounds (5,000 kilograms)

Range: 1,150 miles (1,850 kilometers)

Speed: 9,500 mph (15,300 km/h)

Ceiling: 300 miles (480 meters)

Guidance system: inertial guidance

Propulsion system: Aerojet solid-fuel rockets (two stages)

Warhead: W59 thermonuclear

First tested: 1962

First deployed: never

(Specifications for XAGM-48A)

LIM-49 Nike Zeus/Spartan

The Nike Zeus/Spartan program was a ballistic missile defense project which preceded the Reagan Administration's Strategic Defense Initiative (SDI) by two decades. The idea was to develop a missile that could intercept Soviet ICBMs the way that the Nike Hercules was designed to intercept Soviet bombers.

In 1963, Project Sentinel was authorized, envisioning an anti-ballistic missile to confront enemy ICBMs targeting the highest priority potential targets. Two interceptor missiles were developed as part of the program, the Douglas Nike Zeus and the Martin Marietta Sprint, a smaller, high acceleration missile.

The evolution of the Nike Zeus began with the Nike Zeus A, a missile similar to the Nike Hercules, which first flew in 1960, and progressed to the all-new, three-stage Nike Zeus B. The latter first flew in 1961, and successfully intercepted several inert ICBM reentry vehicles during tests over the next two years. The Nike Zeus B first successfully destroyed an object orbiting in outer space in May 1963.

The Nike Zeus B evolved into the faster reaction Nike X and into the Nike EX (Extended Range), which in turn became the LIM-49A Spartan. The first successful interception of a dummy Minuteman reentry vehicle by a Spartan came in August 1970.

Meanwhile, early in 1969, the incoming Nixon Administration cancelled Project Sentinel, but replaced it a few weeks later with a new anti-ballistic missile program called Project Safeguard. The new program would inherit, and eventually deploy, both the LIM-49A Spartan and never-designated Sprint missile. Safeguard envisioned a dozen missile sites protecting Washington, DC and Minuteman ICBM sites.

However, the Anti-Ballistic Missile Treaty of 1972 between the United States and the Soviet Union permitted each side to keep only a single anti-ballistic missile site. The Soviet Union chose to keep one protecting Moscow, while the United States kept the Safeguard site in North Dakota because it was the nearest to completion at the time. The site went on alert with 100 missiles in October 1975, but a defense budget-cutting Congress ordered it closed almost immediately.

Top right: *A Spartan/Nike Zeus B missile inspected by technicians, circa 1968. By this time, the manufacturer could boast that an LIM-49A launched from the Kwajalein complex had intercepted an orbiting satellite.* (US Army)

Left: *A scale view of the LIM-49A Spartan/Nike Zeus B anti-ballistic missile.* (Author's collection)

Manufacturer: Western Electric and McDonnell Douglas

Length: 55 feet 2 inches (16.79 meters)

Diameter: 43 inches (1.09 meters)

Span (fins): 9 feet 10 inches (3.00 meters)

Weight: 29,000 pounds (13,100 kilograms)

Range: 460 miles (740 kilometers)

Speed: Mach 4

Ceiling: 350 miles (560 kilometers)

Guidance system: radio command remote control

Propulsion system: Thiokol solid-fuel rockets (three stages)

Warhead: W71 thermonuclear

First tested: 1961 (Nike Zeus B)

First deployed: 1975

(Specifications for LIM-49A)

A salvo launch of Spartan/Nike Zeus B missiles from the Kwajalein complex in the Western Pacific. (Author's collection)

An MGM-51 (originally M13) Shillelagh surface-to-surface missile. (Bill Yenne photo)

RIM-50 Typhon LR

Through the 1950s, the US Navy depended on the Terrier, Talos and Tartar systems for shipboard air defense. The Typhon Combat System program was initiated in 1958 as a next generation system that would take advantage of improvements in computing speed to reduce reaction time and permit better multiple-target tracking. There was to have been a Typhon LR (Long Range) to replace Talos and a Typhon MR (Medium Range) to replace the Terrier and Tartar. The LR was originally designated as SAM-N-8 (later RIM-50), while the MR was originally designated as SAM-N-9. It was tentatively redesignated as RIM-55.

The first SAM-N-8 Typhon test launch came in 1961, but while the Navy was pleased with its Mach 4 performance, the service cancelled it in late 1963 to concentrate on the Aegis Combat System and RIM-66 and RIM-67 surface-to-air missiles.

Manufacturer: Bendix

Length: 15 feet 5 inches (4.7 meters)
(with booster: 27 feet 7 inches (8.4 meters))

Diameter: 16 inches (0.41 meters)

Span (fins): 40 inches (1.02 meters)

Weight (with booster): 3,620 pounds (1,650 kilograms)

Range: 230 miles (370 kilometers)

Speed: Mach 4

Ceiling: 95,000 feet (29,000 meters)

Guidance system: inertial guidance

Propulsion system: Bendix ramjet with solid-fuel booster

Warhead: high explosive, blast fragmentation or W60 nuclear

First tested: 1961

First deployed: never

(Specifications for RIM-50A)

MGM-51 Shillelagh

The program originated in 1958 as part of the US Army's broad-ranging Combat Vehicle Weapon System program. Part of this was an effort to develop an anti-tank missile that could be gun-launched from a mobile platform. The platform would be the tank-like M551 Sheridan light armored recon and assault vehicle created for airborne forces. The missile was the M13 guided missile, named Shillelagh, and designed to fit in the 152mm M81 gun of the Sheridan. It was fired by means of a small explosive charge, with the rocket igniting after it left the barrel. The M81 gun could also fire conventional shells.

Initial test-firings of the XM13 Shillelagh took place in 1960, and initial deliveries came in 1964 under the designation MGM-51A. Though improved MGM-51B and MGM-51C variants were introduced later in the decade, the Sheridan was deployed to Vietnam without the Shillelagh. Among the problems were the limited range and large size of the Shillelagh. The latter meant that only a small number could be carried. During the 1970s, experiments were conducted using M60A2 tanks and other platforms to fire Shillelaghs.

Around 88,000 Shillelaghs had been built when production ended in 1971. The Sheridan/Shillelagh combo did see limited service against Iraqi bunkers during Operation Desert Storm in 1991.

Manufacturer: Ford Motor Company, Aeronutronic Division

Length: 3 feet 9.4 inches (1.15 meters)

Diameter: 6 inches (15 meters)

Span (pop-out fins): 11.5 inches (0.15 meters)

Weight: 61 pounds (28 kilograms)

Range: 1.9 miles (3.06 kilometers)

Speed: Mach 3.5

Guidance system: infrared signal link

Propulsion system: Amoco solid-fuel rocket

Warhead: high explosive

First tested: 1960

First deployed: 1964

(Specifications for MGM-51C)

A view of the M81 gun on the M551 Sheridan, used for firing unguided high-explosive anti-tank rounds as well as Shillelaghs. (Bill Yenne photo)

Launching an MGM-51 (M13) Shillelagh from an M551 Sheridan Armored Fighting Vehicle. (US Army)

An XMGM-52B Lance surface-to-surface missile on its mobile launcher, circa 1967. (US Army)

Two MGM-52 Lance missiles are fired A and C Batteries, 1st Battalion, 12th Artillery Regiment at White Sands Missile Range in March 1987. (US Army photo by Frank Trevino)

MGM-52 Lance

As part of a service-wide upgrade of its tactical missiles in the early 1960s, the US Army earmarked the guided Lance to replace its long-serving MGR-1 Honest John unguided artillery rocket. It was to have been used for nuclear as well as conventional warheads.

During tests of the XMGM-52A prototype, which began in 1965, the Army decided to develop a longer range MGM-52B. In turn, as tests of this missile took place through 1971, the Army decided to use the Lance only for nuclear payloads. The resulting MGM-52C was deployed on mobile launchers to Europe in 1973, where it replaced the MGM-29 Sergeant. During nearly two decades of service, some MGM-52Cs were retrofitted to accept conventional warheads. The last of around 2,000 Lances was withdrawn from front line service in 1992, replaced by the MGM-140.

Manufacturer: Ling-Temco-Vought (LTV)

Length: 20 feet (6.01 meters)

Diameter: 22 inches (0.56 meters)

Weight: 2,850 pounds (1,290 kilograms)

Range: 75 miles (120 kilometers)

Speed: Mach 3

Guidance system: inertial guidance

Propulsion system: liquid-fuel rocket

Warhead: W70 nuclear or high explosive

First tested: 1965

First deployed: 1972

(Specifications for MGM-52C)

AGM-53 Condor

The Condor resulted from a US Navy effort to develop a television-guided, long-range, air-to-ground missile. Though the project began in 1962, various technical problems delayed the first flight until 1970, greatly increasing the program cost. It was the latter that eventually sank the program, which was cancelled in 1976 before the Condor became operational.

An EAGM-53A Condor mounted on an A-6A Intruder during tests at the US Navy's China Lake facility in May 1972. (US Navy photo via Gary Verver)

Manufacturer: Rockwell International

Length: 13 feet 10 inches (4.21 meters)

Diameter: 17 inches (0.43 meters)

Span (fins): 4 feet 5 inches (1.35 meters)

Weight: 2,100 pounds (950 kilograms)

Range: 70 miles (110 kilometers)

Speed: Mach 2.9

Ceiling: feet (meters)

Guidance system: television guided

Propulsion system: Rocketdyne solid-fuel rocket

Warhead: high explosive

First tested: 1965

First deployed: never

An AIM-54A Phoenix air-to-air missile mounted on the wing Pave Knife pod of an F-14A Tomcat at NAS Patuxent River in May 1984. (US Navy photo by Don Montgomery)

AIM-54 Phoenix

The longest- range air-to-air missile ever developed by the United States, the Phoenix traces its roots to the late 1950s and a US Navy concept for a fleet air defense system involving a long endurance aircraft armed with very long-range missiles. The envisioned aircraft was the Douglas F6D Missileer, which was cancelled in 1960.

The Defense Department later insisted that the Navy accept a variant of the multirole Tactical Fighter, Experimental (TFX), which entered service as the F-111. Meanwhile, the original missile concept was the Bendix AAM-N-10 Eagle, which was cancelled in favor of the Hughes AAM-N-11 Phoenix, which incorporated some technology that was used in the AIM-47 Falcon. Redesignated as XAIM-54A, the Phoenix was first flight tested in 1965. The Navy TFX, the F-111B, was cancelled in 1969, but the Phoenix remained.

The AIM-54A entered service in 1974, arming the Grumman F-14A Tomcat, the Navy's dedicated fleet interceptor and the only aircraft to carry the Phoenix operationally. The primary mission for the missile was to defend against Soviet air-launched cruise missiles and attack aircraft.

At the same time, Iran became the only export customer for the Tomcat and Phoenix. Deliveries ceased after the Islamic revolution in Iran in 1979.

Though the Phoenix served with the US Navy for 30 years, its only uses in combat were in 1999 while enforcing the No-Fly Zones over Iraq. With Iran, though, both Tomcat and Phoenix saw extensive service during the Iran-Iraq War of the 1980s. Perhaps as many as 70 successful AIM-54A hits were scored by Iranian pilots.

Having phased in the improved longer range AIM-54C after 1986, the US Navy kept the Phoenix in service until 2004. The status of existing Iranian stocks, if any, remained unknown.

Aviation ordnancemen inspect an AIM-54C Phoenix missile on the flight deck of the carrier USS Saratoga during Operation Desert Shield in December 1990. (US Navy photo by CW02 Bailey)

A Fighter Squadron 211 (VF-211) F-14A Tomcat aircraft banks into a turn during a flight from NAS Miramar in 1989 carrying six AIM-54 Phoenix missiles. (US Navy)

A US Navy F-14A Tomcat of Fighter Squadron 21 (VF-21) out of NAS Yokosuka, Japan, fires an AIM-54 Phoenix missile, circa 1991. (US Navy)

Manufacturer: Hughes Aircraft (later Raytheon)

Length: 13 feet 2 inches (4 3.99 meters)

Diameter: 15 inches (0.38 meters)

Span (fins): 36.4 inches (0.93 meters)

Weight: 1,020 pounds (462 kilograms)

Range: 90 miles (150 kilometers)

Speed: Mach 5

Ceiling: 100,000 feet (30,500 meters)

Guidance system: active and semi-active radar homing

Propulsion system: Rocketdyne or Aerojet solid-fuel rocket

Warhead: blast fragmentation

First tested: 1965

First deployed: 1974

(Specifications for AIM-54C)

The Missiles: MGM-1 through MQM-175   **US Guided Missile**

RIM-55 Typhon MR

Through the 1950s, the US Navy depended on the Terrier, Talos and Tartar systems for shipboard air defense. The Typhon program was initiated in 1958 as a next generation system that would take advantage of improvements in computing speed that would reduce reaction time and permit better multiple-target tracking. There was to have been a Typhon LR (Long Range) to replace Talos and a Typhon MR (Medium Range) to replace the Terrier and Tartar. The LR was originally designated as SAM-N-8 (later RIM-50), while the MR was originally designated as SAM-N-9. It was tentatively redesignated as RIM-55.

While the SAM-N-8/RIM-50 was tested in 1961, no SAM-N-9/RIM-55 was ever built. The program was cancelled in late 1963 in favor of the Aegis Combat System and the RIM-66 and RIM-67 surface-to-air missiles.

Manufacturer: Bendix
Length: 15 feet 6 inches (4.72 meters)
Diameter: 13.3 inches (0.34 meters)
Span (fins): 24 inches (0.61 meters)
Weight: 1,700 pounds (770 kilograms)
Range: 47 miles (75 kilometers)
Speed: Mach 4
Ceiling: 90,000 feet (27,400 meters)
Guidance system: inertial guidance
Propulsion system: solid-fuel rocket
Warhead: high explosive
First tested: never
First deployed: never
(Specifications for conceptual RIM-55A)

PQM-56

The PQM-56 was a license-built variant of the CT.41 supersonic target drone originally developed in France by Nord Aviation (Aérospatiale after 1970) in the late 1950s. When the US Navy expressed an interest in the vehicle, Bell acquired the license and built a small number in the United States during the 1960s.

Manufacturer: Bell
Length: 32 feet 1 inch (9.80 meters)
Diameter: 20 inches (0.51 meters)
Wingspan: 12 feet (3.66 meters)
Weight (with booster): 5,620 pounds (2,550 kilograms)
Speed: Mach 3 plus
Ceiling: 65,000 feet (20,000 meters)
Guidance system: radio command remote control
Propulsion system: two ramjets, with two solid-fuel booster rockets
First tested: circa 1959 (in France)
First deployed: circa 1963 (by the US Navy)
(Specifications for PQM-56A)

MQM-57 Falconer

The Falconer was a reconnaissance variant of the MQM-33 target drone which originated in 1955. The aircraft entered service with the US Army in 1959 under the Surveillance Drone designation SD-1. Redesignated in 1963 as MQM-57A or MQM-57B depending on specific guidance configurations, about 1,500 were built. The Falconer continued to remain in service into the 1970s. The payload consisted primarily of still cameras and flash ejectors, but television cameras could also be carried.

Manufacturer: Northrop (Ventura Division)

Length: 13 feet 4 inches (4.01 meters)

Height: 2 feet 7 inches (0.79 meters)

Wingspan: 11 feet 6 inches (3.51 meters)

Weight: 430 pounds (195 kilograms)

Range: 100 miles (160 kilometers)

Speed: 185 mph (300 km/h)

Ceiling: 15,000 feet (4,600 meters)

Guidance system: autopilot with radio-control backup

Propulsion system: McCulloch piston engine, with solid-fuel rocket launcher

First tested: 1955

First deployed: 1959

(Specifications for MQM-57A or MQM-57B)

MQM-58 Overseer

The Overseer was a reconnaissance drone contemporary of the MQM-57 that was created in 1957 by Rheem Manufacturing. Like the Falconer, it was powered by a piston engine, but launched by a solid-fuel rocket and recovered by parachute., The Overseer was acquired by the US Army under the Surveillance Drone designation SD-2, and redesignated as MQM-58 in 1963. Only a few were built, and their use was brief and limited.

Manufacturer: Rheem Manufacturing (Aerojet General after 1959)

Length: 13 feet 5 inches (4.01 meters)

Height: 2 feet 7 inches (0.798 meters)

Wingspan: 11 feet 6 inches (3.51 meters)

Weight: 1,100 pounds (500 kilograms)

Speed: 350 mph (560 km/h)

Guidance system: autopilot with radio-control backup

Propulsion system: Lycoming piston engine, with solid-fuel rocket launcher

First tested: circa 1957

First deployed: circa 1959

(Specifications for MQM-58A)

RGM-59 Taurus

The Taurus project originated in about 1961, and was intended to have been a US Navy ship-launched weapon to be used for onshore bombardment to support Marine amphibious landings. Developed by the Applied Physics Laboratory at Johns Hopkins University, Taurus missiles might have been launched from existing RIM-2 Terrier launchers. The program was cancelled in 1965 while still in the design phase.

Manufacturer: not built

Range: 58 miles (93 kilometers)

Guidance system: inertial guidance

Propulsion system: solid-fuel rocket

Warhead: high explosive

First tested: never

First deployed: never

(Specifications proposed for RGM-59A)

The XQ-5 (later AQM-60A) evolved from the similar X-7 research vehicle. The yellow part is the booster, the orange part is the vehicle. (Lockheed Martin)

AQM-60 Kingfisher

Not to be confused with the AUM Kingfisher family of anti-ship/anti-submarine missiles, this Kingfisher was a latter-day, target drone derivative of the Lockheed X-7 ramjet-powered research vehicle which had first flown in 1951. During nearly a decade of successful X-7 test flights, the US Air Force acquired some under the designation XQ-5 to be used as Mach 3 targets for its Bomarc interceptor missiles. The US Army also used Kingfishers to test its Nike Hercules, and the US Navy to test the Talos missile. Ironically the Kingfisher (AQM-60 after 1963) proved too fast for the interceptors, and it was phased out during the 1960s by a chagrinned Defense Department.

An XQ-5 (later AQM-60A) Kingfisher on the ramp, circa 1959. (Author's collection)

Manufacturer: Lockheed
Length: 38 feet (11.58 meters)
Diameter: 20 inches (0.51 meters)
Wingspan: 10 feet (3.05 meters)
Weight: 8,000 pounds (3,600 kilograms)
Range: 130 miles (210 kilometers)
Speed: Mach 4 plus
Ceiling: 100,000 feet (30,000 meters)
Guidance system: autopilot
Propulsion system: Marquardt ramjet engine, with solid-fuel rocket boosters
First tested: 1951 (X-7)
First deployed: circa late-1950s
(Specifications for XQ-5/AQM-60A)

MQM-61 Cardinal

The V-tailed Beechcraft Model 1001 and 1025 Cardinals were similar unmanned aircraft that were acquired as target drones by the US Navy and US Army respectively. The Model 1001 entered service in 1959 as KDB-1, but was redesignated as MQM-39A in 1963. The Model 1025 entered service in 1958 and was designated as MQM-61A. About 1,300 were delivered.

Manufacturer: Beechcraft
(part of Raytheon after 1980)
Length: 15 feet 1 inch (4.60 meters)
Height: 3 feet 4 inches (1.02 meters)
Wingspan: 13 feet (3.96 meters)
Weight: 660 pounds (300 kilograms)
Range: 300 miles (500 kilometers)
Speed: 300 mph (500 km/h)
Ceiling: 43,000 feet (13,000 meters)
Guidance system: radio command remote control
Propulsion system: McCulloch piston engine
First tested: circa 1957
First deployed: 1958
(Specifications for MQM-61A)

An AGM-62 Walleye glide bomb mounted on the wing pylon of an A-7 Corsair II aircraft at the White Sands Missile Range in 1978. (DoD)

AGM-62 Walleye

Beginning in 1965 with the GBU-1 Paveway I, precision guided munitions (aka "smart bombs") have been designated with the Guided Bomb Unit (GBU) prefix. However, in 1963, the Walleye smart bomb was given an "M for Missile" prefix because it was a guided weapon, despite the fact that it had no powerplant.

The Walleye was a television-guided weapon developed by the Naval Weapons Center at China Lake, California, beginning in 1963 and first deployed on Navy aircraft in 1967. The guidance system was autonomous after a visual lock-on so that the pilot could "fire and forget."

The "M" designator was later dropped. The AGM-62A became the Walleye Mk.1 and later variants, including the extended range Walleye I Mk.3, continued in this fashion.

A Naval Air Warfare Center Aircraft A-6E Intruder flying from NAS Patuxent River releases a Walleye II Extended Range Data Link (ERDL) weapon in February 1994. (US Navy)

Later versions built by Hughes with larger fins and larger conventional payloads were called Walleye II. Notable among these was the Walleye II Mk.6, which carried a low-yield W72 nuclear warhead. The Extended Range Data Link (ERDL) Walleye family began in 1975 with the Mk.21 Walleye I and Mk.23 Walleye II.

Walleyes were used against North Vietnam, initially with less than optimal success, notably failing in efforts to destroy the infamous Thanh Hoa Bridge. Later versions, such as the ERDLs addressed the earlier shortcomings. Walleyes were still in the inventory in 1991 and were used in Operation Desert Storm.

Manufacturer: Martin Marietta (Walleye I), Hughes Aircraft (Walleye II)
Length: 11 feet 4 inches (3.45 meters)
Diameter: 1 foot (0.32 meters)
Span (fins): 3 feet 9.5 inches (1.56 meters)
Weight: 1,125 pounds (510 kilograms)
Range: 19 miles (30 kilometers)
Speed: Mach 0.90
Guidance system: television guidance
Propulsion system: none
Warhead: high explosive
First tested: 1963
First deployed: 1967
(Specifications for AGM-62A)

AGM-63

This designation was set aside in 1963 for an ongoing US Navy project to develop an anti-radar missile with a range four times that of the AGM-45 Shrike. When the project was cancelled without a prototype being designed, the number was not reassigned. The US Air Force had a project with similar objectives, designated as AGM-76, that involved adapting an AIM-4 Falcon.

AGM-64 Hornet

The Hornet was developed to meet a US Air Force requirement for an air-launched anti-armor weapon, a requirement that was later met by the AGM-65 Maverick, a weapon of similar specifications. A prototype XAGM-64A was tested in 1964 before the program was terminated.

Manufacturer: North American Aviation
Guidance system: electro-optical television
Propulsion system: solid-fuel rocket motor
Warhead: high explosive
First tested: 1964
First deployed: never
(Specifications for XAGM-64A)

Ground crewmen move an AGM-65B Maverick air-to-surface missile into position to be mounted on an A-10 Warthog at Cairo West AB during exercise Bright Star '82. (US Air Force)

AGM-65 Maverick

The catalyst for the Maverick program was the poor effectiveness of earlier guided air-to-ground munitions in Vietnam, and it successfully addressed these previous shortcomings. Having entered service in 1972, the Maverick was widely deployed by the US Air Force, Navy and Marines. There were 75,000 built, and Mavericks were still in the American inventory in the twenty-first century. Mavericks have also been in service with most NATO air forces, as well as those of Chile, Egypt, Hungary, Indonesia, Israel, Japan, Jordan, South Korea, Malaysia, Morocco, New Zealand, Pakistan, Poland, Singapore, Sweden, Taiwan, and Thailand, as well as Iran's, having been delivered before the 1979 revolution.

The weapon was originally developed as a Cold War-era "tank buster," and used extensively and with a high success rate against Iraqi targets, especially armor, in 1991 and 2003.

Produced through 1978, the first generation AGM-65A and AGM-65B Mavericks used electro-optical television guidance that were "fire and forget" after the operator achieved lock-on. Introduced in 1978, the AGM-65C was guided by a semi-active laser. It was superseded in 1985 by the AGM-65E, with a more economical laser guidance system along with an improved warhead and motor.

Meanwhile the branch of the Maverick family tree using imaging infrared seekers began when the AGM-65D entered service in 1983. It was in turn superseded later in the decade by the US Navy's AGM-65F and the US Air Force AGM-65G, both of which combined guidance features of the AGM-65D with other features of the AGM-65E. After production ceased at the turn of the century, some earlier Mavericks were retrofitted with charge-coupled device guidance under various designations, especially AGM-65K.

Manufacturer: Hughes Aircraft (Raytheon after 1997)

Length: 8 feet 2 inches (2.49 meters)

Diameter: 12 inches (0.30 meters)

Span (fins): 2 feet 4 inches (0.71 meters)

Weight: 670 pounds (300 kilograms)

Range: 17 miles (27 kilometers)

Speed: Mach 1 plus

Guidance systems: various (see text)

Propulsion system: Thiokol or Aerojet solid-fuel rocket

Warhead: armor penetrating blast fragmentation

First tested: 1969

First deployed: 1972

(Specifications for AGM-65F and AGM-65G)

An F-16C from the 522nd Fighter Squadron fires an AGM-65H Maverick air-to-ground missile at a target on the Utah Test and Training Range near Hill AFB during Exercise Combat Hammer in May 2004. (US Air Force photo by Master Sergeant Michael Ammons)

US Navy Aviation Ordnanceman Airman Cory Smith arms a Maverick missile on an F/A-18 Hornet aircraft assigned to Marine Fighter Attack Squadron 232 aboard the nuclear-powered aircraft carrier USS Nimitz *while under way in the Persian Gulf on July 18, 2007. (US Navy photo by Mass Communication Specialist 3rd Class Gretchen Roth)*

RIM-66 Standard MR/SM-2s, painted blue to indicate they're training missiles, on a Mk.26 launcher. They are aboard the Aegis guided missile cruiser USS Ticonderoga, *sailing from the Atlantic Fleet Weapons Training Facility at Roosevelt Roads, Puerto Rico in April 1983.* (US Navy photo by Don Muhm)

RIM-66 Standard MR

By the end of the 1950s, the US Navy sought to develop a comprehensive shipboard air defense missile system to replace its first generation Terrier, Talos and Tartar missiles. The first attempt was the Typhon Combat System, involving the RIM-50 long-range, and RIM-55 medium-range missiles. This program was terminated in 1963 in favor of the Aegis Combat System (ACS).

The ACS includes an integrated Command & Decision apparatus, with elements linked by robust computers, AN/SPY-1 radar and various weapons, including the Phalanx Close In Weapon System (CIWS) gun, and "Standard" missiles. The latter include the RIM-66 Standard MR and the RIM-67 Standard ER, which are basically the same missile, although the RIM-67 has a booster.

Though the Standard missiles are an integral part of the Aegis system, they were also deployed aboard non-Aegis US Navy ships, replacing existing Tartars but using Tartar fire control. The non-Aegis missiles are called "Standard Missile 1" (SM-1MR), while the ACS RIM-66 missiles are Standard Missile 2 (SM-2MR). (See

Appendix 4 for an overview of the Standard family.)

Testing of the YRIM-66 began in 1965, and the Block I RIM-66A Standard Missile (SM-1MR) entered service in 1967. Incremental improvements came in subsequent production blocks, with extensive upgrades in targeting, propulsion and reaction time coming with the RIM-66B Block V. Meanwhile, the Aegis Standard Missiles (SM-2MR) entered service later, first deployed in 1979 as the RIM-66C, and later the RIM-66D.

The final SM-1MR variant was the RIM-66E, which served with the US Navy from 1983 through 2003, and which continues to be deployed by export customers. The missiles and the ACS are still in service with the US Navy, as well as the navies of Australia, Japan, and South Korea, as well as NATO members Germany, the Netherlands, Norway, and Spain.

Among the SM-2MR variants, the RIM-66L (for use on Mk.26 launchers), and the RIM-66M (for use on Mk.41 launchers), continued in production into the twenty-first century, and were deployed with the Japanese, German and Dutch fleets as well as the US Navy.

A pair of SM-2MRs were used in a July 1988 incident in which the Aegis cruiser USS *Vincennes* shot

A white RIM-66 Standard MR/SM-2 missiles on a Mk.26 launcher, prior to being fired from the Aegis guided missile cruiser USS Ticonderoga *underway in the Atlantic in March 1983. Note the "kill" markings indicating five successful live firings against target drones from this launcher.* (US Navy photo by Don Muhm)

down an Iran Air jetliner over the Straight of Hormuz. The Aegis crew claimed that they mistook the Airbus A300B2 for an Iranian air force F-14.

Until 1992, the Standard missiles were built by the General Dynamics Pomona Division, which was acquired by Hughes, which then formed a consortium with Raytheon to build the Standards. In 1997, Raytheon bought the Hughes missile division.

Though the Standard Missile were developed as surface-to-air missiles, they possess a secondary surface-to-surface capability for use against enemy ships.

Manufacturer: General Dynamics, later Hughes, now Raytheon

Length: 15 feet 6 inches (4.72 meters)

Diameter: 13.5 inches (0.34 meters)

Span (fins): 42.3 inches (1.07 meters)

Weight: 1,560 pounds (700 kilograms)

Range: 46 miles (75 kilometers)

Speed: Mach 3.5

Ceiling: 80,000 feet (24,400 meters)

Guidance system: inertial guidance with semi-active radar homing in terminal phase

Propulsion system: solid-fuel rocket

Warhead: blast fragmentation

First tested: 1965

First deployed: 1967

(Specifications for ACS SM-2 variants)

A RIM-67 Standard SM-2ER is loaded on the missile house rail aboard the guided missile destroyer USS Mahan *in March 1983.* (US Navy)

RIM-67 Standard ER

The RIM-67 Standard Missile is the Extended Range (ER) equivalent of the Medium Range (MR) RIM-66 Standard Missile discussed in the previous section, with the primary difference being that the ER versions have a booster rocket. While the RIM-66 replaced the earlier RIM-24 Tartar missile, the RIM-67 replaced the longer range RIM-2 Terrier. Both missiles had a Standard Missile One (SM-1MR) version, as well as a Standard Missile Two (SM-2MR) version, with the latter being part of the Aegis Combat System (ACS).

Until 1992, the Standard missiles were built by the General Dynamics Pomona Division, which was acquired by Hughes, and which then formed a consortium with Raytheon to build the Standards. In 1997, Raytheon bought the Hughes missile division.

The RIM-67A (SM-1ER) and RIM-67B (SM-2ER) entered service in around 1980, more than a decade after the corresponding Standard MR missiles. This first generation was succeeded by a Block II RIM-67C (SM-2ER) with a Hercules Mk.70 booster, which extended the range from 40 miles to 115 miles.

After 1999, the RIM-67C was augmented by the vertically-launched RIM-156A (SM-2ER Block IV) Standard ER, and will eventually be replaced by the RIM-174 (SM-6) Standard ERAM. The RIM-156A and the similar RIM-161A (SM-3) Standard Missiles are both capable of intercepting ballistic missiles. These successor missiles are discussed later in this book. (See also Appendix 4 for an overview of the Standard family.)

Manufacturer: General Dynamics, later Hughes, now Raytheon

Length: 26 feet 2 inches (7.98 meters) (with booster)

Diameter: 13.5 inches (0.34 meters)

Span (fins): 42.3 inches (1.07 meters)

Weight: 2,960 pounds (1,340 kilograms)

Range: 115 miles (100 kilometers)

Speed: Mach 3.5

Ceiling: 80,000 feet (24,400 meters)

Guidance system: inertial guidance with semi-active radar homing in terminal phase

Propulsion system: solid-fuel rocket, with solid-fuel booster

Warhead: blast fragmentation

First tested: 1965 (RIM-66 Standard)

First deployed: 1980

(Specifications for RIM-67C SM-2ER)

AIM-68 Quetzalcoatl

In 1963, the US Air Force undertook to develop a guided missile successor to its unguided AIR-2 Genie nuclear air-to-air interceptor missile. This work was done internally at the Air Force Weapons Laboratory at Kirtland AFB in New Mexico. A guidance system similar to that used in variants of the AIM-4 Falcon was planned, and the payload was to have been merely half a kiloton, a third the size of the Genie's warhead. The idea was that having a smaller blast radius would make it easier for interceptor pilots to attack closer targets.

Sub-scale variations on the Quetzalcoatl that were test fired at the White Sands Missile Range in 1965, were referred to by the nickname "Little Q." The full scale Quetzalcoatl, known as "Big Q," was apparently never built, and the "AIM-68" designation may not have been officially assigned.

Two AGM-69 SRAM missiles on display at Pease AFB in October 1989. (US Air Force photo by Master Sergeant Ken Hammond)

Manufacturer: Air Force Weapons Laboratory

Length: 9 feet 7 inches (meters)

Diameter: 14 inches (0.35 meters)

Span (fins): 21 inches (0.53 meters)

Weight: 500 pounds (225 kilograms)

Range: 40 miles (65 kilometers)

Speed: Mach 4

Guidance system: semi-active radar and infrared seeker

Propulsion system:

Warhead: W30 nuclear

First tested: 1965 ("Little Q")

First deployed: never

(Specifications for proposed AIM-68)

AGM-69 SRAM

The Short Range Attack Missile (SRAM) was conceived in 1964 as a successor to the AGM-28 Hound Dog as "stand-off" nuclear weapon to allow Strategic Air Command bombers to hit well-defended targets without risking the bomber crews to anti-aircraft defenses.

The range was much less than that of the Hound Dog, but more of the smaller SRAMs could be carried. They could be accommodated aboard a B-52 on underwing pylons like the Hound Dog or the recently terminated Skybolt, as well fitting inside a B-52 bomb bay. The SRAM could also be carried by the FB-111, and was earmarked for use by the Advanced Manned Strategic Aircraft (AMSA) program which evolved into the B-1A.

The first test flight came in July 1969, and the AGM-69A SRAM entered service aboard SAC B-52s in 1972. Boeing built around 1,500 through 1975. Operationally, B-52s could carry eight AGM-69As internally on a rotary launcher, as well as a dozen externally — compared to just two Hound Dogs. The FB-111 could carry six. An AGM-69B (SRAM B) was developed for the B-1A, but this weapon was cancelled when the B-1A was cancelled in 1978.

Having reached a peak number of 1,451 in 1975, there were still more than a thousand in the SAC inventory in 1990 when they were withdrawn from service. A year later, the successor AGM-131 SRAM II was cancelled.

Manufacturer: Boeing

Length: 15 feet 10 inches (4.86 meters)

Diameter: 17.5 inches (0.45 meters)

Wingspan: 2 feet 6 inches (0.76 meters)

Weight: 2,230 pounds (1,000 kilograms)

Range: 100 miles (160 kilometers)

Speed: Mach 3.5

Guidance system: inertial guidance

Propulsion system: Lockheed two-stage solid-fuel rocket

Warhead: W69 thermonuclear

First tested: 1969

First deployed: 1972

(Specifications for AGM-69A)

A maintenance Standardization and Evaluation team inspector observes as members of the 380th Bombardment Wing unstrap an AGM-69 SRAM training missile from a bomb cart during the November 1985 Strategic Air Command Combat Weapons Loading Competition at Ellsworth AFB. (US Air Force photo by Staff Sergeant Rose Reynolds)

AGM-69 SRAMs and Mk.28 thermonuclear bombs (background) in the bomb bay of a B-52H Stratofortress at Ellsworth AFB during Exercise Global Shield in April 1984. (US Air Force photo by Tech Sergeant Boyd Belcher)

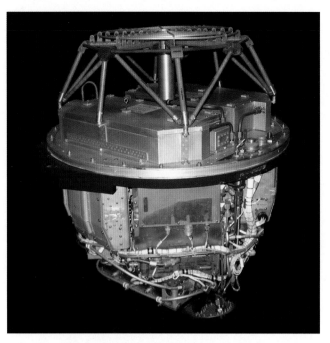

A display of the Emergency Rocket Communications System payload at the National Museum of the United States Air Force. (Public domain image from Wikimedia Commons)

Corporal Matthew Pozorski of from the 26th Marine Expeditionary Unit (MEU) sights an MGM-71 TOW missile at possible targets moving along a hillside at the MEU's forward operating base near Cernica, Kosovo on June 17, 1999. (US Marine photo by Lance Corporal Justin Tyler Watkins)

LEM-70 ERCS

It has been widely speculated without verification that the "70" numeral and the prefix "LEM," meaning "Silo-Launched Electronics Missile," were assigned to, or set aside for, a variant of the Minuteman ICBM. Such a missile would have been part of the Emergency Rocket Communications System (ERCS), a network connecting the National Command Authority with Strategic Air Command control centers and launch sites in time of nuclear attack when land based networks were likely to be destroyed. ERCS existed between the late 1960s and the early 1990s before the era of modern communications satellite capability.

The idea was for such missiles to be based in the Midwest under SAC control at all times, and capable of being launched on a moment's notice. The first generation ERCS, dating to the early 1960s, used an unguided MER-6A Blue Scout vehicle, but modified Minuteman II vehicles came on line in around 1967.

For the specifications, see LGM-30 Minuteman.

BGM-71 TOW

Beginning in the 1950s, the US Army had acquired small, man-portable, wire-guided anti-tank missile systems from Nord Aviation in France, culminating with the MGM-32 ENTAC. In 1963, they contracted with an American company to develop one to match their requirements specifically. The result was one of the most produced and widely deployed missiles in this book, and one which was approaching three quarters of a million units delivered by the turn of the century.

The Tube-launched, Optically-tracked, Wire data link (TOW) missile was originally developed by Hughes to be launched from both helicopters and surface vehicles. The BGM-71A entered production in 1968 and was deployed in 1970. Its first use in combat in Vietnam came in May 1972 when TOWs fired from US Army UH-1 Huey helicopters destroyed North Vietnamese tanks in fighting around An Loc. The TOW was deployed to Europe and Korea during the Cold War and used in the Gulf Wars of 1991 and 2003.

A longer range BGM-71B was introduced in 1976, followed by the BGM-71C Improved TOW (ITOW) with better armor-piercing capability, which reached the force in 1981. The next generation "TOW 2" missiles adopted by the US Army and Marines embodied further warhead enhancements. These included the BGM-71D (TOW 2) of 1983, the BGM-71E (TOW 2A) of 1987, the BGM-71F

Lance Corporal Lopez and his Bravo Company crew fire their ground mounted TOW during a March 1998 exercise at Fort Pickett. (DoD photo by Lance Corporal Timothy Pope)

(TOW 2B) of 1992, and the BGM-71H "Bunker Buster," which was delivered after 2001. Following numerous experiments through the years with various wireless guidance systems, the TOW 2B "Aero" with a radio guidance link system entered service in 2006.

In addition to the US Army and Marine Corps, the TOW has seen service with three-dozen countries worldwide.

Manufacturer: Hughes Aircraft (Raytheon after 1997)

Length: 5 feet (1.5 meters)

Diameter: 6 inches (0.15 meters)

Span (fins): 17.7 inches (0.45 meters)

Weight: 50 pounds (22.6 kilograms)

Range: 2.33 miles (3.75 kilometers)

Speed: 680 mph (1,100 km/h)

Guidance system: optically-tracked, with wire data link

Propulsion system: Hercules solid-fuel rocket

Warhead: shaped charge

First tested: 1963

First deployed: 1970

(Specifications for BGM-71E (TOW 2A) and BGM-71F (TOW 2B))

Troops of the 101st Airborne Division (Air Assault) fire a TOW missile at the building in Mosul, Iraq, where Uday and Qusay Hussein, the Sons of Saddam Hussein, had barricaded themselves on July 22, 2003. (US Army photo by Sergeant Curtis Hargreve)

Marine Lance Corporal Sean Silveraterry of the 4th Marine Regiment fires a TOW missile from a Hum-Vee at Marine Corps Base Camp Fuji in Japan in July 2005. (US Marine photo by Corporal Christopher Rye)

An MIM-72 Chaparral missile is fired from an M54 quad missile launcher mounted on an M730 tracked vehicle. (US Army)

MIM-72 Chaparral

After the cancellation of the costly and disappointing, radar-guided MIM-46 Mauler, the US Army's Forward Area Air Defense (FAAD) program turned in 1965 to the idea of a land-based variation on the successful infrared-guided AIM-9 Sidewinder air-to-air missile. Indeed, the MIM-72A Chaparral was almost identical to the AIM-9D.

XMIM-72As were evaluated in 1967, and operational missiles were deployed to active missile battalions in 1969. The Chaparrals were placed on M54 quad launchers aboard M730 tracked vehicles. Nearly 10,000 MIM-72As and MIM-72B training missiles were built before the introduction of the MIM-72C with improved warhead and guidance in 1976.

Later variants were basically the same as the MIM-72C with minor variations. The MIM-72E and MIM-72F had smokeless motors, and the MIM-72G had the Rosette Scan Seeker to defeat infrared countermeasures. The MIM-72H was the export version of the MIM-72F, and the MIM-72J was the export version of the MIM-72G. The US Navy evaluated but rejected a ship-based RIM-72C "Sea Chaparral" variant. Taiwan did acquire such a missile. Other export customers included Chile, Egypt, Israel, Morocco, Portugal, and Tunisia as production totals topped 20,000 units.

During the 1990s, the US Army slowly phased out the Chaparral in favor of the Avenger system, based on the FIM-92 Stinger.

Manufacturer: Philco Aeronutronic (Division of Ford Motor Co.)

Length: 9 feet 6.5 inches (2.91 meters)

Diameter: 5 inches (0.13 meters)

Span (fins): 24.8 inches (0.63 meters)

Weight: 190 pounds (86 kilograms)

Range: 5.7 miles (9 kilometers)

Speed: Mach 1.5

Ceiling: 10,000 feet (3,000 meters)

Guidance system: infrared

Propulsion system: Hercules solid-fuel rocket

Warhead: blast fragmentation

First tested: circa 1966

First deployed: 1969

(Specifications for MIM-72C and MIM-72G)

March 23, 1979 was marked by the 69th launch of a UGM-73 Poseidon missile. The submerged *launch was from the strategic missile submarine USS* John C. Calhoun. (US Navy)

A UGM-73A Poseidon C-3 fleet ballistic missile lifts off after a May 1979 launch from the submerged nuclear-powered strategic missile submarine USS Ulysses S. Grant. (US Navy)

UGM-73 Poseidon C3

The development program for the successor to the UGM-27 Polaris family of Submarine-Launched Ballistic Missiles (SLBM), was formally initiated by US Navy in January 1965. These studies, which led ultimately to the Poseidon C3, had been ongoing for several years under the Polaris B3 designation, but the new Fleet Ballistic Missile was quite different from its predecessor.

Like Polaris, the Poseidon was a two stage, solid-fuel missile, but it was 15 tons heavier than the largest Polaris. The 74-inch diameter was 20 inches greater than that of the Polaris A3, the last of that family that had been deployed, and the Poseidon was ten percent taller than the Polaris A3. Nevertheless, naval architects were able to redesign existing US Navy ballistic missile submarines to accommodate the larger weapon.

The Poseidon incorporated the large Multiple Independently-targetable Reentry Vehicles (MIRV) that were being developed for the US Air Force Minuteman program, as well as smaller Mk.3 reentry vehicles.

The first Poseidon test launch occurred at Cape Canaveral in August 1968, and the first successful submerged launch was conducted from the USS *James Madison* on July 17, 1970. The initial operational deployment of the UGM-74A was aboard the *James Madison* in March 1971.

Production continued until 1978, with more than 600 Poseidons built. The gradual replacement of the UGM-74A with the UGM-96 Trident C4 began in 1979, with the last Poseidon submarine being decommissioned in 1992.

Manufacturer: Lockheed Missiles & Space Company

Height: 34 feet 1 inch (10.39 meters)

Diameter: 6 feet 2 inches (1.88 meters)

Weight: 64,400 pounds (29,200 kilograms)

Range: 3,300 miles (5,275 kilometers)

Speed: 8,000 mph (12,900 km/h)

Ceiling: 500 miles (800 meters)

Guidance system: inertial navigation

Propulsion system: Hercules/Thiokol solid-fuel rocket First stage), Hercules solid-fuel rocket (second stage)

Warhead: ten W68 thermonuclear

First tested: 1968

First deployed: 1971

(Specifications for UGM-73A)

A BQM-74E Chukar in flight over the Pacific Ocean. (Northrop Grumman)

A DC-130 "mothership" carries a BQM-74E Chukar prior to its being air-launched. (Northrop Grumman)

MQM-74/BQM-74 Chukar

Named for a ground-dwelling game bird indigenous to the Midwestern United States, the Chukar was the last in a lineage of drones that began with those built by the Radioplane Company during World War II, a lineage that included the MQM-33 and MQM-36. The jet-propelled Chukar originated in 1964 in response to a US Navy requirement for an aerial target for anti-aircraft gunnery and missile training.

Designed to be launched from a ship using a rocket assist system, the first MQM-74As were delivered in 1968. An improved MQM-74B was evaluated, but not produced in large numbers. Beginning in 1974, the US Navy started taking delivery of the faster and longer range MQM-74C Chukar II. In the late 1970s both the US Army and the US Air Force studied the Chukar II for possible adaptation as top secret reconnaissance vehicles. The Army version was to have been designated as BQM-74D,

US Navy Aviation Machinist's Mate, Airman Jamar Sharp (right) and other ordnance crew members assigned to Fleet Composite Squadron Six, assemble BQM-74E target drones aboard the Guided Missile Frigate USS Doyle *in preparation for the annual UNITAS live fire exercises in 2002.* (US Navy photo by PH1 Martin Maddock)

but a production model was apparently not built. The Air Force version was evaluated under the Tactical Expendable Drone System (TEDS).

In the meantime, Northrop produced a sizable number of BQM-74Cs, redesignated as "BQM" because they could be air-launched as well as surface-launched. The BQM-74C was also known as the Chukar III, and this name was used by Northrop as the principal designation of the export version of this drone. First deployed by NATO countries in Europe in 1984, the Chukar III was still in service at the turn of the century with France, Spain, and the United Kingdom, as well as Japan, Taiwan, and Singapore. The company produced more than 1,150 Chukars for its international customers.

The BQM-74C incorporated an optional onboard video system for reconnaissance missions, and was designed to be air-launched as well as surface launched. The lighter, air- launched version had a range of more than 500 miles. As with the BQM-34 Firebees, the Chukar IIIs were air launched from Lockheed DC-130 motherships. During Operation Desert Storm, BQM-74Cs, as well as Firebees, were used with reported success as decoy aircraft, drawing Iraqi anti-aircraft fire away from manned strike aircraft.

An estimated 3,200 MQM-74A and MQM-74C drones were produced, and through the turn of the century, about 2,000 BQM-74C and the faster and longer range BQM-74E vehicles had been delivered.

After BQM-74s were used successfully as chaff dispensers during Gulf War II in 2003, plans were accelerated toward a further improved BQM-74F, which first flew in September 2005.

BGM-75 AICBM

Not to be confused with the Douglas SM-75 (PGM-17) Thor, the BGM-75 designation was assigned in 1966 to the Advanced Intercontinental Ballistic Missile (AICBM) program. Also known as Weapons System 120A, AICBM was aimed at a missile that would ultimately replace the Minuteman family. This notional BGM-75 was intended to be armed with up to 20 thermonuclear warheads in Multiple Independently-targetable Reentry Vehicles (MIRV). The "B" in the designation indicates that a variety of launch scenarios were envisioned. Specifically, these included hardened silos like those of the Minuteman, as well as mobile trains, which were also considered for the Minuteman.

The AIBCM program was cancelled in 1967, with much of its content dusted off in 1972 under the Missile Experimental (MX) program that led eventually to the LGM-118 Peacekeeper.

AGM-76 Falcon

This designation was assigned in 1966 to a US Air Force project aimed at adapting a derivative of the Hughes AIM-4 Falcon air-to-air missile to attack North Vietnamese radar sites. Like the US Navy AGM-63 program, the goal was to develop a missile larger and faster than the AGM-45 Shrike. Unlike the AGM-63 project, a few AGM-76A prototypes, probably retrofitted Falcons, were tested.

Manufacturer: Northrop (Ventura Division), Northrop Grumman after

Length: 12 feet 11.5 inches (3.95 meters)

Diameter: 13.9 inches (0.35 meters)

Wingspan: 5 feet 9.4 inches (1.76 meters)

Weight (air-launch): 465 pounds (211 kilograms)

Weight (surface-launch): 595 pounds (270 kilograms)

Range: 735 miles (1,185 kilometers)

Speed: 621 mph (1,000 km/h)

Ceiling: 40,000 feet (12,200 meters)

Guidance system: radio control or autonomously via autopilot

Propulsion system: Williams J400 turbojet

First tested: circa 1964

First deployed: 1968

(Specifications for BQM-74E)

Sighting a McDonnell Douglas M47 (FGM-77) launcher, circa 1991. (Author's collection)

FGM-77 Dragon

A shoulder-fired anti-tank missile system, the Dragon was similar in size and configuration to the earlier FIM-43 Redeye anti-aircraft missile. The idea was to provide US Army infantry units with a man-portable weapon to use against the masses of Soviet armored vehicles expected on a European battlefield if the Cold War turned hot. The Dragon was developed in the mid-1960s, and deployed operationally in 1975.

Through the 1980s, improved Dragon II and Super Dragon variants were introduced, each with incrementally improved penetration capability. These weapons were on hand in time for Operation Desert Storm in 1991. United States forces acquired about 50,000 Dragon missiles (some sources state higher numbers), two-thirds for the Army, and the balance for the Marines. Troops found the noisy, wire-guided Dragon difficult to use because it was hard to keep lined up on the target. Nor was its short range popular when a soldier contemplated attacking a tank.

While many earlier missile systems started out with an "M for Model" designation and were later redesignated with an "M for Missile" prefix, the Dragon went the other way, from FGM-77A to M47. A slow phase-out of the Dragon in favor of the newer FGM-148 Javelin began in the late 1990s.

Meanwhile, the Netherlands, Spain, Switzerland and Thailand also acquired the Dragon. So too did pre-revolution Iran. Later, Iran manufactured a knock-off known as Saeghe (Thunder), which was also delivered to Hezbollah terrorists in Lebanon.

Manufacturer: McDonnell Douglas

Length: 29 feet 4 inches (0.74 meters)

Diameter: 9.8 inches (0.25 meters)

Span (fins): 13.4 inches (0.34 meters)

Weight: 24 pounds (11 kilograms)

Range: 3,300 feet (1,000 meters)
+200 mph (330 km/h)

Guidance system: wire-guided line of sight

Propulsion system: a series of small, solid-fuel rocket motors

Warhead: shaped charge

First tested: 1968

First deployed: 1975

(Specifications for FGM-77A/M47)

Lance Corporal T.A. Moore of the 2nd Marine Regiment with an M47 (FGM-77) Dragon during an April 1997 Combined Arms Exercise at the Marine Corps Air Ground Combat Center at Twentynine Palms, California. (US Marine Corps photo by Lance Corporal E.J. Young)

Below: *A soldier of the 25th Infantry Division fires an M47 (FGM-77) Dragon anti-tank missile during Exercise Cobra Gold at Korat Royal Thai AB in July 1987.* (US Army photo by Staff Sergeant Valentino Gempis)

AGM-78 Standard ARM

The Standard Anti-Radiation Missile (ARM) was an air-launched adaptation of airframe of the ship-launched RIM-66 Standard surface-to-air missile. As such, it joined the AGM-63 and AGM-76 projects among the efforts to create a successor to the disappointing AGM-45 Shrike. Defeating North Vietnamese air defense radar was essential to the strike mission, and developing a weapon that would home on the radar was an obvious solution, but it was an elusive one.

In 1966, the US Navy contracted with General Dynamics to essentially combine a radiation seeker with the existing RIM-66 airframe to save development time. After tests in 1967, the AGM-78A entered service with both the Navy and Air Force in 1968. It was soon followed by an improved AGM-78B with a longer range and larger warhead. The seeker was improved over the Shrike, able to retain its target lock-on even if the enemy shut down its radar emitters after the launch was detected.

Further improvements to the electronics systems led to the deployment of AGM-78C and AGM-78D variants during the 1970s, but by the 1980s, the Standard ARM was phased out in favor of the AGM-88 HARM. (See Appendix 4 for an overview of the Standard family.)

Manufacturer: General Dynamics

Length: 15 feet (4.57 meters)

Diameter: 13.5 inches (0.34 meters)

Span (fins): 42.5 inches (1.08 meters)

Weight: 1,370 pounds (620 kilograms)

Range: 56 miles (90 kilometers)

Speed: Mach 2.5

Guidance system: radar homing

Propulsion system: Aerojet solid-fuel rocket

Warhead: blast fragmentation

First tested: 1968

First deployed: 1969

(Specifications for AGM-78B)

An F-4G "Wild Weasel" Phantom II armed with an AGM-78A Standard ARM, an air-launched variation on the ship-launched RIM-66A fitted with a radiation seeker. (Author's collection)

AGM-79 Blue Eye

The Blue Eye was one of several improved variations on the AGM-12 Bullpup ground attack missile to be evaluated by the US Navy and Air Force. While an AGM-12 operator had to maintain a visual on the target until missile impact, the Blue Eye system achieved target lock-on via a television camera, allowing the pilot to "fire and forget." Test flights of the XAGM-79A, which used an airframe derived from an AGM-12C, occurred in 1968, but the missile never became operational.

Manufacturer: Martin Marietta

Length: 13 feet 7 inches (4.14 meters)

Diameter: 18 inches (0.46 meters)

Span (fins): 4 feet (1.22 meters)

Weight estimate: 1,700 pounds (770 kilograms)

Range estimate: 10 miles (16 kilometers)

Speed: Mach 1.8

Guidance system: television guided

Propulsion system: liquid fuel rocket

Warhead: blast fragmentation

First tested: 1968

First deployed: never

(Specifications for XAGM-78A)

AGM-80 Viper

Like the AGM-79 Blue Eye and the later AGM-83 Bulldog, the Viper was part of an ongoing series of programs aimed at developing a ground attack missile that was an improvement over the AGM-12 Bullpup, but which used the Bullpup as the basis for the new weapon's airframe. Unlike the Blue Eye, the Viper was never tested.

Manufacturer: Chrysler

Dimensions: probably similar to the Bullpup-derived AGM-79

Performance: probably similar to the Bullpup-derived AGM-79

Guidance system: inertial navigation

Warhead: blast fragmentation

First tested: never

First deployed: never

An XAQM-81A Firebolt High Altitude, High Speed Target (HAHST) drone at Eglin AFB in May 1984. (DoD)

AQM-81 Firebolt

The Sandpiper aerial target program is described in an obscure June 1969 report by Franklin Mead and Bernard Bornhorst of the Air Force Rocket Propulsion Lab at Edwards AFB. They wrote that the project was an "in-house exploratory development program [that] was… part of an inter-laboratory team effort to demonstrate the feasibility of hybrid propulsion for the Sandpiper high-performance target."

In this case, "hybrid" means a dual-fuel (solid and liquid) rocket motor. United Technologies built such a motor, which was to be fitted in a variation on the high-performance Beechcraft AQM-37 drone.

The concept was around for a decade when the US Air Force tapped it in 1979 as part of a program that is referred to alternately as High Altitude Supersonic Target (HAST) and High Altitude, High Speed Target (HAHST) program. Because of high estimated program cost from Beechcraft, the Air Force turned to another maker of remotely piloted vehicles, Teledyne Ryan, which developed its Model 305 (a hybrid engine variant of the AQM-37) under the designation AQM-81.

The XAQM-81A flight test program began in 1983, but no operational Firebolts were deployed.

Manufacturer: Ryan Aeronautical (Teledyne Ryan after 1968)

Length: 17 feet (5.18 meters)

Diameter: 13 inches (0.33 meters)

Wingspan: 3 feet 4 inches (1.02 meters)

Weight: 1,230 pounds (560 kilograms)

Speed: Mach 4.3

Ceiling: 103,000 feet (31,400 meters)

Guidance system: telemetry

Propulsion system: United Technology hybrid rocket

First tested: 1983

First deployed: never

(Specifications for XAQM-81A)

AIM-82

In 1969, at a time when the US Air Force was planning ahead for its next generation fighter (which became the F-15), the service thought it would also develop a next generation air-to-air missile. Proposals were submitted by several companies, including General Dynamics, Hughes Aircraft and Philco Aeronutronic (the division of Ford Motor Company that became Ford Aerospace in 1976). However, the program was cancelled in 1970 because the US Navy was then working on the parallel, and nearly identical AIM-95 program. Neither program reached production.

AGM-83 Bulldog

Like the AGM-79 Blue Eye and the AGM-80 Viper, the AGM-83 Bulldog was part of an ongoing series of programs aimed at developing a "fire and forget" ground attack missile that was an improvement over the AGM-12 Bullpup, but which used the Bullpup as the basis for the new weapon's airframe. However, after developing and testing the Bulldog, the US Navy defaulted to acquiring the AGM-65 Maverick, which had been developed for the US Air Force.

Manufacturer: Naval Weapons Center and Texas Instruments

Length: 10 feet 6 inches (3.20 meters)

Diameter: 12 inches (0.30 meters)

Span (fins): 3 feet 1 inch (0.94 meters)

Weight estimate: 620 pounds (280 kilograms)

Range estimate: 7 miles (11 kilometers)

Speed: Mach 1.8

Guidance system: laser guidance

Propulsion system: liquid fuel rocket

Warhead: blast fragmentation

First tested: 1971

First deployed: never

(Specifications for XAGM-83A)

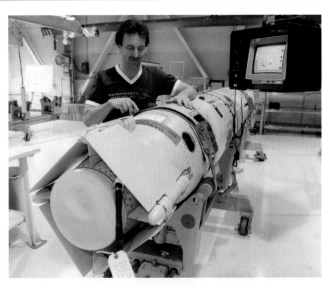

Doing diagnostics work with a nearly completed Harpoon missile on the McDonnell Douglas assembly line at St. Charles, Missouri, circa early 1990s. (McDonnell Douglas)

AGM-84/RGM-84/UGM-84 Harpoon/SLAM

With variants in production for more than three decades, the Harpoon is America's premier anti-ship missile, and it is in service with more than two-dozen foreign countries. Originally developed as an air-launched weapon (AGM-84), the Harpoon has been adapted for surface ship (RGM-84) and submarine (UGM-84) launches. The US Navy has used it operationally a number of times, notably in the sinking of the Iranian frigate *Sahand* during Operation Preying Mantis in 1988. The US Air Force, meanwhile, acquired AGM-84 Harpoons to arm B-52H bombers.

The program originated in 1965 as the US Navy sought a weapon to be used against surfaced submarines, but it gradually morphed to encompass an all-around anti-shipping mission profile. Flight testing began in October 1972, with operational deployments of the RGM-84A in 1977, of the AGM-84A with P-3 patrol planes in 1979, and of the UGM-84A aboard attack submarines in 1981. The United Kingdom deployed a version of the latter as UGM-84B, and has subsequently acquired various models of AGM and RGM Harpoons. Thereafter, McDonnell Douglas introduced the "C Models" of the three types, deployed after 1982, and the "D Models" after 1985. The former was designed for a "sea-skimming" low-altitude mission profile, and the latter had its range capability increased from 60 to 140 miles.

A land attack variant of the Harpoon came about with the second generation AGM-84E Harpoon Stand-off Land Attack Missile (SLAM), which entered service in 1988. It uses inertial guidance until the final leg of the attack, when it is controlled via datalink from the launch aircraft via data from the infrared seeker.

An RGM-84 Harpoon missile is launched from an Antisubmarine Rocket (ASROC) launcher aboard the Knox class frigate USS Badger *in January 1980.* (DoD)

A view of an RGM-84 Harpoon missile being launched from a canister launcher aboard the cruiser USS Leahy *near the Pacific Missile Test Center in the Pacific off California in April 1983.* (DoD)

An ATM-84A Harpoon missile is fitted onto the fuselage of an A-4 Skyhawk aircraft at the Pacific Missile Test Center at Point Mugu in September 1982. The ATM-84A is the training variant of the AGM-84A. (US Navy photo by PH3 Ken Trent)

An AGM-84E Harpoon Block 1E Stand-off Land Attack Missile (SLAM) precision land-attack missile under the wing of an F/A-18C Hornet, circa 1987. (US Navy)

Next in this line of development came the longer-range AGM-84H Stand-off Land Attack Missile-Expanded Response (SLAM-ER), first tested in 1997 and deployed in 1998.

Early in the twenty-first century, Boeing began deliveries of the Harpoon Block II missile, also designated as AGM-84L, RGM-84L and UGM-84L. As the company writes in its literature: "Harpoon Block II expands the capabilities of the Harpoon anti-ship weapon… provides accurate long-range guidance for land and ship targets by incorporating the low-cost inertial measuring unit from the Boeing Joint Direct Attack Munition, or JDAM, program; and the software, mission computer, integrated Global Positioning System/Inertial Navigation System and the GPS antenna and receiver from the SLAM-ER."

Staff Sergeant Richard Pulaski, left, Airman Christian Canada, Airman Vincent Giasco and Sergeant William Reid mount an ATM-84A Harpoon missile on the wings pylon of a 60th Bombardment Squadron B-52G Stratofortress at Andersen AFB in May 1990. The ATM-84A is the training variant of the AGM-84A. (US Air Force photo by Chief Master Sergeant Don Sutherland)

The company adds that: "the 500-pound blast warhead delivers lethal firepower against a wide variety of land-based targets, including coastal defense sites, surface-to-air missile sites, exposed aircraft, port/industrial facilities and ships in port… . Block II improvements maintain Harpoon's high hit probability even against ships very close to land. The multi-mission Block II is deployable from all current Harpoon missile system platforms with either existing command and launch equipment or the new Advanced Harpoon Weapon Control System (AHWCS)."

In addition to the United States, Block II customers included Australia, Canada, Denmark, Egypt, Oman, Pakistan, South Korea and Taiwan.

A contract for the development of the Harpoon Block III RGM-84M was issued in 2008.

Manufacturer: McDonnell Douglas (Boeing after 1997)

Length: 14 feet 9 inches (4.50 meters)

Diameter: 13.5 inches (0.34 meters)

Span (fins): 3 feet (0.91 meters)

Weight: 1,385 pounds (627 kilograms)

Range: 60 miles (93 kilometers)

Speed: Mach 0.85

Guidance system: infrared seeker, automatic target acquisition (air-to-air) with optional operator override

Propulsion system: Teledyne turbojet (RGM-84 and UGM-84 incorporate solid-fuel rocket booster)

Warhead: blast fragmentation

First tested: 1972

First deployed: 1977

(Specifications for AGM-84E SLAM-ER)

RIM-85

This designation was assigned to a US Navy project initiated in 1968 and aimed at developing a surface-to-air missile capable of engaging both aircraft and missiles. The program was apparently terminated before the design phase.

A Boeing Aerospace Company technician assembles an AGM-86B Air Launched Cruise Missile (ALCM) at the company's production line at the Boeing Space Center in Kent, Washington, circa 1983. This missile was one of 40 being produced each month at that time. (Courtesy of William A. Rice, Boeing)

AGM-86 ALCM and CALCM

Though such weapons date back to Germany's World War II V-1, the term "cruise missile" entered the vernacular in the early 1980s as the world became aware of Boeing's Air-Launched Cruise Missile (ALCM).

The ALCM traces its roots to the 1968 US Air Force Subsonic Cruise Aircraft Decoy (SCAD), conceptually an improvement over the ADM-20 Quail. In 1973, the Air Force officially scrapped the SCAD concept and reoriented the program toward the goal of a strategic nuclear strike cruise missile. First tested in 1976, the AGM-86A was quickly superseded by the development of the larger AGM-86B with double the range.

The first AGM-86B ALCMs became operational in December 1982, with the 416th Bombardment Wing at Griffiss AFB in New York. Production of a total of 1,715 missiles was completed in October 1986.

The rapid evolution of data processing technology made it possible to improve the ALCM beyond what was previously imagined. One of the major technological

breakthroughs of this period was Terrain Contour Matching (TERCOM), a revolutionary guidance system that could allow a cruise missile to navigate autonomously in three dimensions at low level.

In June 1986 a small number of AGM-86B missiles were converted to conventional weapons. Their nuclear warheads were replaced by a high-explosive blast fragmentation warhead, and they were redesignated as the AGM-86C Conventional Air-Launched Cruise Missile (CALCM). This modification also replaced the AGM-86B's terrain contour-matching guidance system with an internal Global Positioning System (GPS) capability within the existing inertial navigation computer system. The later AGM-86D Block II CALCM is equipped to penetrate hardened targets.

The CALCM became operational in January 1991 at the onset of Operation Desert Storm. Seven Boeing B-52s from Barksdale AFB launched 35 AGM-86Cs at designated high-priority targets in Iraq, marking the beginning of the Desert Storm air campaign. CALCMs were next used against Iraq in September 1996 during Operation Desert Strike.

An AGM-86 Air Launched Cruise Missile in flight over the Utah Test and Training Range near Hill AFB in 1980. (DoD photo by R.L. House)

A specially designed remote control hydraulic trailer is used to attach a pylon carrying six AGM-86B ALCMs to the wing of a B-52G at Fairchild AFB in May 1984. (US Air Force photo by Staff Sergeant Bob Simons)

Members of the 92nd Bombardment Wing load AGM-86B ALCMs aboard a B-52G during the November 1985 Strategic Air Command Combat Weapons Loading Competition at Ellsworth AFB. (US Air Force photo by Staff Sergeant Rose Reynolds)

A May 1984 view of Staff Sergeant Craig Van Wagenen of the 92nd Bomb Wing at Fairchild AFB working at the left side station of a B-52G ALCM control panel. (US Air Force photo by Staff Sergeant Bob Simons)

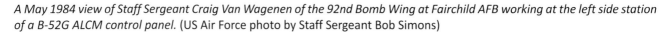

Both ALCMs and CALCMs are air-launched by B-52H bombers, which can carry eight on an internal rotary launcher, plus six externally under each wing.

During the 1990s, the Air Force augmented its cruise missile fleet with the stealthy AGM-129A. Like the ALCM, it was designed for nuclear strike mission, but was adapted for conventional explosives. Both were used in the Gulf Wars of 1991 and 2003, as well as in the Balkans in 1999.

Rather than replacing the AGM-86B with the AGM-129A, the Air Force decided in 2007 to retire all 486 AGM-129As. At the same time, the Air Force announced the reduction of its nuclear-armed ALCM fleet from 1,140 to 528.

Manufacturer: Boeing

Length: 20 feet 9 inches (6.32 meters)

Diameter: 24.5 inches (0.62 meters)

Wingspan: 12 feet (3.66 meters)

Weight: 3,200 pounds (kilograms)

Range: 1,500 miles (2,400 kilometers)

Speed: 500 mph (800 km/h)

Guidance system: inertial navigation supplemented with TERCOM, and later by GPS

Propulsion system: Williams F107 turbofan engine

Warhead: W80 thermonuclear (AGM-86B), blast fragmentation (AGM-86C), AUP-3 hardened target penetrator (AGM-86D)

First tested: 1976

First deployed: 1982

(Specifications for AGM-86B)

A close-up view of eight AGM-86B Air-Launched Cruise Missiles loaded on the rotary launcher in the bomb bay of a B-52G Stratofortress aircraft. (US Air Force)

AGM-87 Focus

The US Navy Focus program involved the modification of an unknown number of AIM-9B Sidewinders from their air-to-air configuration to a ground attack mission. The weapon was developed by the Naval Weapons Center at China Lake, and production work was done by General Electric. Beginning in about 1969, a few were used nocturnally in Southeast Asia against targets that emitted an infrared signature

Manufacturer: General Electric

Specifications: Same as AIM-9 Sidewinder

Guidance system: infrared heat seeking

Propulsion system: Thiokol solid-fuel rocket

Warhead: blast fragmentation

First tested: circa 1969

First deployed: 1969

(Specifications for AGM-87A)

A September 1985 side view of an AGM-88A HARM attached to the wing pylon of an F-4G Phantom II Wild Weasel aircraft. (US Air Force)

A March 1986 close-up of an AGM-88A High-speed Anti-Radiation Missile (HARM) mounted on the wing pylon of an A-7E Corsair II aboard the aircraft carrier USS Saratoga. (US Navy photo by PH1 Shayka)

AGM-88 HARM

When it was deployed, the High-Speed Anti-Radiation Missile (HARM) capped a two-decade quest for a missile that could successfully destroy enemy radar sites by homing on their own emissions. Both the AGM-45 Shrike and AGM-78 Standard ARM had been used against North Vietnamese targets in the 1960s, but both left much to be desired in terms of reliability and ease of use. While the Vietnam War still raged, the Naval Weapons Center at China Lake was working on a replacement that addressed these shortcomings. High speed was a caveat given the need to lock on to the target before the operator shut down the radar emitter.

During the flight test program, which began in 1975, various problems with the target seeker, guidance and other systems were identified and overcome. Built by Texas Instruments, production AGM-88As first reached the US Navy in 1983, and were operational with the US Air Force by 1987. In the meantime, HARMs had their baptism of fire against Libyan radar sites in March 1986, and again during Operation El Dorado Canyon a month later. Interestingly, Shrikes were also used in the latter mission.

Incremental improvements to the seeker, data processing and warhead marked the later AGM-88B (Block II), introduced in 1987, and the AGM-88C (Block IV), introduced in 1993.

During the March 2003 Air-to-Ground Weapons System Evaluation Program Combat Hammer, Captain Thomas Seymour of the 86th Fighter Weapons Squadron at Eglin AFB fires an AGM-88 HARM from his F-16C. (US Air Force photo by Tech Sergeant Michael Ammons)

A 522nd Fighter Squadron F-16C fires an AGM-88 HARM at a target on the Utah Test and Training Range near Hill AFB during Exercise Combat Hammer in May 2004. (US Air Force photo by Tech Sergeant Michael Ammons)

A substantially new missile is the AGM-88E Advanced Anti Radiation Guided Missile (AARGM), introduced in 2010. Built by Alliant Techsystems, it was developed jointly for the United States and Italy for use by F/A-18 variants, Tornado ECRs and F-35s.

According to Alliant, the AGM-88E's advanced multi-sensor system includes a global positioning system/inertial navigation system seeker and a millimeter wave terminal seeker that can counter radar shutdown tactics, or operate in a stand-alone mode to guide to non-emitting targets.

Manufacturer: Texas Instruments (Raytheon after 1997), Alliant Techsystems (AGM-88E)

Length: 13 feet 8 inches (4.2 meters)

Diameter: 10 inches (0.25 meters)

Span (fins): 2 feet (0.61 meters)

Weight: 800 pounds (360 kilograms)

Range: 90 miles (160 kilometers)

Speed: Mach 2

Guidance system: radar homing

Propulsion system: solid-fuel rocket

Warhead: blast fragmentation

First tested: 1975

First deployed: 1983

(Specifications for AGM-88A)

UGM-89 Perseus

The US Navy's Perseus program was initiated in the late 1960s as part of an effort to develop an elaborate submarine/cruise missile capability to complement the Submarine-Launched Ballistic Missile (SLBM) fleet. The project was known variously as the Submarine Tactical Missile (STAM) and the Submarine Anti-ship Weapon System (STAWS), and involved a new class of nuclear attack submarines as well as the missiles.

Because the missiles were too large in diameter for a conventional torpedo tube, the plan was for them to be launched vertically like SLBMs. The UGM-89 Perseus program was cancelled in 1973, and the even more costly submarine project a year later. Vestiges of the work done on the STAWS mission of the Perseus program were later recycled in the UUM-125 Sea Lance program.

The US Navy soon got its cruise missiles, albeit with torpedo tube diameter, with the UGM-84 Harpoon and BGM-109 Tomahawk.

Manufacturer: Lockheed Missiles & Space Company

Length: 25 feet (7.62 meters)

Diameter: 30 inches (0.76 meters)

Weight: 6,000 pounds (2,700 kilograms)

Range: 35 miles (55 kilometers)

Propulsion system: solid-fuel rocket

Warhead: high explosive

First tested: never

First deployed: never

BQM-90

The designation was allocated to a US Navy project involving the development of a Mach 3 target drone for testing surface-to-air missiles and anti-missile missiles. The subject of design studies between 1970 and 1973, this notional target missile was also to have had the ability to fly very low, simulating the flight profile of an anti-ship missile.

Designated as AQM-91A, Teledyne Ryan's Model 154 Firefly reconnaissance drone was a waypoint on the technological evolution from the Model 147/AQM-34 Firebee family and the larger YQM-98 Compass Cope aircraft. (Author's collection)

AQM-91 Firefly

A stealthy aircraft developed before the term "stealth" entered the lexicon, the Ryan Model 154/AQM-91 Firefly evolved from the Ryan Model 147/BQM-34 Firebee both in terms of is airframe and its mission. The Compass Arrow program envisioned an unmanned, remotely-piloted vehicle (RPV) with range sufficient to fly reconnaissance missions over China and North Korea that were too dangerous for a manned U-2.

The aircraft looked like a scaled-up Firebee, with the engine rotated to the top of the fuselage to minimize detection from the ground. Its fuselage was also coated with radar absorbing materials.

Designated as AQM-91A, the Firefly first flew under a veil of secrecy in 1968, and was acknowledged only after a 1969 crash. Like the Lightning Bug drones then active over Southeast Asia, it was air-launched from a DC-130 and it was recovered with the Mid-Air Retrieval System. Nearly two-dozen production series AQM-91s were built, but the program was reportedly terminated in 1973 without becoming operational. Technically, it

was a stepping stone to the Compass Cope program's Ryan YQM-98 Tern, and eventually even to the Ryan/Northrop RQ-4 Global Hawk.

Manufacturer: Teledyne Ryan (Ryan Aeronautical before 1969)

Length: 34 feet (10.36 meters)

Wingspan: 48 feet (14.63 meters)

Weight: 5,245 pounds (2,375 kilograms)

Range: 2,300 miles (3,700 kilometers)

Speed: Mach 0.8

Ceiling: 78,000 feet (24,000 meters)

Guidance system: radio link remote control

Propulsion system: General Electric J97 turbojet

First tested: 1968

First deployed: never acknowledged

(Specifications for AQM-91A)

A US Marine with a field radio relays the direction of aircraft approaching the Crow Valley Electronic Warfare Tactical Range in the Philippines to the operator of an FIM-92 Stinger missile launcher during Exercise Cope Thunder in September 1984. (US Marine photo by Staff Sergeant Danny Perez)

FIM-92 Stinger

One of the most successful and widely-used man-portable anti-aircraft missiles in the world, the Stinger has accounted for nearly 300 interceptions, and is in service with about 30 countries around the world. The program began in 1967 when the US Army was seeking a successor to the FIM-43 Redeye, and in the beginning, the system was called Redeye II.

The XFIM-92A development process was lengthy and laden with teething troubles. Indeed, tests of shoulder-fired Stingers did not occur until 1975, and the FIM-92A did not enter service until 1981. From that point, however, use of the Stinger spread quickly. The principal improvements of the Stinger over the Redeye include its ability to attack from the front, rather than only the exhaust of an attacking aircraft, and its ability to lock-on and follow an aircraft taking tight evasive action.

Stingers were first used in combat by British forces in the 1982 Falklands War, who scored the first Stinger kill against an Argentine Pucara on May 21. During the 1980s, they were supplied by the United States to UNITA rebels fighting the communists in Angola, as well as to

Mujahideen insurgents fighting the Soviets in Afghanistan. In the latter instance, they are said to have been a decisive weapon. Stingers also found their way into the hands of participants in the Balkan Wars of the 1990s.

With the introduction of the FIM-92B in 1983, the Stinger had a passive optical seeker that allowed it to discriminate against ground clutter. The FIM-92C of 1987 had reprogrammable software that could be updated. Some such missiles when updated were redesignated as FIM-92D. The FIM-92E and FIM-92F, embodying further refinements and upgraded software, appeared at the turn of the century.

In addition to the United States and most NATO countries, Stingers have served with countries such as Bangladesh, Chad, Chile, Egypt, Israel, Japan, South Korea, Taiwan, Latvia, Lithuania, Pakistan, Slovenia, and Switzerland. They are also reportedly in the arsenal of the United States Secret Service.

Though designed to be shoulder-launched, Stingers also arm launchers on a variety of vehicles. In American service, these include the M6 Linebacker, a derivative of the M2A2 Bradley, as well as the Hum-Vee as part of the Avenger Air Defense System.

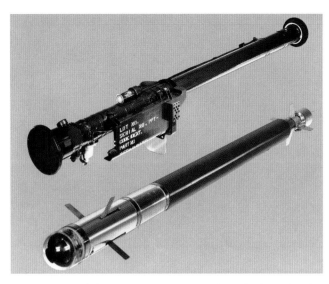

A 1987 view of the FIM-92 Stinger missile and a launch tube, a lightweight, portable, shoulder-fired, surface-to-air defense system. (General Dynamics via DoD)

A view of an Avenger air defense system deployed with the US Army during Operation Desert Shield in 1991. Carried by a Hum-Vee, the Avenger consists of a four-tube Stinger launcher mounted on each side of an operator's station on a pedestal. (US Army photo by Sergeant Brian Cumper)

Marine Corp personnel from the 3rd Low Altitude Air Defense Battalion launch an FIM-92 Stinger at Twentynine Palms. (US Marine photo by Lance Corporal Manuel Valdez)

An air-launched AIM-92 Stinger was first tested by the US Army in 1996. These have subsequently been widely deployed aboard many helicopter types, including the OH-58 Kiowa, UH-60 Black Hawk and AH-64 Apache, as well as aboard MQ-1 Predator drones.

Manufacturer: originally General Dynamics, Hughes Aircraft 1992-1997, Raytheon thereafter (also under license by EADS in Germany and Roketsan in Turkey)

Length: 5 feet (1.52 meters)

Diameter: 2.75 inches (0.07 meters)

Span (fins): 3.6 inches (0.09 meters)

Weight: 22.3 pounds (10 kilograms)

Range: 3 miles (4.8 kilometers)

Speed: Mach 2.2

Ceiling: 26,000 feet (3,800 meters)

Guidance system: infrared homing

Propulsion system: Atlantic Research solid-fuel rocket

Warhead: blast fragmentation

First tested: 1973

First deployed: 1981

(Specifications for FIM-92C)

GQM-93 Compass Dwell

Like the Compass Arrow program which led to the AQM-91, the Compass Dwell program was a secret effort to develop a very long endurance, unmanned surveillance platform. While Compass Arrow involved a jet, the aircraft evaluated under Compass Dwell were powered by piston engines. These included the Martin Marietta Model 845A and the E-Systems Model L450F, which were flight tested in early 1972. Both were variations on Schweizer SGS gliders. The program was reportedly cancelled later in 1972, but the Model L450F was retroactively designated as XGQ-93A at least two years afterward.

Manufacturer: E-Systems (later Raytheon)

Length: 29 feet 7 inches (9.02 meters)

Height: 10 feet 8 inches (3.25 meters)

Wingspan: 57 feet (17.37 meters)

Weight: 5,300 pounds (2,400 kilograms)

Range: 5,200 miles (8,300 kilometers)

Speed: 230 mph (370 km/h)

Ceiling: 50,000 feet (15,200 meters)

Guidance system: radio command remote control

Propulsion system: Pratt & Whitney Canada turboprop

First tested: 1972

First deployed: never

(Specifications for XAQM-93A)

A hangar view of the Boeing YQM-94 Gull. The aircraft was built as Boeing Model 901 for the US Air Force Compass Cope program. (Author's collection)

YQM-94 Gull (Compass Cope B)

The US Air Force Compass Cope program of 1971 envisioned a remotely piloted vehicle (RPV) roughly analogous in range and performance to the manned Lockheed U-2 spyplane. As with the U-2, Compass Cope was a slow aircraft with an emphasis on very long endurance (up to 24 hours) at very high altitudes. Compass Cope control would be by way of a real-time television data link to a ground-based operator. In addition to reconnaissance, the platform could be tasked with communications relay and atmospheric sampling. Unlike the air-launched AQM-91 Compass Arrow, Compass Cope aircraft were intended to take off and land on runways.

There were two aircraft types built as flight test vehicles under the program. Originally planned as the sole Compass Cope aircraft was the Boeing Model 901, ordered in 1971 as the YQM-94A Gull (Compass Cope-B). However, the Teledyne Ryan Model 235 was ordered in 1972 as the YQM-98A Tern (Compass Cope-R). Both aircraft, like the AQM-91, had engines mounted atop their fuselage to make them harder to detect from the ground. Both had a "YQM" rather than the "YGQM" prefix which would have fit the nomenclature paradigm for such craft.

The first prototype Boeing YQM-94A Gull made its debut flight in July 1973, but crashed a few days later on its second flight. The flight test program continued,

with the second YQM-94A, until November 1974. During this time, the YQM-94A demonstrated an endurance of more than 17 hours.

In August 1976, the Boeing YQM-94A was chosen over the YQM-98A and a production contract was issued for a series of larger YQM-94B aircraft. However, the program was cancelled in July 1977 before any further aircraft were built.

Manufacturer: Boeing

Length: 40 feet (12.19 meters)

Height: 12 feet 8 inches (3.86 meters)

Wingspan: 90 feet (27.43 meters)

Weight: 14,400 pounds (6,520 kilograms)

Speed: Mach 0.6

Ceiling: 55,000 feet (16,700 meters)

Guidance system: television datalink remote control

Propulsion system: General Electric TF34 turbofan

First tested: 1973

First deployed: never

(Specifications for YQM-94A)

Long of wing and ahead of its time, the YQM-94A Gull prepares for its debut flight in 1973. (Author's collection)

AIM-95 Agile

At the end of the 1960s, both the US Air Force and US Navy toyed with the idea of replacing the AIM-9 Sidewinder air-to-air missile. The Air Force entertained various industry proposals for a notional AIM-82 missile, while the Naval Weapons Center at China Lake began working on the Agile concept in 1968. The AIM-82 was cancelled in 1970 because of perceived duplication of effort, and the Defense Department decided that both services would acquire the Agile as the AIM-95A. However, this program was cancelled in 1975 before reaching production. The replacement for the early AIM-9 Sidewinder was ultimately a series of more refined AIM-9 Sidewinders.

A naval aviator poses with an unmarked AIM-95A Agile at the Naval Weapons Center at China Lake, circa 1970. (US Navy)

Trident I C4, which had the same dimensions as the Poseidon, and which therefore could fit in existing launch tubes. The second step, which began in 1983, would be the larger Trident II D5 (UGM-133).

With a first test launch in January 1977, the UGM-96 was first deployed in October 1979 aboard the USS *Francis Scott Key*, the first of 12 Poseidon submarines retrofitted for the Trident I. Meanwhile, the Navy was building the new Ohio Class (aka "Trident" Class) boats, the first eight of which were designed to carry the Trident I, and later transition to the Trident II. The USS *Ohio* went to sea with the Trident I in November 1981. Britain's Royal Navy ordered the Trident I in 1980, but soon switched their procurement to the Trident II.

Compared to the Poseidon, the Trident I had three, rather than two, solid-fuel engine stages, greater range and greater kilotonnage in its multiple independently targeted reentry vehicles (MIRV). UGM-96s remained in production until 1986, and in service until 2007, although their gradual replacement by the Trident II began in 1990. The last UGM-96A Trident I test launch occurred in 2001.

The seventeenth land pad launch of a Trident missile took place at Cape Canaveral on December 16, 1978. (DoD)

UGM-96 Trident I C4

The objective of a successor to the US Navy's UGM-73 Poseidon Submarine-Launched Ballistic Missile (SLBM) fleet was first addressed in November 1971, just eight months after the Poseidon was first deployed. The idea was to create a missile with nearly double the range of the Poseidon, but this goal would be reached in a lengthy two-step process. With development getting underway in 1974, the first step would be the UGM-96

A demonstration and shakedown operation launch of a UGM-96A Trident SLBM from the nuclear-powered strategic missile submarine USS Michigan *in November 1982.* (DoD)

A UGM-96A Trident I (C-4) fleet ballistic missile is loaded aboard the nuclear-powered strategic missile submarine USS Ohio *at Cape Canaveral in 1982.* (DoD)

Manufacturer: Lockheed Missiles & Space Company

Height: 34 feet 1 inche(10.39 meters)

Diameter: 6 feet 2 inches (1.88 meters)

Weight: 73,000 pounds (33,000 kilograms)

Range: 4,600 miles (7,400 kilometers)

Guidance system: electronic star-sighting inertial guidance

Propulsion system: Thiokol (first stage), Hercules (second stage), United Technologies (third stage) solid-fuel rockets

Warhead: multiple warhead W76 thermonuclear

First tested: 1977

First deployed: 1979

(Specifications for UGM-96A)

AIM-97 Seekbat

As the name suggests, the Seekbat program was directed at the development of an air-to-air missile that could counter the theoretically unstoppable Soviet MiG-25 'Foxbat' high-altitude, Mach 3 interceptor. Beginning in 1972, the program sought to adapt the airframe of the AGM-78 Standard anti-radar missile for the new task. Testing of the XAIM-97A took place between 1972 and 1976, but the missile was apparently never deployed operationally.

Manufacturer: General Dynamics

Length: 15 feet (4.57 meters)

Diameter: 13.5 inches (0.34 meters)

Span (fins): 42.5 inches (1.08 meters)

Weight: 1,300 pounds (600 kilograms)

Speed: Mach 3

Ceiling: tested at 80,000 feet (24,000 meters)

Guidance system: passive infrared homing

Propulsion system: Aerojet solid-fuel rocket

Warhead: blast fragmentation

First tested: 1972

First deployed: never

(Specifications for XAIM-97A)

The YQM-98A Tern, seen here circa 1974, was the Teledyne Ryan entry in the US Air Force Compass Cope high-altitude UAV evaluation program. (Author's collection)

YQM-98 Tern (Compass Cope-R)

As described under YQM-94 above, the Compass Cope program of 1971 envisioned a remotely piloted vehicle (RPV) roughly analogous in range and performance to the manned Lockheed U-2 spyplane. The two aircraft flight tested were the Boeing Model 901, ordered in 1971 as the YQM-94A Gull (Compass Cope-B), and the Teledyne Ryan Model 235, was ordered in 1972 as the YQM-98A Tern (Compass Cope-R).

The YQM-98A made its first flight in August 1974, and went on to set a world endurance record for an unmanned, unrefueled aircraft, of 28 hours 11 minutes.

In August 1976, the Gull was chosen over the Tern for a production contract. Teledyne Ryan then lodged a protest with the US Air Force, arguing that it had produced a superior (albeit more expensive) aircraft. It was a moot point, as the Air Force cancelled the Compass Cope project in July 1977 before any further aircraft were built. Ryan later went on to bigger and better things in the world of unmanned reconnaissance aircraft, specifically to the RQ-4 Global Hawk, which first flew in 1998.

Manufacturer: Teledyne Ryan
Length: 37 feet 4 inches (11.38 meters)
Height: 8 feet (2.44 meters)
Wingspan: 81 feet 2.5 inches (24.75 meters)
Weight: 14,310 pounds (6,480 kilograms)
Range: 9,500 miles (15,000 kilometers)
Speed: Mach 0.6
Ceiling: 70,000 feet (21,000 meters)
Guidance system: television datalink remote control
Propulsion system: Garrett YF104 turbofan
First tested: 1974
First deployed: never
(Specifications for YQM-98A)

LIM-99

Little is known about the US Army's LIM-99 and LIM-100 projects other than they originated in the 1972 time frame and that they were apparently ballistic missile interceptors in the vein of the MIM-49 Spartan. Either or neither designation may have been associated with the otherwise undesignated Martin Marietta Sprint interceptor missile.

LIM-100

Little is known about the US Army's LIM-99 and LIM-100 projects other than that they originated in the 1972 time frame and that they were apparently ballistic missile interceptors in the vein of the MIM-49 Spartan. Either or neither designation may have been associated with the otherwise undesignated Martin Marietta Sprint interceptor missile.

AIM-101 Sparrow III

The AIM-101A designation was assigned as an interim designation for the AIM-7D (formerly AAM-N-6) Sparrow III. Some sources mention a RIM-101, which may or may not have been an interim designation for the RIM-7 Sea Sparrow.

A PQM-102A drone, converted from an F-102A Delta Dagger interceptor, seen here near Tyndall AFB in 1980. (DoD)

PQM-102 Pave Deuce

First flown in 1953, the F-102 Delta Dagger entered service in 1956 and served as a front line manned interceptor with the US Air Force Air Defense Command (and later the Air National Guard) for two decades. In 1973, as some F-102s were still flying with the Air Guard, the Air Force decided to convert some of the retired interceptors to unmanned aerial targets. The McDonnell Douglas F-15 was beginning to be developed, and after the Vietnam experience, air-to-air combat was again a high priority in the development of fighter aircraft. In order to refine the F-15 as a fighter, it would need something to fight.

Under the Pave Deuce program, managed at the Armament Development & Test Center at Eglin AFB in Florida, surplus Delta Daggers were converted to simulate the flight profile of the MiG-21. In April 1973, Sperry Rand received a contract to modify F-102s into two remotely piloted aircraft types. Those which retained controls so that a human pilot could fly them, were designated as QF-102. Others had the human component deleted and were given the coincidental, but conveniently available "102" missile designation as PQM-102A.

The initial PQM-102A flight came in August 1974, and the first of about 200 became operational with the US Air

Force two months later. The conversions continued until 1982, with the PQM-102A drones being joined by PQM-102Bs, which were capable of operating at altitudes as low as 200 feet. Intercepted by AIM-7s, AIM-9s, FIM-92s and MIM-104s, the Pave Deuces dwindled in number gradually until the last one was shot down in 1985.

Manufacturer: Convair Division of General Dynamics

Length: 68 feet 5 inches (20.85 meters)

Wingspan: 38 feet 1 inch (11.61 meters)

Height: 21 feet 2.5 inches (6.46 meters)

Weight: 31,500 pounds (14,300 kilograms)

Range: 200 miles (320 kilometers)

Speed: 605 mph (975 km/h)

Ceiling: 53,400 feet (16,287 meters)

Guidance system: radio command remote control, as well as autonomous flight control

Propulsion system: Pratt & Whitney J57-P-23 turbojet

First tested: 1973

First deployed: 1974

(Specifications for F-102A)

AQM-103

The XAQM-103A designation (originally XQM-103A) was assigned to a single Ryan Model 147G Firebee (see BQM-34) that was modified in 1974 to make extremely high *g* turns to simulate the capability of manned fighters.

Length: 29 feet (8.84 meters)

Height: 6 feet 8 inches (2.03 meters)

Wingspan: 27 feet (8.23 meters)

Weight: 3,000 pounds (1,350 kilograms)

Speed: 600 mph (960 km/h)

Ceiling: 50,000 feet (15,000 meters)

Guidance system: radio command remote control

Propulsion system: Continental J68 turbojet

First tested: 1974

First deployed: probably never

(Specifications for Model 147G)

An MIM-104 Patriot Missile is fired at the White Sands Missile Range by members of the 43rd Air Defense Artillery in April 1987. (US Army photo by Frank Trevino)

MIM-104 Patriot

Developed as a battlefield air defense weapon during the Cold War, the Patriot became an anti-ballistic missile weapon, earning household name status in 1991 during Operation Desert Storm as it intercepted Scud surface-to-surface missiles being launched from Iraq.

In the 1960s, the US Army sought to develop a weapon more sophisticated than the MIM-23 Hawk to defend forces in the field against potential Soviet tactical missile attacks. After initial studies and proposal evaluation, the Army contracted with Raytheon to build such a weapon under the designation SAM-D. First tested at the White Sands Missile Range in 1969, the program evolved considerably over the next several years, including the adoption in the mid-1970s of Track-Via-Missile (TVM) guidance, a system combining aspects of semi-active radar homing with radio command guidance. In 1976, the SAM-D became the XMIM-104A Patriot.

The MIM-104A reached its IOC with the US Army in 1984, and the MIM-104B with stand-off jamming countermeasures was introduced shortly thereafter.

Subsequent incremental software and systems upgrades were undertaken under the Patriot Advanced Capability (PAC) program, which gave the Patriot its anti-ballistic missile capability. PAC-1 was fielded in 1988, and PAC-2 became operational in 1990. PAC-2 features, along with a deadlier conventional warhead, were signature features of the MIM-104C.

During Operation Desert Storm in January-February 1991, PAC-2 Patriots became the first missiles used operationally against enemy ballistic missiles. First

A view of a 7th Air Defense Artillery Brigade Patriot tactical air defense system MIM-104 Patriot missile launcher deployed during Operation Desert Shield in January 1991. Another Patriot launcher is in the background. (US Army photo by Sergeant Brian Cumper)

deployed to Saudi Arabia in 1990 to protect American and Coalition troops, they were also rushed to Israel as Iraq targeted that country. The US Army stated that 53 Soviet-made Scud tactical ballistic missiles were engaged by Patriots, but their success rate is mired in controversy.

According to GlobalSecurity.org, "Patriot success was initially believed to be over 70 percent in Saudi Arabia and over 40 percent in Israel [later these figures were reduced]. Public statements made by Congressman John Conyers and MIT Professor Theodore Postol both suggested that Raytheon 'misrepresented' the Patriot's Gulf War performance."

At the two extremes, President George H.W. Bush claimed a 98 percent success rate during a speech at the Raytheon plant, while Postol claimed a success rate of ten percent or less in his Congressional testimony.

Raytheon's current official Patriot fact sheet gives no data, but states "Patriot performance against Iraqi SCUD missile attacks was impressive, even though these SCUD missiles exceeded Patriot's design threat."

Notable was the incident on February 25, when an unintercepted Scud hit an American base at Dhahran, killing 28.

After these experiences, Raytheon developed the MIM-104D PAC-2 Guidance Enhanced Missile (GEM), which

was built after 1994. The PAC-2 GEM was superseded by the more advanced PAC-3 configuration, for which Lockheed Martin Missiles & Fire Control was the primary contractor for the upgrade. Though the PAC-3 is associated by some sources with the designation "MIM-104F," it is referenced in DOD and industry documents only by the PAC-3 designation. Another, similar Lockheed Martin weapon without an "M For Missile" designation is the Theater High Altitude Area Defense (THAAD) missile described in Addendum 1.

The PAC-3 was flight tested in 2001 after several years of delays, and reached IOC in 2003 in time for Operation Iraqi Freedom. During that conflict, Patriots were used successfully against Iraqi missiles, including the advanced Al-Samoud type. However, the story was marred by two deadly friendly fire incidents in which an American F/A-18 and a British Tornado were shot down.

There was at least one notable success. As described in a CNN report, the Patriot's greatest moment came when "the Iraqi military came within seconds of possibly wiping out the headquarters of the coalition ground forces [at Camp Doha] with a missile on March 27, US military officials said. The missile was intercepted and destroyed by a US Patriot missile shortly before it could have hit its target."

Lockheed Martin Missiles and Fire Control developed the Patriot Advanced Capability (PAC-3) missile, a small, highly agile, kinetic kill interceptor for defense against tactical ballistic missiles, cruise missiles and air-breathing threats. (Lockheed Martin)

Left: *The Missile Segment Enhancement (MSE), Lockheed Martin's enhanced version of the combat-proven PAC-3 Missile. On February, 17, 2010, this PAC-3 MSE successfully intercepted a target representative tactical ballistic missile at White Sands Missile Range.* (Lockheed Martin photo)

Above: *US Army Pfc. Robert Pearl, left, and Specialist Atlee Steever, both with 1st Battalion 43rd Air Defense Artillery, power up a MIM-104 Patriot surface-to-air missile system at an undisclosed location in Southwest Asia in August 2009.* (US Air Force photo by Staff Sergeant Robert Barney)

An artist's conception of the Medium Extended Air Defense System (MEADS). a mobile air and missile defense system designed to replace Patriot systems in the United States and Germany and Nike Hercules systems in Italy. The MEADS interceptor is the Lockheed Martin PAC-3 Missile Segment Enhancement (MSE), which increases the engagement envelope and defended area over the PAC-3 Missile. MEADS is designed to provide "enhanced force protection against a broad array of third dimension threats." Note the NATO logo subtly forming in the clouds. (MEADS International)

PAC-3 improvements continued thereafter, with highlights including the 2007 PAC-3 Missile Segment Enhancement (MSE), which involved a more robust engine and more finally tuned controls. In turn, the PAC-3 MSE was incorporated into the joint American and European Medium Extended Air Defense System (MEADS).

In addition to the US Army, Patriots have been or are operated by the armed forces of Germany, Greece, Netherlands, Spain, Bahrain, Egypt, Israel, Japan, Kuwait, Taiwan, Saudi Arabia, and South Korea.

Manufacturer: Raytheon and later Lockheed Martin (PAC-3)

Length: 17 feet 1 inches (5.21 meters)

Diameter: 10 inches (0.25 meters)

Span (fins): 20 inches (0.5 meters)

Weight: 700 pounds (320 kilograms)

Range: 12 miles (20 kilometers)

Speed: Mach 5 plus

Ceiling: 50,000 feet (15,000 meters)

Guidance system: Track-Via-Missile (see text)

Propulsion system: solid-fuel rocket

Warhead: blast fragmentation/kinetic energy

First tested: 1969 (SAM-D)

First deployed: 1984 (MIM-104A)

(Specifications PAC-3)

Preparing a Lockheed YMQM-105A Aquila for a test flight. The first launch of an Aquila took place here at Fort Huachuca, Arizona in July 1982 and flights continued into 1987. (Lockheed)

MQM-105 Aquila

In the early 1970s the US Army undertook development of a remotely powered air vehicle under its Target Acquisition, Designation & Aerial Reconnaissance (TADAR) program. The objective was to provide battlefield commanders with a light, easy-to-use observation platform, that could also be used as an over-the-horizon artillery target designator.

To address this requirement, Lockheed developed its Aquila (Eagle), which first flew in 1975 under the designation AMQM-105A. Lockheed received the full-scale development contract in 1979 and a 17-flight test program involving the YMQM-105 prototype occurred at Fort Huachuca, Arizona during the summer and fall of 1982.

It was catapult-launched from a truck and recovered aboard a truck using a large nylon net. It also carried a parachute for emergency landings. The Aquila was equipped with a Westinghouse electro-optical payload that included a stabilized laser artillery designator. However, problems with the systems and systems integration led to delays, and ultimately to the cancellation of the program. The US Army had originally planned to achieve an initial operating capability with the first of 995 MQM-105s by

1985, but this didn't happen and the program was terminated in 1987. Lockheed's plans for an export version of the Aquila, known as Altair, also died along with the YMQM-105 program.

Manufacturer: Lockheed Missiles & Space Company

Length: 6 feet 10 inches (2.08 meters)

Wingspan: 12 feet 9 inches (3.89 meters)

Weight: 265 pounds (120 kilograms)

Range: 280 miles (450 kilometers)

Speed: 80 mph (130 km/h) (while on station)

Ceiling: 14,000 feet (4,500 meters)

Guidance system: radio command, or preprogrammed autonomous operation

Propulsion system: piston engine driving a pusher propeller

First tested: 1982 (YMQM-105A)

First deployed: never

(Specifications for YMQM-105A)

BQM-106 Teleplane

The XBQM-106 designation did not describe a single aircraft type, but rather two dozen different, small, remotely piloted vehicles that were built and tested between 1975 and 1986. Run by the Flight Dynamics Laboratory as FDL-33, the Teleplane project was not aimed at an operational aircraft, but rather as an experimental program designed to study many aspects of airframe design by building what amounted to a bunch of radio-controlled models built of composite materials. There were high-wing Teleplanes and low-wing Teleplanes, ones with differing types of tails and differing types of fuselages. Some were designed by Teledyne Ryan, and the XBQM-106A described below was by Digital Design.

Manufacturer: Flight Dynamics Laboratory (US Air Force)

Length: 10 feet 1 inches (3 meters)

Height: 2 feet 9 inches (0.84 meters)

Wingspan: 11 feet 11 inches (3.63 meters)

Weight: 235 pounds (106 kilograms)

Range: 575 miles (925 kilometers)

Speed: 115 mph (185 km/h)

Ceiling: 10,000 feet (3,000 meters)

Guidance system: radio command remote control

Propulsion system: piston engine

First tested: 1975 (Teleplane program beginning)

First deployed: never

(Specifications for Digital Design XBQM-106A, other aircraft differed but were similar in size and performance)

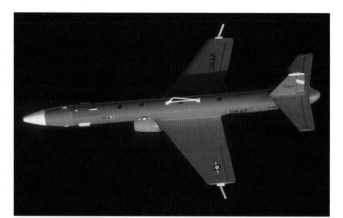

An MQM-107E Streaker from the 82nd Aerial Targets Squadron at Tyndall AFB descends for recovery after a Combat Archer Air-to-Air Weapons System Evaluation Program mission over the Gulf of Mexico in September 2003. The MQM-107E is used to support a variety of air-to-air and surface-to-air missions requiring aerial targets and is typically recovered after each mission, refurbished and reused for future missions. (US Air Force photo by Master Sergeant Michael Ammons)

MQM-107 Streaker

Having produced several early piston-engine target drones, Beechcraft proposed its Model 1089 jet-propelled drone for the US Army's Variable Speed Training Target (VSTT) program. Having been acquired by the Army to challenge MIM-23 Hawks and MIM-104 Patriots, it was also used by the US Air Force as an air-to-air missile target.

First tested in 1974, the Streaker was initially ordered into production in 1975 as the MQM-107A. Incremental improvements in engine technology and other refinements led in turn to introduction of the MQM-107B in 1982, and the MQM-107D in 1987. The final production variant was the MQM-107E, built by British Aerospace) now BAE Systems, which first flew in 1992 and remained in production until 2003.

According to *Forecast International* (April 2008), the MQM-107E, called "Super MQM," is "an improved version of the MQM-107D designed to meet the greater speed and high-*g* maneuvers required by the US Air Force and Navy for air-to-air combat training. This variant is expected to be lighter, faster, and more maneuverable than the standard MQM-107. The MQM-107E had the following improvements: a reshaped rudder and elevators; decreased horizontal stabilizer incidence; reshaped wing leading edges; and a digital autopilot (faster response, magnetometer heading hold, preprogrammed maneuvers, and low-altitude capability)."

Forecast International lists total production at 2,236 Streakers, including 244 MQM-107Bs and 1,916 MQM-107D/E vehicles.

Major Pete Davey, of the 428th Fighter Squadron (the "Buccaneers" from Cannon AFB) flies his F-16C in formation with an MQM-107E Streaker drone during a Combat Archer mission over the Gulf of Mexico in April 2004. (US Air Force photo by Mater Sergeant Michael Ammons)

In addition to the MQM-107s in the American armed forces, Export Model 999 Streakers have served or still serve with the militaries of Egypt, Iran, Jordan, South Korea, Sweden, Taiwan, Turkey and the United Arab Emirates. Australia operates the MQM-107E as the N28 Kalkara.

Manufacturer: Beechcraft
(part of Raytheon, 1980-2007), and BAE Systems
(British Aerospace 1977-1999) (MQM-107E)

Length: 18 feet 9 inches (5.75 meters)

Height: 5 feet (1.52 meters)

Diameter: 15 inches (0.38 meters)

Wingspan: 9 feet 11 inches (3.02 meters)

Weight: 1,460 pounds (662 kilograms)

Range: 1,450 miles (2,330 kilometers)

Speed: 630 mph (1,015 km/h)

Ceiling: 40,000 feet (12,200 meters)

Guidance system: preprogrammed, or radio control override

Propulsion system: Teledyne or Microturbo turbojet, with solid-fuel rocket booster

First tested: 1974

First deployed: 1975

(Specifications for MQM-107E)

BQM-108

The XBQM-108A was a single hybrid research vehicle built by the Naval Weapons Center at China Lake in about 1975, using the fuselage and tail of an MQM-74, to which a delta wing was retrofitted. The purpose was to set the winged drone on its tail and test it in Vertical Take-off and Landing (VTOL) mode. For this, thrust-vectoring tail surfaces were attached. Apparently the only test flights were short lift-offs with the vehicle securely tethered.

Manufacturer: Naval Weapons Center

Length: 12 feet (3.66 meters)

Diameter: 14 inches (0.36 meters)

Wingspan: 7 feet 3 inches (2.21 meters)

Weight: 560 pounds (254 kilograms)

Guidance system: tethered flight

Propulsion system: Teledyne YJ402 turbojet

First tested: 1976

First deployed: never

(Specifications for XBQM-108A)

A test firing of a BQM-109 Ground Launch Cruise Missile (GLCM) painted in early development colors. (Author's collection)

BGM-109 Tomahawk and Gryphon

A nuclear strike weapon, the BGM-109 originated with the US Navy, but also served briefly as one of the most important late Cold War weapons in the US Air Force arsenal. As the popular legend goes, if there was a single weapon which ended the Cold War, this was it. When large numbers of the BGM-109G ground-launched variant were deployed to continental Europe in the late 1980s, Mikhail Gorbachev and his military commanders are said to have consciously realized that it was impossible to defend against these weapons, so they threw in the towel. Even if this legend about a single-handed victory is mere hyperbole, the BGM-109 variants certainly played an important role in the demise of the Cold War.

The original idea was to create a Submarine-Launched Cruise Missile that could be fired from the same launch tubes that were used by the Polaris SLBM. In the 1950s, the US Navy had abandoned the Regulus cruise missile in favor of the Polaris and later SLBMs, but two decades later, technology had evolved to a point where they were ready to revisit the cruise missile concept. Comparative flight tests of the General

Dynamics YBGM-109 and the Ling Temco Vought YBGM-110 during 1976 led the Navy to select the former for a production contract. The new missile would be used aboard surface ships as well as submarines.

Meanwhile, the Department of Defense insisted that both the Air Force AGM-86 and Navy BGM-109 production-series missiles be powered by the Williams F107 turbofan engine and guided by the McDonnell Douglas AN/DPW-23 Terrain Contour Matching (TERCOM) navigation system.

After a series of operational evaluations, the Tomahawk entered service in 1983. Initially, there were four parallel variants, the BGM-109A Tomahawk Land Attack Missile-Nuclear (TLAM-N), and three conventionally armed missiles. These were the BGM-109B Tomahawk Anti-Ship Missile (TASM), the BGM-109C Tomahawk Land Attack Missile-Conventional (TLAM-C), and the BGM-109D Tomahawk Land Attack Missile-Dispenser (TLAM-D) which carried a payload of small submunitions, rather than a single warhead. In 1986, ship-launched conventional TASMs and TLAMs had their prefixes changed to RGM, and submarine-launched ones to UGM.

Members of the 487th Tactical Missile Wing raise the launch tubes of a Ground GLCM launcher during a field training deployment in November 1983. (US Air Force photo by Tech Sergeant Rob Marshall)

Ship-launched Tomahawks are launched using the modular Mk.41 Vertical Launching System (VLS). First deployed in the 1980s, VLS is easy to use, has a faster reaction time than turret or rail launchers, and has long since become the world's standard shipboard launch platform for many missile types.

An air-launched AGM-109 variant was considered by the Air Force, but rejected because the AGM-86 ALCM was already in service.

A Block III upgrade of these variants, which achieved IOC in 1993, included a more compact warhead and added GPS capability to the navigation system. The further improved, albeit cheaper, RGM/UGM-109E TLAM Block IV Tactical Tomahawk (TacTom) was first tested in 2003 and reached IOC in 2004. The RGM/UGM-109H TacTom, with a penetrator warhead for hardened targets, was tested in 2003.

The TLAM had its baptism of fire during Operation Desert Storm in 1991, and was used extensively during further conflicts in the 1990s. According to data compiled by Jane's Information Group, 264 TLAM-Cs and 27 TLAM-Ds missiles were used in Desert Storm, with a further 99 against Iraq in 1993-1996. During actions in the Balkans between 1995 and 1999, at least 338 Block III TLAMs were used. Strikes against terrorist targets in Sudan and Afghanistan in 1998 accounted for 79 Block III TLAM strikes.

Jane's estimates that at least 50 TLAMs were used in Operation Enduring Freedom in October 2001, and about 800 against Iraq in March-April 2003. Among the latter were some fired by British Royal Navy submarines, which first received TLAMs in 1998.

Meanwhile, the BGM-109G Ground-Launched Cruise Missile (GLCM) was the US Air Force version of the US Navy Tomahawk. It was officially named "Gryphon," but best known as "Glick-Um" after its acronym.

During the 1950s, the Air Force had fielded small numbers of ground launched Matador and Mace tactical cruise missiles in Europe. Both were withdrawn from service by the mid 1960s, and replacing them was given a low priority and constantly postponed. Finally, in 1977, the Air Force chose to move forward with the BGM-109G.

Overleaf: *Building Tomahawk cruise missiles at the General Dynamics Convair Division factory in San Diego, circa the mid-1980s.* (Convair via Author's collection)

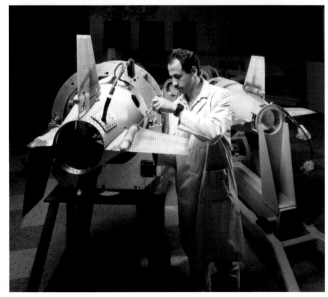

Major James Blondin, an instructor with the 868th Tactical Missile Training Squadron, in the missile launch commander's position in the GLCM training simulator. He is going over missile status checking procedures and the environmental control board during GLCM training. It is interesting to see how computers have evolved, and to imagine how computing power has expanded since 1983. (US Air Force photo by Tech Sergeant Rob Marshall)

The catalyst was the deployment of the Soviet RSD-10 Pioneer, known as the SS-20 Saber in NATO nomenclature. This mobile IRBM had the range to easily deliver a nuclear strike against any target in Western Europe. Both Britain and West Germany were anxious for the United States to do something to counter this threat and to give Western Europe a tactical nuclear deterrent force. The United States answer would be to deploy a combination of US Army Pershing II and US Air Force GLCMs.

Physically, the BGM-109G was roughly the same size and weight as the Tomahawk, and its W84 thermonuclear warhead had the same yield as the TLAM-N's W80.

The first GLCM test launch was in 1980, with the first missiles deployed to RAF Greenham Common in England in 1983. By August 1987, a total of 464 GLCMs were fielded in Belgium, West Germany, the Netherlands, Sicily, and the United Kingdom. The plan was for the GLCMs to be as mobile as Soviet IRBMs, so they were mounted on tractor-trailer trucks, each with four launch tubes.

Documents recovered from Soviet archives after the end of the Cold War show that the Soviet leadership reacted to the GLCMs with an unusually high level of concern. The TERCOM capability of both TLAM and GLCM allowed the missiles to fly so low that detecting and intercepting them would have been virtually impossible. It is now known that the Soviet Union greeted the deployment of the GLCMs almost as a strategic checkmate.

In the West, those favoring a continuation of Mutual Assured Destruction through the ongoing Nuclear Freeze movement, also reacted with a singularly elevated degree of distress. A large number of vociferous protesters descended upon the perimeter fence at Greenham Common to establish a semipermanent "Peace Camp." Strangely, these individuals launched no similar protest to the widespread deployment of the Soviet IRBMs which were aimed *at* the United Kingdom.

In the United States, Paul Warnke, who had been director of the Arms Control & Disarmament Agency under Jimmy Carter Administration, insisted in a counterintuitive *Washington Post* op-ed piece that the United States unilaterally halt deployment of the GLCM, regardless of the Soviet deployment of the RSD-10, or else "the United States will face a further deterioration in its relations with the Soviet Union, and Western Europe's confidence in American leadership will decline."

Above: *An AGM-109 Tomahawk air-launched cruise missile is unloaded from a B-52 aircraft in April 1979.* (DoD)

Left: *An inside view of AGM-109 Tomahawk air-launched cruise missiles mounted on a rotary missile launcher in the bomb bay of a B-52 in April 1979.* (DoD)

A Tomahawk from one of the eight armored box launchers aboard the battleship USS New Jersey is fired off the coast of Southern California in May 1983. It traveled about 500 miles to its target at the Tonopah Test Range in Nevada. (DoD)

A BGM-109D Tomahawk Land-Attack Missile (TLAM) during a development flight, circa 1987. (Author's collection)

Warnke was right insofar as the fact that the Soviet Union *was* angry about the GLCM, but the result was just the opposite of what he predicted.

When Warnke complained that the GLCM had "no military justification," he could not have been farther from the truth. The nuclear checkmate afforded by GLCM compelled the Soviet Union to go to the bargaining table for the talks that led to the Intermediate-Range and Shorter-Range Nuclear Forces (INF) Treaty that went into effect in 1988. The United States agreed to withdraw the GLCMs only in exchange for parallel demobilization of Soviet weapons in Eastern Europe. The Cold War was one step closer to a conclusion.

After their short-lived, but pivotal, deployment in Europe, the Glick-Ums were removed from Europe between 1988 and 1991.

Manufacturer: General Dynamics

Length (all variants): 18 feet 3 inches (5.56 meters)

Length (all variants, with booster): 20 feet 6 inches (6.25 meters)

Diameter (Tomahawk variants): 20.9 inches (0.53 meters)

Diameter (GLCM): 20.4 inches (0.52 meters)

Wingspan (all variants): 8 feet 7 inches (2.6 meters)

Weight (TLAM-N): 2,600 pounds (1,180 kilograms)

Weight (TLAM-N with booster): 3,200 pounds (1,450 kilograms)

Weight (TLAM-C): 2,700 pounds (1,220 kilograms)

Weight (TLAM-C with booster): 3,300 pounds (1,490 kilograms)

Weight (GLCM): 2,650 pounds (1,200 kilograms)

Weight (GLCM with booster): 3,250 pounds (1,470 kilograms)

Range (TLAM-N): 1,550 miles (2,500 kilometers)

Range (TLAM-C): 540 miles (870 kilometers)

Range (GLCM): 1,550 miles (2,500 kilometers)

Speed: 550 mph (880 k/ph)

Guidance system: Terrain Contour Matching (TERCOM), later incorporating GPS

Propulsion system: Williams F107 turbofan

Warhead: conventional or thermonuclear (see text)

First tested: 1976 (Tomahawk), 1980 (GLCM)

First deployed: 1983 (Tomahawk), 1983 (GLCM)

A BGM-109 TLAM is launched toward a target in Iraq from the port side Mk.143 Armored Box Launcher on the stern of the nuclear-powered guided missile cruiser USS Mississippi *during Operation Desert Storm in January 1991.* (US Navy photo by MMCS Henderlite)

The nuclear attack submarine USS Santa Fe *in February 1994, with the doors of its Mk.36 Vertical Launch System for Tomahawk missiles in the open position.* (US Navy photo by OS2 John Bouvia)

A Block IV Tactical Tomahawk, the "next generation" Tomahawk, during a November 2002 flight test over the Pacific. In this flight, the missile successfully completed a vertical underwater launch, flew a fully guided 780-mile course, and impacted a designated target structure as planned. (US Navy)

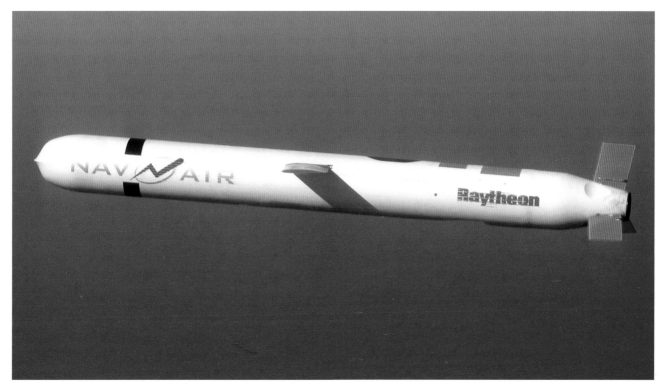

BGM-110

This missile was the now-forgotten LTV entry in the US Navy Submarine-Launched Cruise Missile (SLCM) competition that was won by the BGM-109 Tomahawk. It was even being considered in an air-launched configuration. Had the YBGM-110A not botched a February 1976 submarine torpedo tube launch test, there might have been more of a competition, but the failure doomed the LTV missile and the Tomahawk was ordered a month later.

Manufacturer: Ling-Temco-Vought (LTV)

Length: 17 feet 10 inches (5.43 meters), with booster: 20 feet 6 inches (6.25 meters)

Diameter: 21 inches (0.53 meters)

Wingspan: 10 feet 6 inches (3.20 meters)

Range: 1,500 miles (2,400 kilometers)

Speed: Mach 0.7

Guidance system: Terrain Contour Matching (TERCOM)

Propulsion system: Teledyne J471 turbojet

Warhead: W80 Thermonuclear

First tested: circa 1975

First deployed: never

(Specifications for YBGM-110A)

BQM-111 Firebrand

Initiated in 1977, Firebrand was the result of an effort to create a target drone to test US Navy shipboard surface-to-air missiles against low-level anti-ship missiles. The contract went to Ryan with its extensive remotely piloted vehicle experience gained in the earlier Firebee and Firefly programs. Like earlier drones with a similar mission profile, Firebrand was to be air-launched from a DC-130. At least one was built, but the project fell to the budget-cutter's axe, apparently before any flight tests. The Navy made do with MQM-7 Vandals (converted RIM-7 Taloses), while waiting for the next generation AQM-127, which would also be cancelled.

Manufacturer: Teledyne Ryan

Length: 34 feet (10.4 meters)

Diameter: 28 inches (0.71 meters)

Wingspan: 9 feet (2.74 meters)

Weight: 6,200 pounds (2,800 kilograms)

Speed: Mach 2.1

Ceiling: 40,000 feet (12,200 meters)

Guidance system: preprogrammed, or radio control override

Propulsion system: two Marquardt ramjets with Thiokol solid-fuel rocket boosters

First tested: never

First deployed: never

(Specifications for ZBQM-111A)

The AGM-112 designation was considered, but not used, for the unpowered GBU-15 electro-optically guided glide bombs. (US Air Force)

AGM-112

The AGM-112A and AGM-112B designations were originally set aside for variants of the GBU-15 glide bomb unit. Like the AGM-62 Walleye, the weapon was guided, but unpowered, and therefore not a missile. While the Walleye retained its missile nomenclature, the AGM-112 designation was never officially assigned. A version of the GBU-15 with a "strap-on" rocket motor was developed and deployed in 1994, but under the designation AGM-130.

The GBU-15 is essentially a Mk.84 general purpose bomb, with a guidance unit attached. Later GBU-15s were adapted from BLU-109 penetrating bombs. The GBU-15 has been and continues to be a widely used "smart bomb," having seen service in both Gulf Wars.

RIM-113

The US Navy's Shipboard Intermediate Range Combat System (SIRCS) program was initiated in 1976 in an effort to develop a cruise missile defense system for surface ships. The system itself involved radar and fire control, as well as a missile component. The Navy wished to develop an all-new missile, and assigned the designation XRIM-113A. However, Congressional budget-cutters asked why the RIM-7 Sea Sparrow could not be satisfactorily upgraded. Not receiving an answer which they deemed satisfactory, Congress terminated the notional RIM-113A program before a contractor had been selected and a design developed.

Manufacturer: Rockwell International, later Boeing and Raytheon

Length: 12 feet 10.5 inches (3.92 meters)

Diameter: 18 inches (0.46 meters)

Span (fins): 4 feet 11 inches (1.50 meters)

Weight: 2,450 pounds (1,100 kilograms)

Range: 15 miles (24 kilometers)

Guidance system: television and infrared variants

Propulsion system: none

Warhead: high explosive

First tested: 1975

First deployed: circa 1981

(Specifications for GBU-15)

A YAH-64 Apache helicopter prototype during a March 1982 demonstration flight at Fort Belvoir. It was armed with an M230A1 30mm automatic cannon and early AGM-114A Hellfire missiles. (US Army photo by Robert Ward)

AGM-114 Hellfire

The program began in 1971 as the US Army sought a lightweight, fire-and-forget, anti-tank missile that could be used to arm attack helicopters. The resulting weapon was named "Hellfire," a Biblical term which is also considered an acronym for "HELicopter-Launched FIRE-and-forget missile."

Beginning in 1976, the Hellfire program was developed jointly by Rockwell, who built the missile and Martin, who built the laser seeker. Tests of the YAGM-114A prototype took place between 1978 and 1981, and the AGM-114A achieved IOC with Army AH-64 attack helicopters in 1985. Meanwhile, the similar AGM-114B with a less smoky motor and a shipboard safety system was acquired by the US Navy and Marine Corps. The next variant to enter production was the AGM-114F, which was designed with dual warheads to pierce reactive armor.

New generation Hellfire II missiles were developed between 1989 and 1994, incorporating improvements deemed necessary by the experience of Operation Desert Storm in 1991. The Hellfire II package included the dual warhead similar to that of the AGM-114F, as well as a new autopilot, and more flexibility in reprogramming the system software in the field. The AGM-114K Hellfire II entered service 1994.

Deployed since 1998, a derivative of the AGM-114K is the AGM-114L Longbow Hellfire which includes an active radar seeker working in concert with the radar of the AH-64D Apache Longbow helicopter.

Other Hellfire II variants include the AGM-114M, designed with blast fragmentation warhead for use against unarmored vehicles or urban targets, and the AGM-114N, which is armed with a thermobaric (fuel-air explosive) long-duration blast warhead.

The principal platforms from which Hellfires are launched include Army AH-64, Marine AH-1 and Navy SH-60 helicopters. However, they are also used routinely by many other helicopter and fixed wing aircraft. Land and sea launch platforms have also been evaluated.

Beginning in 2001, the US Air Force and the CIA have used Hellfires to arm RQ-1/MQ-1 Predator unmanned aerial vehicles (UAV), giving this surveillance platform an attack capability. The MQ-9 Reaper UAV, which entered combat in 2007, was designed with an inherent offensive capability and the Hellfire as a standard weapon. These Hellfire-armed drones have been especially effective hunting high value targets in Afghanistan and Pakistan.

A tight close-up of an AGM-114 Hellfire missile hung on the rail of a US Air Force MQ-1L Predator Unmanned Aerial Vehicle (UAV) at Balad AB, Iraq in June 2004. It is inscribed with, "in memory of Honorable Ronald Reagan." (US Air Force photo by Tech Sergeant Scot Reed)

An AGM-114 Hellfire II launched by a Marine Corps AH-1Z Venom gunship. (Lockheed Martin Photo)

US Marines assigned to Light Attack Helicopter Squadron 169 offload an AGM-114 Hellfire missile from an AH-1 Super Cobra helicopter on Camp Taqaddum, Iraq on May 10, 2006. (US Marine Corps photo by Cpl. Trenton E. Harris)

A Lockheed Martin's public affairs team puts it, the "Manned HELLFIRE Turret System (MHTS) brings attack helicopter capability to ground combat." (Lockheed Martin photo)

The high-altitude AGM-114P and bunker-busting AGM-114R were developed specifically for arming UAVs.

In addition to American armed services, Hellfires have been or are in service with the forces of Australia, Egypt, France, Greece, India, Iraq, Israel, Italy, Japan, Jordan, Kuwait, Lebanon, the Netherlands, Norway, Taiwan , Saudi Arabia, Singapore, Sweden, Turkey, the United Arab Emirates, and the United Kingdom.

A derivative of the Hellfire, called Brimstone (another Biblical term), was developed in the United Kingdom by Matra-BAe Dynamics-Alenia (MBDA) (a missile consortium with operations in Britain, France, Germany, and Italy) in cooperation with Boeing. Brimstone became operational with the Royal Air Force in 2005.

Manufacturer: Originally Martin Marietta and Rockwell International,
now Lockheed Martin and Boeing

Length: 5 feet 10 inches (1.78 meters)

Diameter: 7 inches (0.18 meters)

Span (fins): 13 inches (0.33 meters)

Weight: 110 pounds (50 kilograms)

Range: 5.6 miles (9 kilometers)

Speed: Mach 1.3

Guidance system: semi-active laser homing, or active radar seeker (AGM-114L)

Propulsion system: Thiokol solid-fuel rocket

Warhead: primarily anti-armor explosive (see text)

First tested: 1978

First deployed: 1985 (Hellfire II in 1994)

(Specifications for AGM-114L Hellfire II)

A dramatic artist conception of the AGM-114L Longbow Hellfire, which uses a millimeter wave Fire Control Radar mounted above the helicopter's main rotor to provide targeting data to a matched millimeter wave seeker in the nose of the fire-and-forget missile. (Lockheed Martin photo)

A truck-mounted MIM-115 Roland low-altitude surface-to-air missile is fired from Launch Complex 32 at White Sands Missile Range in February 1984. The Army originally mounted the Roland system on an M109 tracked chassis, but later adopted a modified M812A1 five-ton truck as the Roland vehicle. (US Army photo by James Cloyd)

MIM-115 Roland

Though it was smaller and had a shorter range than the MIM-23 Hawk, the US Army acquired around 600 examples of the European Roland surface-to-air missile as a potential short-range air defense weapon.

The subject of a lengthy development process between 1964 and 1977, the Roland was a product of Euromissile, a joint venture of Nord Aviation (Aérospatiale after 1970) in France and Messerschmitt-Bölkow-Blohm in Germany. It entered service with the French army in 1977, seven years behind schedule, while the all-weather Roland II variant joined the German army in 1978.

US Army evaluation of the missile began in 1974, with licensed production in the United States undertaken by Hughes and Boeing. The first test launch of an American XMIM-115A Roland II came in 1978. Though the program was terminated in 1981, production continued through 1985. Due to technical issues, the Roland II never officially became operational with the regular US Army, but one Army National Guard air defense battalion was active with the MIM-115A and large numbers remained in the inventory until 1988.

Elsewhere, Roland variants remained in service past the turn of the century in France, as well as Argentina, Brazil, Iraq, Nigeria, Qatar, Slovenia, Spain, and Venezuela. A

decade into the twenty-first century, the German Army replaced its Rolands with the *Lenkflugkörper Neue Generation* (Guided Missile, New Generation).

Through the decades, Rolands have been credited with at least two kills. Argentina downed a British Harrier in 1982, and Iraq downed an American A-10 in 2003.

Manufacturer: Boeing and Hughes

Length: 7 feet 10.5 inches (2.4 meters)

Diameter: 6.3 inches (0.16 meters)

Span (fins): 20 inches (0.51 meters)

Weight: 148 pounds (67 kilograms)

Range: 5 miles (8 kilometers)

Mach: 1.6

Ceiling: 18,000 feet (5,500 meters)

Guidance system: line of sight radio command

Propulsion system: solid-fuel rocket

Warhead: high explosive

First tested: 1968 (European version), 1978 (American version)

First deployed: not officially in the United States

(Specifications for MIM-115A)

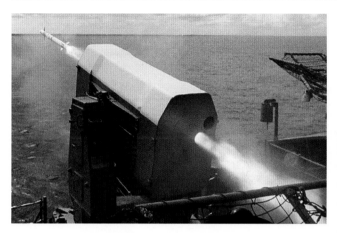

Above: *The launch of a RIM-116 Rolling Airframe Missile (RAM), circa May 2005.* (Raytheon)

Right: *Sailors download the rolling airframe missile system aboard the Nimitz-class aircraft carrier USS* Harry S. Truman, *May 2008.* (US Navy photo by Mass Communication Specialist Third Class Ann Marie Lazarek)

RIM-116 Rolling Airframe Missile

Given the serious potential of cruise missile attacks against ships, one would assume that more urgency would have been devoted to a missile system to defend against them. One would also expect a faster turn around in a missile that used off-the-shelf components from existing missiles. In this case, the warhead was from an AIM-9, the motor from the MIM-72 and the infrared seeker from the FIM-92. Nevertheless, the development process of the RIM-116 unfolded over a period of 16 years.

The program began in 1976, and the first test flight of the XRIM-116A came in 1978. However, even though intercept tests in the early 1980s were successful, the RIM-116A was not operational until 1992. (Meanwhile, the entire operational career from first flight to retirement, of the decisive BGM-109G cruise missile took place within this time frame!)

Once operational, the missile was widely deployed. The US Navy went on to install RIM-116 launchers aboard more than 80 ships, including amphibious assault ships, frigates, transports and Nimitz Class aircraft carriers. The German Navy armed 'Braunschweig' Class corvettes with them, and early in the twenty-first century made a point of installing them on all new vessels. which mount two RAM launchers per ship. The navies of Egypt, Greece, Turkey, and South Korea have all added the RIM-116 to their arsenals. The typical launch system is the 21-tube Mk.49 "box" launcher.

The missile is a joint venture of American and German contractors, specifically Diehl Stiftung (and successor companies) in Germany, and a succession of the American companies. Originally, it was General

Dynamics, whose missile business was acquired Hughes Aircraft in 1992, and whose missile business was in turn acquired by Raytheon in 1997.

Because it is spin-stabilized, the RIM-116 is known as the Rolling Airframe Missile (RAM). For guidance, the RIM-116A (Block 0) relied on tracking radar emissions from the target, using infrared for terminal homing. The RIM-116B (Block 1), developed in the 1990s, uses infrared-only guidance, homing on targets with no radar emissions.

First installed in 2008, the Block 1B SeaRAM combines the missile into a coordinated, radar-sharing air defense system along with the Raytheon Phalanx Close-In Weapon System (CIWS), a 20mm multi-barrel rapid-fire gun.

Manufacturer: Diehl BGT and Raytheon (see text)

Length: 9 feet 4 inches (2.82 meters)

Diameter: 5 inches (0.13 meter)

Span (fins): 17.5 inches (0.45 meters)

Weight: 162 pounds (73.5 kilograms)

Range: 4.7 miles (7.5 kilometers)

Speed: Mach 2 plus

Guidance system: passive radar seeking, infrared homing

Propulsion system: solid-fuel rocket

Warhead: blast fragmentation

First tested: 1978

First deployed: 1992

(Specifications for RIM-116B)

Both the RS-Systems FQM-117 and Continental MQM-143 Remote-Controlled Miniature Aerial Target (RCMAT) drones are piston-engine powered scale models of Soviet era warplanes, which are used as targets for FIM-92 Stinger missiles. The "B" Model of each replicates the Su-25. (US Marine Corps photo by Manuel Valdez)

FQM-117

The FQM-117 is unique in that there are no other vehicles in the "M for Missile" list that can be acquired legally and in fully operable condition for around $200.

This family of Radio-Controlled Miniature Aerial Targets (RCMAT) were small, wood and styrofoam, radio-controlled aircraft on the scale of hobby-shop RC models that were acquired by the US Army in the early 1980s for use in surface-to-air gunnery training. The FQM-117A was a simple, delta-winged craft, while the FQM-117B and FQM-117C were 1/9th scale models of MiG-27 and F-16 aircraft. Other aircraft were also simulated in other FQM-117 variants.

An estimated 100,000 of these aircraft were made, with roughly half of them being the FQM-117B. They were phased out in the 1990s and superseded by the MQM-143A, which are 1/5th-scale replicas of Su-25 aircraft and Mi-24 helicopters. Surplus FQM-117s are often seen for sale on model airplane websites.

Manufacturer: RS-Systems
Length: 6 feet (1.83 meters)
Wingspan: 5 feet 6 inches (1.68 meters)
Weight: 8 pounds (3.6 kilograms)
Range: 15 miles (18 kilometers)
Speed: 75 mph (120 km/h)
Ceiling: 10,000 feet (meters)
Guidance system: radio control
Propulsion system: piston engine
First tested: circa 1979
First deployed: circa 1980
(Specifications for FQM-117B)

LGM-118 Peacekeeper

The Peacekeeper was the culmination of efforts to develop a successor to the Minuteman as America's primary ICBM. However, after 14 years of development and 19 years of deployment, the Peacekeeper went away and the Minuteman remained.

Within a few years of initial Minuteman deployment in 1963, the US Air Force considered and then rejected the BGM-75 as a potential successor. The idea was revisited again in 1972 against the backdrop of an overwhelming lead the Soviet Union was taking in the deployment of newer multiple-warhead Soviet ICBMs. Throughout the decade, studies were conducted of various configurations for the new ICBM, which was given the notional designation "MX" (missile, experimental).

In 1979, the missile was designated as MGM-118, though it was later redesignated as LGM-118 or LG-118. In 1982, it was named "Peacekeeper" by President Ronald Reagan. The Peacekeeper was powered by three solid-fuel stages plus a liquid-fuel post-boost stage. Whereas the MIRVed Minuteman III had three warheads, the MIRVed Peacekeeper had ten Avco Mk.21 reentry vehicles, each with a 300-kiloton W87 nuclear warhead.

The first successful launch occurred in June 1983 at Vandenberg AFB in California, dropping a test payload 4,190 miles downrange near Kwajalein.

In the meantime, the basing scenario was the subject of great controversy. The obvious idea of basing them in existing Minuteman silos was rejected early on, and in 1979, the Carter administration proposed the "Racetrack System." Under this idea, the MGM-118s would be hauled on a vast network of roads or railways built beneath hundreds of acres of Utah and Nevada desert. They would be randomly moved through these tunnels so that the Soviets would be uncertain where they were, compelling them to expend numerous warheads in a first strike and still not be sure that they had gotten all the missiles.

After rejecting the expense of the Racetrack, the Department of Defense considered the Multiple Protective Shelter (MPS) scheme, involving a large number of shelters from which the missiles could be moved randomly — like peas in a shell game.

In October 1982, the Reagan administration proposed Closely Spaced Basing (CSB), nicknamed "Dense Pack," in which all Peacekeeper missiles would be based together in one field at SAC's 5,872-acre Francis E. Warren AFB in Wyoming. The rationale for Dense Pack was that with all the missiles so close together, at least some would survive a direct hit. Nevertheless, survivability under the CSB came into serious question, so it was back to the drawing board once again.

Shock-absorbing pads fall away from the surface of an MGM-118A Peacekeeper ICBM as it emerges from its launch canister in the first test launch of the missile at Vandenberg AFB in June 1983. (DoD)

Above: *An MGM-118 Peacekeeper ICBM climbs away from the test launch site during a February 1985 test flight at Vandenberg AFB.* (DoD)

Left: *A view of an MGM-118A Peacekeeper ICBM being assembled at Vandenberg AFB in August 1983,* (DoD)

above: *An aerial view of an LGM-118A Peacekeeper ICBM being fired from a launch tube during a test at Mercury Proving Grounds in April 1986.* (DoD photo by Garfield Jones)

left: *A close-up look at four Multiple Independently-targeted Reentry Vehicles (MIRV) such as were the payload of the Peacekeeper ICBM.* (DoD)

Captains Mark Schuler and Shane Clark from the 90th Operations Group Evaluations/Peacekeeper Crew, input case data into the magnetic drum for transmission to the Launch Facility in the Missile Procedures Trainer at F.E. Warren AFB in March 1996. (US Air Force photo by Senior Airman Tracy Reisinger)

In May 1983 the Congress had come back to the previously rejected idea of basing the Peacekeeper in former Minuteman silos at Warren AFB. The first ten were on alert by December 1986, and a final total of 50 were installed by 1988. Meanwhile, the Department of Defense announced that an additional 50 Peacekeepers would be deployed in a mobile scenario that was known as "Rail Garrison." By the end of 1992, the missiles would be loaded, two each, on 25 trains that would be parked at Warren AFB, as well as at five other bases from Spokane to Baton Rouge.

In April 1989, however, Congress decided to limit Peacekeeper acquisition to the 50 missiles already delivered. There were plans to pull these missiles out of the silos and put them into the Rail Garrison, but the Cold War ended before this happened. A total of 114 Peacekeepers were built, with over half expended in testing or otherwise not deployed.

Between 2003 and September 2005, the Peacekeepers were gradually pulled out of their silos and decommissioned.

Manufacturer: Martin Marietta (Lockheed Martin after 1995)

Height: 71 feet 6 inches (21.79 meters)

Diameter: 7 feet 7 inches (2.31 meters)

Weight: 195,000 pounds (88,300 kilograms)

Range: more than 6,800 miles (10,900 kilometers)

Speed: 15,000 mph (24,000 km/h)

Ceiling: 500 miles (800 kilometers)

Guidance system: inertial guidance (Advanced Inertial Reference Sphere)

Propulsion system: Thiokol solid-fuel rocket (first stage), Aerojet solid-fuel rocket (second stage), Hercules solid-fuel rocket (third stage), Rocketdyne liquid-fuel rocket (post-boost upper stage),

Warhead: ten W87 thermonuclear

First tested: 1983

First deployed: 1986

(Specifications for LGM-118A)

An AGM-119 Penguin anti-ship missile is fired from an SH-60B Sea Hawk helicopter during aircrew weapon certifications over the Pacific Ocean off the Coast of Okinawa in July 2002. (US Navy photo by Photographer's Mate 2nd Class Lisa Aman)

AGM-119 Penguin

An anti-ship missile developed in by Kongsberg in Norway in the 1970s, the Penguin has been in service with the navies of Norway and Turkey since 1972, and with Greece and Sweden since 1980. Originally created as a ship-launched missile, it later became available in an air-launched variant, and this version was first acquired by the US Navy in 1994.

The original Mk.1 variant was superseded by the longer range Mk.2 in 1980 and augmented by the air-launched Mk.3, which first entered service aboard Norwegian F-16s in 1987. The Mk.3 was acquired by the US Navy as AGM-119A, but passed over in favor of the Mk.2/Modification 7, which incorporates features from the two marks. This entered service with the US Navy as the AGM-119B, mainly as armament for SH-60 Seahawk helicopters. The Australian Navy has also used Penguins as helicopter armament since 2003.

As a Penguin successor, Kongsberg has marketed its newer Naval Strike Missile (NSM) since 2007.

Manufacturer: Kongsberg Defence & Aerospace
Length: 9 feet 8.5 inches (2.96 meters)
Diameter: 11 inches (0.28 meters)
Span (fins): 4 feet 8 inches (1.42 meters)
Weight: 800 pounds (365 kilograms)
Range: 18 miles (28 kilometers)
Speed: Mach 0.8
Guidance system: passive infrared
Propulsion system: solid-fuel rocket
Warhead: armor piercing
First tested: circa 1970
First deployed: 1972 (Norway), 1994 (US Navy)
(Specifications for AGM-119B)

An F-16C from the 21st Fighter Squadron launches an AIM-120 AMRAAM over the Gulf of Mexico during the Air-to-Air Weapons System Evaluation Program Combat Archer in November 2003. (US Air Force photo by Michael Ammons)

AIM-120 AMRAAM

The AIM-120 Advanced Medium-Range Air-to-Air Missile (AMRAAM) was developed in the 1980s and deployed in 1991 as the eventual successor to the AIM-7 Sparrow, although the two missiles have coexisted in the US Navy and US Air Force for two decades.

Similar in appearance to the Sparrow, the all-weather AMRAAM is smaller and faster with active radar that allows the pilot to "fire-and-forget" several missiles simultaneously. The AMRAAM can also engage low-altitude targets and can home on the same jamming signals that a target aircraft would use to jam the radar of an air-to-air missile.

In the late 1970s, the Navy and Air Force jointly evaluated air-to-air missiles and tactics in their Air Intercept Missile Evaluation (AIMVAL) and Air Combat Evaluation (ACEVAL) fly-off programs. From this, the AIM-9 Sidewinder was confirmed in its short-range (circa 10 miles) role, while the momentum toward a medium-range (circa 40 miles, or "beyond-visual-range") missile began rolling toward the AMRAAM.

After initial tests, the first launch of an AMRAAM in operational configuration came in 1984, with the first AIM-120As delivered to the Air Force in 1988. The missile reached IOC with the Air Force in 1991 and with the Navy in 1993. Deliveries of the successor AIM-120B began in 1994, and the AIM-120C (with the range increased from 45 to 65 miles) was deployed after 1996. The AIM-120D, first tested in 2008, offered a half again greater range than the AIM-120C.

In addition to the United States armed forces, the AMRAAM has been exported to more than 30 countries, including most NATO members, as well as Australia, Chile, Israel, Japan, Jordan, Kuwait, Malaysia, Oman, Pakistan, Saudi Arabia, Singapore, South Korea, Sweden, Switzerland, and the United Arab Emirates.

The AMRAAM was first used in combat in 1992 and 1993, when US Air Force F-16s shot down two Iraqi MiGs during Operation Southern Watch. In 1994, an American F-15 accidentally downed two American Black Hawk helicopters. Subsequently, one Netherlands and six American AMRAAMs scored victories in the Balkans.

A crewman with the 157th Aircraft Maintenance inspects an AIM-120 AMRAAM prior to a combat sortie launch of an F-16CJ Fighting Falcon at a forward deployed location during Operation Iraqi Freedom in April 2003. (US Air Force photo by Senior Master Sergeant Edward Snyder)

The US Army has evaluated ground-launched AMRAAM variants, including the Hum-Vee-launched HUMRAAM, since the 1990s. So too did the Marine Corps in their Complementary Low-Altitude Weapon System (CLAWS) program. In 2009, the Surface-Launched version (SLAMRAAM) was test-fired by a High Mobility Artillery Rocket System (HIMARS) launcher from a modified Army Tactical Missile System (ATACMS).

Manufacturer: Hughes Aircraft (Raytheon after 1997)

Length: 12 feet (3.66 meters)

Diameter: 7 inches (0.18 meters)

Span (fins): 17.6 inches (0.45 meters)

Weight: 345 pounds (157 kilograms)

Range: 65 miles (105 kilometers)

Speed: Mach 4

Guidance system: inertial guidance, with active radar homing

Propulsion system: solid-fuel rocket

Warhead: blast fragmentation

First tested: 1984 (in operational configuration)

First deployed: 1991

(Specifications for AIM-120C)

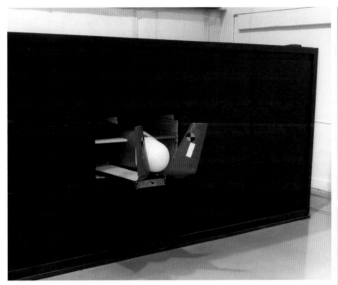

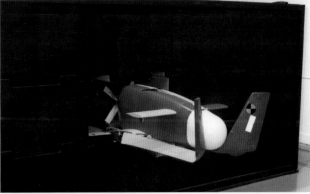

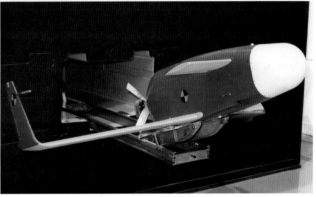

The unique storage module designed for housing Boeing YCQM-121A Pave Tiger attack drones had the appearance of something like the coin lockers at a bus station, or perhaps like a morgue. The UAVs were designed to be packed into a 15-locker module and shipped to Central Europe. If World War III had started, they would be unpacked, unfolded, and launched as a swarm to attack Soviet air defenses. (US Air Force)

CQM-121 Pave Tiger/Seek Spinner

In 1979, Boeing began an internally-funded project aimed at the creation of an inexpensive craft, known as the Boeing Robotic Air Vehicle (BRAVE-200), which could function either as a cruise missile or as a recoverable, multi-mission drone. In the same size class as the Lockheed MQM-105, it was a compact, tailless drone with swept wings and a pusher propeller.

In 1983, the Air Force ordered the BRAVE-200 under the designation YCQM-121A and it was named Pave Tiger. The plan at the time was to deploy as many as a thousand of them into Germany by 1987 for defense against a potential Warsaw Pact invasion. Operationally, the little Tigers would be packed in boxes until use and then launched with a small rocket booster and recovered – if possible – with a parachute.

After limited flight testing, the Pave Tiger program was cancelled in 1984. The problems in the program were said by the Air Force to have been due to "underestimating the complexity" of integrating the airframe and the targeting system. This phrase could easily have been worked into the cancellation explanation for a lot of programs during the Cold War.

Despite this, there was still interest being expressed in 1986 by the German government in buying several thousand of them. The Germans continued to look into using the BRAVE-200 as an anti-radar system, although in Germany, it was competing with the German Messerschmitt-Bölkow-Blohm Tucan UAV. The Pave Tiger concept was revived briefly between 1987 and 1989 as the YCGM-121B under the Air Force Seek Spinner program. The YCGM-121B was considered as a weapon to attack enemy radar sites.

Boeing later developed and tested a jet-propelled BRAVE-3000, but found no customer interest.

Manufacturer: Boeing

Length: 6 feet 11 inches (2.12 meters)

Height: 2 feet (0.61 meters)

Wingspan: 8 feet 5 inches (2.57 meters)

Weight: 280 pounds (130 kilograms)

Range: 500 miles (800 kilometers)

Speed: 200 mph (320 km/h)

Ceiling: 10,000 feet (3,000 meters)

Guidance system: preprogrammed autopilot (YCQM-121A) radar homing (YCGM-121B)

Propulsion system: piston engine, with solid rocket booster for launch

Warhead: high explosive

First tested: 1983

First deployed: never

(Specifications for CQM-121A)

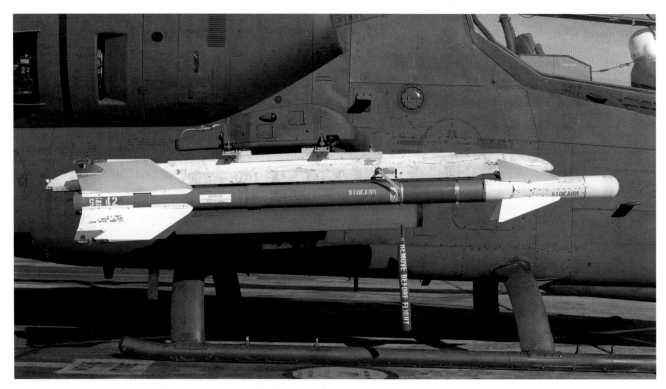

An AGM-122 Sidearm mounted on an AH-1T Sea Cobra during testing at the US Navy facility at China Lake in October 1981. (Photo from Wayne Mutza collection via Gary Verver)

AGM-122 Sidearm

As the name suggests, the idea behind this weapon was to develop an anti-radiation missile (ARM) based on the airframe of the AIM-9 Sidewinder. Because existing hardware was used, it would theoretically be much less expensive that an all-new missile or existing AGM-88s. The Sidearm was developed by the Naval Weapons Center at China Lake and a contract was issued to Motorola to convert around 700 existing AIM-9Cs into AGM-122As for use by the Marine Corps. Production of newly built AGM-122Bs was considered but it never happened.

Manufacturer: Motorola

Length: 9 feet 5 inches (2.87 meters)

Diameter: 5 inches (0.13 meters)

Span (fins): 24.8 inches (0.63 meters)

Weight: 195 pounds (88 kilograms)

Range: 10.2 miles (16.5 kilometers)

Speed: Mach 2.5

Propulsion system: Hercules solid-fuel rocket

Warhead: blast fragmentation

First tested: 1981

First deployed: 1986

(Specifications for AGM-122A)

An AGM-123A Skipper II mounted on the wing pylon of an A-7 Corsair aircraft at the Naval Weapons Center in 1985. (DoD)

AGM-123 Skipper II

The AGM-123 was designed by the Naval Weapons Center at China Lake as a low-cost anti-ship weapon, and a contract was issued to Emerson to build about 2,500 units. Just as the unpowered GBU-15 guided bomb was briefly given the missile designation AGM-112, the AGM-123 designation was assigned to the Texas Instruments GBU-16 Paveway II laser-guided bomb when it was fitted with a strap-on rocket motor. (As the GBU-15 is a Mk.84 bomb with a guidance unit attached, the GBU-16 is a Mk.83 bomb with a guidance unit attached.)

The name "Skipper" was derived from a flight path reminiscent of a flat rock skipping across the surface of a body of water. The "II" was derived from the Paveway II designation. There was apparently never a "Skipper I."

Manufacturer: Emerson Electric
Length: 14 feet 1inch (4.29 meters)
Diameter: 19.6 inches (0.50 meters)
Weight: 1,283 pounds (582 kilograms)
Range: 15.5 miles (25 kilometers)
Speed: 680 mph (1,100 km/h)
Guidance system: laser guidance
Propulsion system: Aerojet solid-fuel rocket
Warhead: high explosive (Mk.83 bomb)
First tested: 1980
First deployed: 1985
(Specifications for AGM-123A)

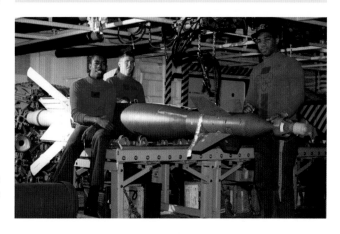

Ordnancemen pose with an AGM-123A Skipper II aboard the carrier USS Dwight D. Eisenhower *in 1988.* (US Navy photo by PH2 Tracy Lee Didas)

AGM-124 Wasp

During the Cold War, NATO conventional land forces were greatly outnumbered by Warsaw Pact armies, especially with regard to numbers of tanks. To offset this, the US Air Force turned to technology, specifically to ways that airpower could kill large numbers of tanks efficiently. Cluster bombs were among such weapons, and "cluster missiles" were also considered. Boeing and Hughes submitted proposals, and the latter won a development contract under the AGM-124A designation. The scenario imagined "swarms" of "Wasps" launched from 12-round launch pods carried by aircraft such as the A-10. The program was cancelled in 1983 shortly after its first flight test.

Manufacturer: Hughes Aircraft

Length: 5 feet (1.52 meters)

Diameter: 8 inches (0.20 meters)

Span (fins): 20 inches (0.51 meters)

Weight: 125 pounds (57 kilograms)

Range: 6.2 miles (10 kilometers)

Guidance system: preprogrammed autopilot with infrared terminal guidance

Propulsion system: solid-fuel rocket

Warhead: shaped charge

First tested: 1983

First deployed: never

(Specifications for AGM-124A)

UUM-125 Sea Lance

The idea was to develop a successor to the UUM-44 SUBmarine ROCket (SUBROC) that could also replace the RUR-5 Anti-Submarine ROCket (ASROC). Boeing undertook the project in 1982, but the complexities of shoe-horning two very different missions into one missile became apparent, and the two were divorced in 1983. While Boeing continued with the torpedo-tube-launched UUM-125A Sea Lance, Lockheed was given the task of developing the ASROC replacement as RUM-139A. After numerous technical delays, the Sea Lance fell to the budget-cutter's axe in 1990 without being flight tested. In the meantime, non-nuclear UUM-125B and RIM-125B variants were proposed and rejected.

Manufacturer: Boeing

Length: 20 feet 6 inches (6.25 meters)

Diameter (launch capsule): 21 inches (0.53 meters)

Weight: 3,086 pounds (1,400 kilograms)

Range: 115 miles (185 kilometers)

Speed: Mach 1.5

Guidance system: inertial guidance

Propulsion system: Hercules solid-fuel rocket

Warhead: W89 Thermonuclear

First tested: never

First deployed: never

(Specifications for UUM-125A)

BQM-126

Developed to meet a US Navy requirement, the Beechcraft Model 997 was essentially a twin-tailed variant of the company's Model 1089 Streaker target drone, which had entered service with the US Army as MQM-107. First flown in 1984, it was ordered as BQM-126A. However, the program was terminated for cost reasons before production began.

Manufacturer: Beechcraft (part of Raytheon, 1980-2007)

Length: 18 feet 6 inches (5.64 meters)

Diameter: 15 inches (0.38 meters)

Wingspan: 10 feet (3.05 meters)

Weight: 1,400 pounds (630 kilograms)

Range: 1,000 miles (621 kilometers)

Speed: 668 mph (1,075 km/h)

Ceiling: 40,000 feet (12,200 meters)

Guidance system: preprogrammed, or radio control override

Propulsion system: Microturbo J403 turbojet

First tested: 1984

First deployed: never

(Specifications for YBQM-126A)

AQM-127 SLAT

Throughout the 1970s and early 1980s, the US Navy attempted without success to develop a target drone that would simulate a supersonic, sea-skimming cruise missile. Two such projects, the BQM-90 and BQM-111, went far enough to be designated, but neither entered service. The effort was revived again in 1983 as the Supersonic Low-Altitude Target (SLAT) program. In 1984, Martin received a contract to build an air-launched SLAT missile under the YAQM-127A designation. Flight tests began in 1987, but technical issues, delays and costs led to Congressional termination of SLAT in 1991. In the meantime, the Navy continued to use the MQM-8 Vandal for this purpose until the arrival of the GQM-163 Coyote early in the twenty-first century.

Manufacturer: Martin Marietta

Length: 17 feet 11.5 inches (5.47 meters)

Diameter: 1 foot 9.25 inches (0.54 meters)

Weight: 2,400 pounds (1,090 kilograms)

Range: 62 miles (100 kilometers)

Speed: Mach 2.5

Guidance system: preprogrammed autopilot with manual override

Propulsion system: Marquardt ramjet, with Thiokol solid-fuel rocket booster

First tested: 1987

First deployed: never

(Specifications for YAQM-127A)

A 1985 artist conception of a Martin Marietta YAQM-127A Supersonic Low-Altitude Target (SLAT) simulating an enemy strike missile in flight. In the distance, a Standard Missile rises to the occasion. (Martin Marietta)

Martin Marietta technicians working on a YAQM-127A Supersonic Low-Altitude Target (SLAT) in 1986. (Martin Marietta)

AQM-128

The YAQM-128A designation was reportedly assigned in 1984 to a US Navy air-launched drone project that never resulted in a vehicle being either designed or built.

AGM-129 ACM

With the successful deployment of the AGM-86 ALCM, the US Air Force turned to developing a successor that could come on-line when the ALCM grew obsolescent. Work on the Advanced Cruise Missile (ACM), embodying stealth characteristics, began in 1982. The debut flight of the General Dynamics YAGM-129A came in July 1985, and operational ACMs were first deployed in 1990.

Though the AGM-129A, with its stealthy profile and forward swept wings, is different in appearance to the AGM-86, it carries the same warhead and is powered by a similar engine. Like the AGM-86 missiles, the ACM was designed to be air-launched by B-52H bombers, which could carry eight on an internal rotary launcher, plus six externally under each wing.

The initial acquisition plan for 2,500 ACMs was scaled back several times, and terminated in 1993 after about 460 AGM-129As were delivered. Plans for an AGM-129B were apparently shelved. Because of maintenance costs and reliability issues, the Air Force decided in 2007 to gradually phase out the ACM, while retaining the AGM-86 variants.

An AGM-129 Advanced Cruise Missile during an early test flight. (McDonnell Douglas)

Technicians swarm over an AGM-129 on the factory floor of the General Dynamics Convair Division factory in San Diego. (Convair)

Avionics assembly for the AGM-129 program in Building 33 at the General Dynamics Convair Division factory in San Diego. (Convair)

A vintage 1980s McDonnell Douglas advertisement describing the AGM-129 Advanced Cruise Missile. (McDonnell Douglas)

Manufacturer: originally General Dynamics, Hughes Aircraft 1992-1997, Raytheon thereafter

Length: 20 feet 10 inches (6.35 meters)

Diameter: 2 feet 5 inches (0.74 meters)

Wingspan: 10 feet 2 inches (3.10 meters)

Weight: 3,500 pounds (1,334 kilograms)

Range: 2,300 miles (3,700 kilometers)

Speed: 500 mph (800 km/h)

Guidance system: inertial navigation supplemented with TERCOM

Propulsion system: Williams F112 turbofan

Warhead: W80 thermonuclear

First tested: 1985

First deployed: 1990

(Specifications for AGM-129A)

Above top: *A side view of an AGM-130 air-to-surface missile.* (DoD)

Above: *An F-15E Strike Eagle of the 494th Fighter Squadron releases a specially painted AGM-130 Missile over the Utah Test and Training Range during Exercise Combat Hammer in August 2002.* (US Air Force photo by Tech Sergeant Michael Ammons)

AGM-130

Like the AGM-123, the AGM-130 is a guided bomb with a rocket motor strapped on to make it into a missile. Indeed, AGM-130 missiles are literally existing bombs retrofitted with motors.

To simplify the story, you attach a guidance unit to a Mk.83 bomb, and you have a GBU-16 Paveway II. Add a motor, and you have an AGM-123A. Attach a guidance unit to a Mk.84 bomb, and you have a GBU-15. Add a motor, and you have an AGM-130A, although later AGM-130 variants flowed from bomb types other than the Mk.84. The AGM-130C was based on a 2,000-pound BLU-109 penetrator bomb, and the AGM-130D used the BLU-118 thermobaric (fuel-air explosive) weapon. The never-deployed AGM-130B would have been based on a SUU-54, dispensing multiple submunitions.

The AGM-130A was first tested in 1985 and reached IOC in 1994. AGM-130s were used in the Balkans in the 1990s, and have been used against targets in Iraq and Afghanistan. They are typically carried by F-15E Strike Eagles.

Manufacturer: Rockwell International, later Boeing and Raytheon

Length: 12 feet 10.5 inches (3.92 meters)

Diameter: 18 inches (0.46 meters)

Span (fins): 4 feet 11 inches (1.50 meters)

Weight: 2,450 pounds (1,100 kilograms)

Range: 40 miles (60 kilometers) plus

Guidance system: inertial guidance aided by GPS

Propulsion system: Alliant Techsystems solid-fuel rocket

Warhead: high explosive or other conventional munitions

First tested: 1985

First deployed: circa 1994

(Specifications for AGM-130A)

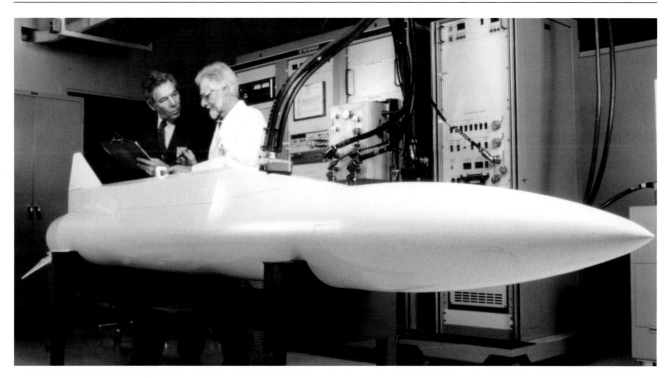

This photograph shows a full-scale mock-up of the AGM-131 SRAM II positioned for a checkout with the Boeing-built Electronic Systems Test Set. (DoD)

AGM-131 SRAM II

As the name suggests, the SRAM II was the intended successor to the AGM-69A Short-Range Attack Missile (SRAM). The AGM-69B SRAM B had been cancelled along with the B-1A bomber in 1978, but when the B-1B variant was resurrected in 1981, the US Air Force decided to go with an all-new SRAM II. Originally, the AGM-131A was to have been smaller than the AGM-69A so that 36, rather than 24, could be carried. However, the final configuration was about the same size. A tactical AGM-131B (SRAM T) with a smaller nuclear payload was also planned to equip F-15Es.

Though both AGM-131A and AGM-131B prototypes were tested, the program was cancelled in 1991 before either was deployed.

Manufacturer: Boeing

Length: 10 feet 5 inches (3.18 meters)

Diameter: 15.3 inches (0.439 meters)

Weight: 2,000 pounds (900 kilograms)

Range: 250 miles (400 kilometers)

Speed: Mach 2

Guidance system:

Propulsion system: Thiokol solid-fuel rocket

Warhead: W89 thermonuclear (AGM-131A), W91 thermonuclear (AGM-131B)

First tested: circa 1988

First deployed: never

(Specifications for AGM-131A)

This artist's concept shows two Tactical Short Range Attack Missiles (SRAM T) after being fired from US Air Force F-15Es. The SRAM T, a variant of the SRAM II, was created to be carried by tactical aircraft, including the F-111, F-16 and Tornado fighter-bombers. (DoD)

Though assigned the designation AIM-132A, the Advanced Short Range Air-to-Air Missile (ASRAAM) was not acquired operationally by the United States. It has been called by its manufacturer "the most agile, modern air-to-air missile designed to dominate the combat mission from Within Visual Range to near Beyond Visual Range." (MBDA)

AIM-132 ASRAAM

The AIM-132 Advanced Short-Range Air-to-Air Missile (ASRAAM) was developed concurrently with the AIM-120 Advanced Medium-Range Air-to-Air Missile (AMRAAM) in the 1980s. The original plan called for missiles used jointly by the United States and Europe, with the Americans handling the beyond-visual range AMRAAM, and the Europeans creating the complementary ASRAAM. It was imagined that the ASRAAM would replace the AIM-9 Sidewinder. However, the scheme fell apart when Canada, Germany, Norway and the United States dropped out of the ASRAAM project in 1989-1990.

As the Americans then proceeded with the AMRAAM, the British proceeded essentially alone with the ASRAAM based on earlier air-to-air missiles studies done in the United Kingdom. Testing of the YAGM-132A began in 1994, though it was not adopted by the Royal Air Force until 2002. In the meantime, it became operational with Australia in 1998. Despite the continued use of the American AIM-132 designation, there has been no United States ASRAAM procurement. The Americans prefer the AIM-9X.

Manufacturer: originally British Aerospace (BAe), Matra-BAe Dynamics-Alenia (MBDA) since 1996.

Length: 9 feet 6 inches (2.90 meters)

Diameter: 6.5 inches (0.17 meters)

Span (fins): 17.7 inches (0.45 meters)

Weight: 192 pounds (87 kilograms)

Range: 9 miles (15 kilometers)

Speed: Mach 3 plus

Guidance system: imaging infra-red, with lock-on after launch (LOAL) capability

Propulsion system: solid-thrust rocket

Warhead: blast fragmentation

First tested: 1994

First deployed: 1998

(Specifications for AIM-132A)

ASRAAMs being carried by a Royal Air Force Typhoon. Developed by Matra BAe Dynamics Alenia (MBDA), the missile is in service with Britain, France, Germany, and Italy. (MBDA)

A UGM-133 Trident II D-5 missile on a flat pad at Cape Canaveral before launching during a US Navy developmental test flight in August 1987. (Lockheed)

The first developmental flight test model of the UGM-133 Trident II D5X-1 missile is launched from a flat pad at Cape Canaveral in January 1987. (DoD)

UGM-133 Trident II D5

As noted in the earlier section on the UGM-96 Trident I C4, the US Navy's effort to supersede the UGM-73 Poseidon Submarine-Launched Ballistic Missile (SLBM) fleet was a two-step process beginning with the Trident I, first deployed in 1979. The green light for the next step, the larger Trident II D5 was given in 1983 when President Ronald Reagan called for a modernization of the United States strategic forces.

While the Trident I was the same size as the earlier Poseidon, the Trident II was an all-new missile in many respects. It featured improvements in all of its systems, including guidance and reentry, fire control and navigation. This would lead to a weapon with a heavier payload, additional range and enhanced accuracy.

The initial flight of the Trident II occurred in January 1987, and the 15-launch test program continued through September 1988. The first deployment of UGM-133A Trident II was in 1990 aboard the USS *Tennessee*, an Ohio Class submarine. The gradual replacement of the Trident I missiles continued until 2007. In all, 14 Ohio Class boats were each armed with 24 Trident IIs, while four British Vanguard Class submarines were each armed with 16. These submarines and the Trident II will continue to be the principal nuclear strike capability of their respective navies well into the twenty-first century.

A 1990s submerged launch of a UGM-133 Trident II D5 Fleet Ballistic Missile from a US Navy Ohio-Class submarine. (DoD)

Manufacturer: Lockheed Missiles & Space Company (Lockheed Martin Space Systems after 1995)

Height: 44 feet 7 inches (13.59 meters)

Diameter: 6 feet 11 inches (2.11 meters)

Weight: 129,000 pounds (58,500 kilograms)

Range: 7,000 miles (11,100 kilometers)

Speed: 13,600 mph (22,000 km/h)

Guidance system: electronic star-sighting inertial guidance

Propulsion system: Alliant Techsystems (incorporating Thiokol and Hercules) (first and second stages), United Technologies (third stage) solid-fuel rockets

Warhead: multiple warhead W88 thermonuclear

First tested: 1987

First deployed: 1990

(Specifications for UGM-133A)

MGM-134 SICBM

The idea behind the Small Intercontinental Ballistic Missile (SICBM) was for a smaller scale complement to the Minuteman and Peacekeeper ICBMs. Nicknamed "Midgetman" as a pun on the name "Minuteman," the MGM-134 was not a simpler "budget model" missile, but a serious effort to create a weapon less vulnerable to attack than the existing ICBMs. Nor was the 46-foot SICBM truly "small." The key to the concept was mobility. As with the mobile V-2s of 1944 or tactical missiles since the 1950s, a constantly moving launch site is hard to target. By the 1980s, the Soviet Union had been developing RT-23 (SS-24) and RT-2PM (SS-25) mobile ICBMs which could be hauled by rail and road, and in the chess game of the Cold War arms race, the MGM-134 was the counter-piece.

Rail mobility had been earlier considered and rejected for both Minuteman and Peacekeeper, so the SICBM concept embraced road mobility and the development by Boeing of a large, 120-ton transporter truck called a Hard Mobile Launcher to carry it.

Work on the project began in 1984, but the first successful test flight of the missile did not occur until 1991. By this time, the Cold War was over and the MGM-134A SICBM program was terminated in 1992.

Manufacturer: Martin Marietta

Length: 46 feet (14.02 meters)

Diameter: 3 feet 10 inches (1.17 meters)

Weight: 30,000 pounds (13,600 kilograms)

Range: 6,800 miles (11,000 kilometers)

Guidance system: inertial guidance

Propulsion system: compressed gas "cold" launch, with solid-fuel rockets (three stages)

Warhead: W87 thermonuclear

First tested: 1989

First deployed: never

(Specifications for XMGM-134A)

Right: *Inspectors examine a Martin Marietta MGM-134A Midgetman, the weapon originally known as the "Small Intercontinental Ballistic Missile"* (SICBM). *(Martin Marietta)*

Overleaf: *A 1988 test of a Martin Marietta MGM-134A Midgetman. (Martin Marietta)*

Note the tail insignia of the F-15A "Celestial Eagle," seen here armed with an ASM-135 ASAT. On September 13, 1985, Major Doug Pearson launched the missile from this aircraft at 38,100 feet, destroying the Solwind P78-1 satellite, then at an altitude of 345 miles. (DoD)

ASM-135 ASAT

The idea of using an air-launched missile to destroy an orbiting satellite dates back to the early years of satellite launches themselves, though the ASM-135 program, begun in 1977, was the first with an operational designation.

In October 1959, a Martin Bold Orion missile, air-launched from a B-47 destroyed the American Explorer 6 spacecraft, becoming the first American weapon known to have downed a satellite. Bold Orion was an experimental vehicle developed under the Air Force Weapon System 199 (WS-199) program. This was actually an air-launched ballistic missile proof-of-concept project, but the weapons were adapted as anti-satellite (ASAT) weapons. The long list of other experimental ASAT weapons included Air Force Projects 437 and 505, which were based on Thor and Nike Zeus vehicles. Both weapons would have carried a nuclear warhead if they had become operational.

However, because of the delicacy of satellites, destroying them requires no warhead. If they can be struck by a fast-moving object, even an inert one, they can be demolished or knocked out of orbit. Therefore, the ASM-135 Anti-Satellite Missile (ASAT) was conceived as a kinetic energy ("hit-to-kill") projectile with no explosive warhead.

Nor did it need to be a large weapon. Like the MGM-134 was given the harmless-sounding nickname "Midgetman," the ASM-135 was also identified innocently as the Air-Launched Miniature Vehicle (ALMV), though technically, the small homing stage was the "miniature" portion of the system.

In 1979, Vought (Ling Temco Vought until 1976) was given a contract to build this kinetic-energy ASAT. It was based on a Boeing AGM-69 SRAM airframe with an LTV Altair second stage, also known as the Miniature Homing Vehicle (MHV).

On September 13, 1985, an ASM-135A fired from an F-15 fighter successfully destroyed the American Solwind solar research satellite. Solwind was picked because its useful life was determined to be nearing an end.

Seen here in 1959, the Bold Orion (Weapon System 119B) was a conceptual precursor to the ASM-135. Air-launched from a B-47 Stratojet, it was successfully tested in October 1959 against the Explorer 6 satellite. (Lockheed)

Nearing an end too were the ASM-135 and the ASAT concept. A congressional ban on such tests took effect a month later.

Manufacturer: Vought Aerospace

Length: 17 feet 9.5 inches (5.42 meters)

Diameter: 20 inches (0.5 meters)

Weight: 2,600 pounds (1,180 kilograms)

Speed: 15,000 mph (24,000 km/h)

Ceiling: 350 miles (560 kilometers)

Guidance system: infrared homing

Propulsion system: two solid-fuel rocket stages

Warhead: kinetic energy

First tested: 1984 (initial flight tests)

First deployed: never

(Specifications for ASM-135A)

An AGM-136A Tacit Rainbow anti radar missile descends over the mountains in search of a ground radar target at the Naval Weapons Center Test Range at China Lake in California, circa 1990. (US Air Force)

AGM-136 Tacit Rainbow

The top secret Tacit Rainbow anti-radar missile project originated in the early 1980s as the flip side of the AGM-88 HARM. With the latter, high speed was a means of locking on to the target before the operator turned *off* the radar emitter. Tacit Rainbow, meanwhile, was a slower cruise missile whose mission was to loiter in a target area waiting for the emitters to be turned *on*. The plan was for large numbers to fly into the target area ahead of the bombers and pick off the radar sites as they prepared to track the bombers.

The first US Air Force AGM-136A air-launched test flight occurred in 1984, but cost overruns led to its cancellation in 1991. A proposed BGM-136B US Army ground-launched variant was never built.

Manufacturer: Northrop

Length: 8 feet 4 inches (2.54 meters)

Diameter: 27 inches (0.69 meters)

Wingspan: 5 feet 2 inches (1.58 meters)

Weight: 430 pounds (195 kilograms)

Range: 270 miles (430 kilometers)

Speed: Mach 0.9

Guidance system: radar homing

Propulsion system: Williams turbofan

Warhead: blast fragmentation

First tested: 1984

First deployed: never

(Specifications for AGM-136A)

An AGM-136A Tacit Rainbow is inspected and tested by Northrop Corporation technicians at the company's Ventura Division, circa March 1990. The vehicle's unique pivoting wing design permitted more missiles to be carried by the launch aircraft than would be possible with a fixed-wing weapon. The wing pivoted into flight position after launch, enabling the missile to loiter on its own in flight for long periods, then automatically attack and disable hostile radar on land or sea. (US Air Force)

AGM-137 TSSAM

The 1980s were the time when tactical aircraft with "stealthy" (low radar observable) characteristics were a sought-after technological breakthrough. As the US Air Force and US Navy were developing such aircraft, it was only natural to consider a stealthy air-launched tactical missile, and work began on the top secret Tri-Service Stand-off Attack Missile (TSSAM) in 1986. The Air Force and Navy planned to acquire their air-launched TSSAM as AGM-137A, the US Army a ground-launched MGM-137B. The project was cancelled in 1994 without having been flown, and the Air Force and Navy had refocused their attention on the Joint Air-to-Surface Stand-off Missile (JASSM) program, for which the AGM-158 and AGM-159 were contenders.

A series of views of the RUM-139 Vertical Launch ASROC (VLA) missile as it is fired from its Vertical Launch System (VLS) during tests at the Naval Weapons Center in July 1984. (DoD)

Manufacturer: Northrop

Length: 14 feet (4.27 meters)

Wingspan: 8 feet 4 inches (2.54 meters)

Weight: circa 2,000 pounds (907 kilograms)

Range: 115 miles (185 kilometers)

Speed: circa Mach 0.9

Guidance system: inertial navigation with GPS while inflight, and infrared target homing

Propulsion system: Williams turbofan

Warhead: high-explosive penetrating munition, or submunitions

First tested: never

First deployed: never

(Specifications for AGM-137A)

RUM-139 ASROC

In the 1960s, the US Navy deployed the unguided, nuclear-armed, ship-launched RUR-5 Anti-Submarine ROCket (ASROC). Two decades later, it was time for a new, guided replacement weapon. This weapon would be the RUM-139 Vertical Launch (VL) ASROC. Similar in size to the RUR-5, the RUM-139 carries a conventional, rather than nuclear warhead. This is contained within a Mk.46 torpedo, which is released by the missile as it nears the target.

Development of the RUM-139 proceeded in fits and starts from 1983, and although the RUR-5 was retired in 1989, the RUM-139 was not deployed until 1993. Initial RUM-138As were upgraded to RUM-139B standard by 2001, and the RUM-139C with a Mk.54 torpedo was introduced in 2004. Through the first decade of the twenty-first century, nearly 500 VL-ASROCs were built.

CEM-138 Pave Cricket

Designated as YCEM-138A, the Pave Cricket was actually a variant of the Boeing YCQM-121A Pave Tiger that was equipped with radar jamming equipment. It was test flown for about a year, beginning in 1987, but apparently never deployed.

Manufacturer: Goodyear Aerospace (Loral after 1986, Lockheed Martin after 1996)

Height: 16 feet (4.88 meters)

Diameter: 14 inches (0.36 meters)

Span (fins): 27 inches (0.7 meters)

Weight: 1,400 pounds (630 kilograms)

Range: 17 miles (28 kilometers)

Speed: Mach 1

Guidance system: inertial guidance

Propulsion system: solid-fuel rocket

Warhead: high explosive

First tested: 1986

First deployed: 1993

(Specifications for RUM-139B)

A 1995 test of an LTV (later Lockheed Martin) MGM-140A Army Tactical Missile System (ATACMS). (Lockheed Martin)

Right: *An MGM-140 Army Tactical Missile System (ATACMS) weapon fired from an M270 Multiple Launch Rocket System (MLRS) vehicle.* (Lockheed Martin)

MGM-140 ATACMS "Steel Rain"

The MGM-140 is the missile component of the M39 US Army Tactical Missile System (Army TACMS or ATACMS), which also includes the M270 Multiple Launch Rocket System (MLRS) vehicle. Born of the 1978, Cold War-era "Assault Breaker" technology demonstration program, the system earned the nickname "Steel Rain" from Iraqi field commanders in the 1991 Gulf War.

Looking to replace the MGM-52 Lance SRBM, the Army considered a number of options, including the Corps Support Weapon System and the tri-service MGM-137B TSSAM, before focusing on the M39 TACMS after 1984.

Though originally intended for deployment in 1991, delivery was accelerated. The first M39s went overseas to the Middle East in 1990, and were available for Operation Desert Storm. Deployed by VII Corps, 20 M39s had 105 MGM-140As at their disposal in 1991. Lockheed Martin reports that 450 ATACMS missiles were fired during Operation Iraqi Freedom in 2003.

First tested in 1994, the GPS-guided MGM-140B was deployed in 1998. The MGM-140C Block II ATACMS, with guided submunitions, was redesignated as MGM-164A, while the single-warhead MGM-140E ATACMS Block IA Unitary was redesignated as MGM-168A. An ATACMS Block III with a hard-target penetrating warhead was tested in 2004, but reportedly cancelled. More than 2,000 A and B model ATACMS were built through the first decade of the twenty-first century.

In addition to the MGM-140 and MGM-168 guided missiles, the MLRS can also be armed with unguided M26, M30 and M31 ballistic rockets, as well as the M27 and M28 training rockets and the M131 "retaliatory chemical" rocket.

ATACMS is also compatible with the US Army's High Mobility Artillery Rocket System (HIMARS) a light, truck-mounted multiple rocket launch system. HIMARS carries six rockets or one ATACMS, and can use all MLRS munitions. HIMARS was first operationally deployed with the 14th Marine Regiment in 2007 in Iraq's Al Anbar province.

Manufacturer: Ling Temco Vought (LTV) (Loral Vought Systems after 1992, Lockheed Martin after 1996)

Length: 13 feet (3.97 meters)

Diameter: 2 feet (0.61 meters)

Span (fins): 4 feet 7 inches (1.40 meters)

Weight: 2,900 pounds (1,320 kilograms)

Range: 186 miles (300 kilometers)

Guidance system: inertial guidance (MGM-140A), inertial guidance aided by GPS (later variants)

Propulsion system: solid-fuel rocket

Warhead: 275 submunitions

First tested: 1988

First deployed: 1991

(Specifications for MGM-140B)

An F-14A Tomcat of the Strike Aircraft Test Directorate of the Naval Air Warfare Center Aircraft Division at NAS Patuxent River is shown, circa early 1994, conducting a separation test of the Tactical Air Launched Decoy (TALD). (US Navy photo by Vernon Pugh)

ADM-141 TALD

The ADM-141 Tactical Air-Launched Decoy (TALD) was intended to be deployed in large numbers to overwhelm enemy radar systems ahead of a bomber attack.

An unpowered TALD predecessor, called Samson, was originally built in the United States by the Brunswick Corporation (better known for their bowling alley pin-setters) for the Israeli Air Force, but later versions, including the ADM-141, have been built for the US Navy by Israel Military Industries (IMI), who acquired the manufacturing license from Brunswick in the 1990s.

Israel began acquiring Brunswick gliders in the 1970s. Based on Israeli experience, the US Navy began deploying the decoys in 1987. They were used to great effect in Operation Desert Storm, and are still standard equipment, carried by F/A-18s.

The basic, unpowered TALDs are the ADM-141A and ADM-141B. Both carry radar enhancers to make them noticeable, and the ADM-141B carries chaff to simulate a real aircraft attempting to defend against surface-to-air missiles. The ADM-141C is a powered TALD introduced in 1996.

Manufacturer: Brunswick Corporation and (IMI)

Length: 7 feet 8 inches (2.34 meters)

Wingspan: 15 feet 1 inch (4.60 meters)

Weight: 400 pounds (180 kilograms) (without engine)

Range: 190 miles (300 kilometers)

Speed: Mach 0.8

Guidance system: pre-programmed autopilot

Propulsion system: Teledyne turbojet

Warhead: radar enhancers

First tested: circa 1987 (US Navy)

First deployed: circa 1987 (US Navy)

(Specifications for ADM-141C)

Air to air view of an AGM-142 Have Nap precision-guided missile on an F-16 flying from Eglin AFB in April 1996. (US Air Force photo by Cindy Farmer)r

AGM-142 Popeye/Have Nap

A field-programmable, long-range air-to-ground missile, the Popeye was developed in Israel and acquired by the US Air Force as the AGM-142A under its Have Nap program. The idea was to extend the conventional stand-off reach of the B-52H fleet. These were first used in combat in Afghanistan in 2001.

The generally similar variants include the AGM-142A with an electro-optical seeker, the AGM-142B with an infrared seeker, the AGM-142C with an electro-optical seeker and a hardened target penetrating warhead, and the AGM-142D with an infrared seeker and the penetrating warhead.

According to *Jane's Missiles and Rockets* (January 22, 2003), a "lightened, smaller version of the AGM-142 Have

Nap missile," called Have Lite, was successfully tested by the US Air Force. It was "fired at an altitude of 8,700 feet and a speed of Mach 0.7, and the trials demonstrated that the pilot of a single-seat fighter could launch and control the weapon while also flying the aircraft."

In addition to the original users, Popeye/Have Nap weapons have been acquired by Australia, India and South Korea. Rafael supplied Popeyes to Turkey, and established a joint production program with Turkish Aerospace Industries.

A Have Lite weapon on the wing pylon of a US Air Force F-16. This precision guided missile weapon is produced by Precision Guided Systems United States (PGSUS) of Orlando, Florida. (Lockheed Martin)

An Eglin AFB F-16 releases a Have Lite weapon. The base is home to the Air Force's Air Armament Center, the umbrella organization for the Precision Strike System Program Office that manages Have Lite. (Lockheed Martin)

Manufacturer: Precision Guided Systems United States (a joint venture of Rafael in Israel and Lockheed Martin)

Length: 15 feet 10 inches (4.83 meters)

Diameter: 21 inches (0.53 meters)

Span (fins): 5 feet 8 inches (1.73 meters)

Weight: 3,000 pounds (1,360 kilograms)

Range: 50 miles (80 kilometers)

Speed: circa Mach 1

Guidance system: electro-optical or infrared

Propulsion system: solid-fuel rocket

Warhead: penetrator or blast fragmentation

First tested: circa 1988

First deployed: 1988 (Israel), 1992 (US Air Force)

(Specifications for AGM-142C and AGM-142D)

MQM-143

Developed in the 1980s, the MQM-143 family of Remotely Piloted Vehicle Target (RPVT) aircraft are a complement to the smaller FQM-117 family of Radio-Controlled Miniature Aerial Targets (RCMAT). All of these aircraft are radio-controlled planes reminiscent of hobby-shop RC models. While the FQM-117s are one-ninth scale and hand-launched, the MQM-143s are one-fifth scale and launched pneumatically from mobile launchers.

These targets are used mainly by the US Army, but also by other services, to train troops to recognize and intercept enemy aircraft with weapons such as the FIM-92 Stinger man-portable and vehicle-launched anti-aircraft weapon.

Among the variants are the MQM-143A, which replicates a MiG-27; the MQM-143B, which replicates a Su-25; and the MQM-143, which is a replica of the Mi-24 helicopter.

Manufacturer: Continental

Length: 11 feet 2 inches (3.40 meters)

Wingspan: 9 feet 10 inches (3.00 meters)

Weight: 60 pounds (27 kilograms)

Speed: 130 mph (210 km/h)

Guidance system: radio control

Propulsion system: piston engine

First tested: circa 1983

First deployed: circa 1984

(Specifications for MQM-143A/MiG-27 replica)

ADM-144

Little is known about the ADM-144 other than that it was an air-launched decoy project under consideration in about 1989, but apparently never built.

The BQM-145A Peregrine (Teledyne Ryan Model 350) was a derivative of the company's similar Model 324, which was produced between 1984 and 1993 and operational with Egyptian forces under the name Scarab. The DoD issued a contract for the Peregrine in 1989, but the program was cancelled without becoming operational. (Northrop Grumman)

BQM-145 Peregrine

After two decades of experience with BQM-34 Firebee UAVs, the Peregrine was one of the last major programs undertaken by Teledyne Ryan before its 1999 acquisition by Northrop Grumman.

In 1988, the Department of Defense issued a request for a joint-service UAV that could be either air or surface launched, and which could be used as an aerial target or as a reconnaissance platform. This effort would later be designated as the Unmanned Aerial Vehicle, Medium Range (UAV-MR) program. In May 1989, Teledyne Ryan was selected to develop their Model 350, a derivative of the Model 324 Scarab that the company had built for Egypt. As with the Scarab and other Ryan drones back through the Firebee, it was recoverable by parachute or in mid-air by aircraft outfitted with the Mid-Air Retrieval System (MARS).

The first flight of the YBQM-145A came in May 1992, but the program was cancelled 17 months later when both the Navy and Marine Corps dropped out. Only six of a planned 500 production Peregrines were built, and they were not flown until 1997.

Manufacturer: Teledyne Ryan
Length: 18 feet 4 inches (5.59 meters)
Wingspan: 10 feet 6 inches (3.20 meters)
Weight: 2,160 pounds (980 kilograms)
Mission radius: 400 miles (650 kilometers)
Speed: Mach 8.5
Ceiling: 40,000 feet (12,200 meters)
Guidance system: preprogrammed, GPS-supported autonomous operation, with optional radio command interface
Propulsion system: Teledyne Continental turbofan
First tested: 1992
First deployed: 1997
(Specifications for BQM-145A)

An artist conception of an MIM-146A Air-Defense Anti-Tank System (ADATS) missile, circa 1980. (Martin Marietta)

MIM-146 ADATS

The story of the US Army's quest for Forward Area Air Defense (FAAD) weapons is studded with failures and disappointments and the great success of the FIM-92 Stinger. The failures included the MIM-46 Mauler and the M247 Sergeant York Division Air Defense (DIVAD) gun system. While not really a disappointment, the later MIM-72 Chaparral was greatly overshadowed by the highly successful Stinger system in the 1980s.

In the meantime, the US Army was attracted to the multi-mission concept, setting its sights on a FAAD weapon with a parallel anti-tank role. This resulted in the Air Defense Anti-Tank System (ADATS) program. As a specific weapon, the Army chose a missile created in Switzerland by Oerlikon, a company with a long history of anti-aircraft systems. Martin Marietta received a contract in 1979 to build the missile in the United States under the designation MIM-146A. Like the Mauler, the launchers were mounted on an armored, tracked M113 chassis.

It was intended for the MIM-46A to replace the Chaparral and supplement the Stinger. However, after a decade of testing, the army added it to the disappointment list and cancelled ADATS in 1992.

However, Canada made it work successfully. Having adopted it in 1988, Canadian Forces continued to use it into the twenty-first century. In 2005, these launchers were moved to an LAV armored, wheeled vehicle designated as the Multi-Mission Effects Vehicle (MMEV). Thailand, meanwhile, deployed a few MIM-146s in fixed air defense sites.

Manufacturer: Lockheed

Length: 6 feet 9 inches (2.06 meters)

Diameter: 6 inches (0.15 meters)

Span (fins): 19.5 inches (0.50 meters)

Weight: 112 pounds (51 kilograms)

Range: 6 miles (10 kilometers)

Speed: Mach 3

Ceiling: 23,000 feet (7,000 meters)

Guidance system: passive electro-optical tracking, laser beam director

Propulsion system: solid-fuel rocket

Warhead: blast fragmentation

First tested: 1981

First deployed: never for the US Army, but 1988 in Canada

(Specifications for MIM-146A)

The MIM-146A Air-Defense Anti-Tank System (ADATS) was fired from an eight-missile turret mounted on a vehicle modified from an M113A2 armored personnel carrier. (Martin Marietta)

Widely used in Operation Desert Storm, BQM-147A Exdrones have been upgraded since 1998 to the improved Dragon Drone configuration as seen here. (DoD)

BQM-147 Exdrone and Dragon Drone

Having been instrumental in the development of such tactical missile programs as the Regulus, Lacrosse and Taurus in the 1950s and 1960s, the Applied Physics Laboratory (APL) at Johns Hopkins University in Baltimore was called upon once again in 1986 by the US Marine Corps. The objective was to develop a small, low-cost, radio-controlled, remote control aerial vehicle specifically tasked with communications jamming. A simple craft in the same class as target drones such as the MQM-143, the new drone was considered to be expendable, hence the original name, "ExJam," and the later name, "ExDrone."

It is axiomatic within the military that simple machines tasked with explicit missions are often seen as a nearly blank slate on which creative minds seek to add "just one more" purpose or task, then one more, then another.

APL became overwhelmed with demands for new applications, and the Marines turned the program over to BAI Aerosystems, a division of Texas-based L-3 Communications, which designs, manufactures, and integrates small (less than 500-pound) unmanned aircraft systems. Later BQM-147s were delivered with progressively more sophisticated reconnaissance and sensor packages. In 1996, an improved variant known as the Dragon Drone — now too sophisticated to be considered expendable — was introduced. Earlier ExDrones were also retrofitted with the Dragon Drone equipment. Uniquely, the flying-wing-shaped Dragon Drone can routinely fly upside down to the extent that it has no up or down.

BQM-147s were used during Operation Desert Storm, as well as in Operation Iraqi Freedom in 2003, and were adopted by the US Army as well as the Marines. The US Coast Guard is also acquiring an extended range variant of the vehicle under the name Condor. It will equip ocean-going patrol ships and will be launched and recovered by means of a parasail.

Manufacturer: BAI Aerosystems

Length: 5 feet 4 inches (1.62 meters)

Wingspan: 8 feet 2 inches (2.49 meters)

Weight: 95 pounds (43 kilograms)

Range: 240 miles (300 kilometers)

Speed: 80 mph (130 km/h)

Ceiling: 10,000 feet (3,000 meters)

Guidance system: preprogrammed autopilot, or radio control

Propulsion system: piston engine

First tested: circa 1987

First deployed: circa 1991

(Specifications for Dragon Drone)

In full-rate production since 1994, the FGM-148A Javelin was conceived as a lightweight, man-portable, shoulder-fired, "fire-and-forget" medium antitank weapon that would be superior to the FGM-77 Dragon. (Lockheed Martin)

A good, stop-action view of an FGM-148A Javelin emerging from its launch tube. It was combat-proven during Operation Iraqi Freedom in its intended anti-tank role and as an urban assault weapon against alternative targets. (Lockheed Martin)

FGM-148 Javelin

In the late 1970s, the FGM-77 (aka M47) Dragon gave American ground troops a guided, man-portable, anti-tank weapon for the first time. It added a guidance system to the old aim-and-fire technology of the World War II bazooka, but it required the operator to maintain visual contact with the target until impact. The FGM-148 Javelin added the dimension of a fire-and-forget lock-on for the seeker, so that the operator could take cover as the missile traveled to the target.

As important as such a weapon would seem to be, progress was slow. The Defense Department began studies of various proposals and configurations in 1983 and issued the development contract in 1989. The first test launch came in 1991, and the Javelin was finally deployed to field units in 1996.

Among other features, the Javelin has a tandem warhead, the first exploding on contact with reactive armor, and the second blowing a hole in base armor. Javelins proved extremely effective against Iraqi tanks during operations in 2003.

The FGM-148 has a longer range than the earlier Dragon and it is much easier to use than the BGM-71 TOW. However, the sighting system is very complex, and the 50-pound weight of missile plus launcher pushes the limits of the definition of "man-portable."

In addition to the US Army and Marine Corps, major users of the Javelin include the armed forces of Australia, France, Jordan, Norway, Taiwan and the United Kingdom.

Manufacturer: Martin Marietta (Lockheed Martin after 1995) and Texas Instruments (Raytheon after 1997)
Length: 3 feet 7 inches (1.10 meters)
Diameter: 5 inches (0.13 meters)
Span (fins): 15 inches (0.384 meters)
Weight: 26 pounds (11.8 kilograms)
Range: 1.6 miles (2.5 kilometers)
Guidance system: imaging infrared seeker
Propulsion system: cold launch ejection, then two-stage solid-fuel rocket
Warhead: tandem high explosive anti-tank (HEAT)
First tested: 1991
First deployed: 1996
(Specifications for FGM-148A)

A McDonnell Douglas "PQM-149" Sky Owl parked on the desert floor during flight testing in 1991. (McDonnell Douglas)

PQM-149 UAV-SR

The UAV-Short Range (UAV-SR) program originated circa 1989 as an effort to develop a multi-service unmanned aerial vehicle that could be used by field units for both reconnaissance and for targeting.

As such, it was a precursor to late twentieth and early twenty-first century American "Q for Drone" UAVs such as the RQ-1 Predator, RQ-2 Pioneer, RQ-5 Hunter and the RQ-7 Shadow, which have fulfilled these roles since the late 1990s. Indeed, the Hunter originated as a UAV-SR aircraft, and was originally given the "M For Missile" designation BQM-155A.

A 12-month "fly-off" evaluation took place in 1991-1992 between the Hunter and the McDonnell Douglas Sky Owl. The latter is occasionally mentioned in the same breath with the Defense Department designation YPQM-149A, but, while this designation was officially reserved for *one of* the UAV-SR contestants, it was apparently not assigned to *any* aircraft. The same was the case with the unassigned YPQM-150A designation.

The Sky Owl was a derivative of the earlier Model R4 series SkyEye, created by Developmental Sciences, a company that became the Astronautics Division of Lear Siegler in 1984. The SkyEye was first flown experimentally in 1973, and demonstrated to the US Army in 1979. It was used extensively by the US Army in Central America during the 1980s to track guerilla infiltration into Honduras from Nicaragua.

The McDonnell Douglas Sky Owl, which made its first flight in June 1991, was constructed with landing gear for take-offs and landings from runways, but it was also configured for a catapult launch and a parachute recovery. It was radio controlled, but also had a programmable

guidance system. In June 1992, after a year of flight testing, the Hunter was for chosen over the Sky Owl for operational deployment.

Manufacturer: McDonnell Douglas (based on the Lear Siegler precursor)

Length: 13 feet 6 inches (4.12 meters)

Wingspan: 24 feet (7.32 meters)

Weight: 1,250 pounds (566 kilograms)

Range: 115 miles (185 kilometers)

Speed: 125 mph (200 km/h)

Ceiling: 16,000 feet (4,900 meters)

Guidance system: radio control with programmable autopilot

Propulsion system: rotary engine

First tested: 1991

First deployed: never

(Specifications for Sky Owl)

Recovering a McDonnell Douglas "PQM-149" Sky Owl following a December 1991 test flight. Though the vehicle was equipped with a centerline landing skid, the preferable means of recovering the McDonnell Douglas Sky Owl was by way of a parasail device. (McDonnell Douglas)

PQM-150 UAV-SR

For the evaluation of air vehicles in the UAV-Short Range (UAV-SR) program evaluation of 1991-1992, there were apparently three designations set aside by the Defense Department – YPQM-149A, YPQ-150A and (Y)BQM-155A. The latter was assigned to the Hunter, while the other two are not believed to have been officially assigned to anything. As noted in the previous section, the Sky Owl is often informally associated with the YPQM-149A designation, but there is no known aircraft associated with YPQ-150A. It may have been, but probably was not, reserved originally for the Hunter.

FQM-151 Pointer

First flown in 1988, the Pointer is a precursor to the myriad of small battlefield UAVs, such as the ScanEagle and RQ-11 Raven, which have proliferated within the United States armed forces in the twenty-first century.

Used by the United States Army and Marine Corps for battlefield surveillance, it was designed by AeroVironment Incorporated, which was run by the late Paul MacCready, famous for such pioneering aircraft as the human-powered Gossamer Condor and a robotic flying pterodactyl replica. Having been developed with company funds, the Pointer was acquired by the US Army and Marine Corps after 1990.

The radio-controlled Pointer was built mostly of high-impact Kevlar, resembling a hobbyist's RC sailplane with a small engine added. A lithium battery pack powered the UAV's compact electric motor to drive the propeller. The little Pointer was hand-launched, and recovered by simply putting it into a flat spin, allowing it to flutter down to the ground.

The FQM-151A carried a CCD camera fixed in its nose, meaning it had to be directly pointed at its target to see it, which is how the machine got its name. The ground station recorded flight imagery on an eight-millimeter video cassette recorder. Digital compass headings were superimposed on the imagery and the controller could add verbal comments. The imagery could be inspected with normal, freeze-frame, fast, or slow-motion replay. The aircraft system and the ground control station were carried in separate backpacks. It required a pilot and an observer, though Pointers were later upgraded with a GPS-INS capability.

Pointers saw action in Afghanistan from 2001, and were deployed to front-line troops in Iraq, beginning in 2003. They will gradually be replaced by the RQ-11.

The small AeroVironment FQM-151 surveillance UAV, used in Operation Desert Storm, was a direct predecessor of the company's similar RQ-11 Raven, widely deployed in Iraq and Afghanistan since 2003. (US Army photo by Specialist Venessa Hernandez)

Manufacturer: AeroVironment
Length: 6 feet (1.83 meters)
Wingspan: 9 feet (2.74 meters)
Weight: 9 pounds (4 kilograms)
Range: circa 50 miles (75 kilometers)
Speed: 46 mph (73 km/h)
Ceiling: 1,000 feet (300 meters)
Guidance system: radio control, supported by inertial navigation and GPS
Propulsion system: electric motor
First tested: 1988
First deployed: 1990
(Specifications for FQM-151A)

An artist concept, circa 1989, of the Hughes/Raytheon YAIM-152A Advanced Air-to-Air Missile (AAAM) in flight. (Author's collection)

AIM-152 AAAM

The Advanced Air-to-Air Missile (AAAM) Program was initiated in the 1980s by the Naval Weapons Center at China Lake to develop a Mach 3 successor to the AIM-54 Phoenix very long range interceptor missile. Two teams of contractors were selected in 1987, and they developed quite dissimilar competing missile designs to satisfy the requirement. However, neither weapon was ready for testing when the Cold War ended, and the AAAM program was cancelled in 1992.

Manufacturer: General Dynamics and Westinghouse

Length: 12 feet (3.66 meters)

Diameter: 5.5 inches (0.14 meters)

Weight: approximately 380 pounds (170 kilograms)

Range: 115 miles (185 kilometers)

Speed: Mach 3 plus

Guidance system: inertial guidance with radar midcourse correction and electro-optical homing

Propulsion system: solid-fuel rocket

Warhead: blast fragmentation

First tested: never

First deployed: never

(Specifications for proposed YAIM-152A concept)

AGM-153

In 1992, the US Air Force initiated a short-lived study of a potential new low-level ground-attack missile. It was to have been a multi-mission weapon, with the AGM-153A variant being a hard-target penetrator, and the AGM-153B having a blast fragmentation warhead. Both infrared and electro-optical guidance were considered, as was the potential of switching between the two systems in the field. Ultimately, the Air Force chose not to proceed with the project, apparently because the AGM-153 was not sufficiently dissimilar to missiles already in the inventory.

Manufacturer: Hughes and Raytheon

Length: 12 feet (3.66 meters)

Diameter: 9 inches (0.23 meters)

Weight: approximately 660 pounds (300 kilograms)

Range: 115 miles (185 kilometers)

Speed: Mach 3 plus

Guidance system: inertial guidance with active radar for terminal phase

Propulsion system: ramjet and solid-fuel rocket hybrid

Warhead: blast fragmentation

First tested: never

First deployed: never

(Specifications for proposed YAIM-152A concept)

Circa 1989, this folding-wing McDonnell Douglas weapon was developed for the US Navy's Advanced Interdiction Weapon System (AIWS) program, a precursor to the Joint Standoff Weapon (JSOW) program that led to the very similar AGM-154. (DoD)

AGM-154 JSOW

The Joint Stand-Off Weapon (JSOW) program was a collaborative effort between the US Navy and Air Force to develop a precision, fire-and-forget guided bomb. Though given an "M For Missile" designation, it is unpowered. A turbojet variant has been considered.

JSOW evolved out of a Navy program begun in 1986, and became "joint" in 1992 when the Air Force saw the weapon as addressing its needs as well. Test drops began in 1994 and the AGM-154A became operational in 1999. The program received notice in procurement circles for its having stayed *ahead* of schedule during development.

The AGM-154A was first used in combat in 1999 against Iraqi targets during Operation Southern Watch. It was subsequently used in the Balkans, Afghanistan and during Operation Iraqi Freedom in 2003.

Export customers for the JSOW include Australia, Greece, the Netherlands, Poland, Turkey, and Singapore.

The AGM-154A JSOW A uses inertial guidance and GPS for targeting, and is armed with 145 BLU-97 submunitions. An AGM-154B with anti-armor submunitions was considered, but not deployed.

The AGM-154C JSOW C, which entered service in 2005 with the US Navy only, has the same guidance system, but uses an infrared seeker for targeting. The AGM-154C is armed with British-developed Bomb Royal Ordnance Augmented CHarge (BROACH) penetrating warhead, whose creators can be acknowledged at least for going to great lengths to make an acronym work. These creators are BAE Systems, QinetiQ and Thales Missile Electronics. BROACH has two stages. The first blows a hole in a hardened target, allowing the second to pass through.

A quartet of AGM-154 Joint Standoff Weapons (JSOW) aboard an F/A-18. (DoD)

Manufacturer: Texas Instruments (Raytheon after 1997)

Length: 13 feet 4 inches (4.06 meters)

Diameter: 13 inches (0.33 meters)

Wingspan: 8 feet 10 inches (2.69 meters)

Weight: 1,065 pounds (483 kilograms)

Range: 14 miles (22 kilometers) in a low altitude launch, 81 miles (130 kilometers) at high altitude

Guidance system: inertial navigation combined with GPS

Propulsion system: none (turbojet proposed for AGM-154D)

Warhead: see text

First tested: 1994

First deployed: 1999

(Specifications for AGM-154A)

Army personnel position a BQM-155 Hunter UAV for takeoff at Petrovec Airfield at Skopje, Macedonia in 2001 in support of Task Force Harvest. (US Air Force photo by Staff Sergeant Jocelyn Broussard)

BQM-155 (RQ-5 after 1997) Hunter

The winner of the Defense Department's Unmanned Aerial Vehicle, Short Range (UAV-SR) competition of 1991-1992, the Hunter is a reconnaissance and targeting platform equipped with Low-Light Television (LLTV) and Forward-Looking Infrared (FLIR) systems. It was officially ordered by the US Army in February 1993 under the designation BQM-155A. Though it began life designated as an "M For Missile" system, the Hunter was appropriately redesignated as RQ-5 under the new "Q for Drone" nomenclature.

The Hunter was originally designed by the Malat component of Israel Aircraft Industries (IAI), and was assembled in the United States by TRW until 2003, when the program was acquired by Northrop Grumman.

The Hunter's successful career almost didn't happen. After a series of crashes in 1995, the Army terminated acquisition and sidelined the BQM-155A fleet. However, it was taken out of mothballs in 1999 for operations in Kosovo, where, thanks to various improvements, the Hunter redeemed itself monitoring infiltrations by rebel fighters.

In subsequent operations in Iraq, the Hunter (now RQ-5A) continued to prove useful. Since 2003, armed Hunters are designated as MQ-5A, and in 2005, Northrop Grumman rolled out an improved, armed, multi-mission MQ-5B Hunter. The designated successor to the Hunter family is the similar RQ-7 Shadow.

Manufacturer: TRW (Northrop Grumman since 2003)
Length: 22 feet 10 inches (6.96 meters)
Wingspan: 29 feet 2 inches (8.89 meters)
Weight: 1,600 pounds (727 kilograms)
Range: 185 miles (300 kilometers)
Speed: 122 mph (196 km/h)
Ceiling: 15,000 feet (4,570 meters)
Guidance system: radio control, or preprogrammed autopilot
Propulsion system: two piston engines
(later RQ-5As and MQ-5B carry GBU-44 munitions)
First tested: 1991
(US Army evaluation of the IAI Hunter)
First deployed: 1994
(Specifications for BQM-155A)

RIM-156 SM-2ER Block IV

The US Navy's RIM-156 Standard Missile 2, Extended Range (SM-2ER) is an upgraded and more compact version of the RIM-67 SM-1ER ship-launched anti-aircraft and anti-ship missile of the 1980s. First tested in 1992, the RIM-156A became operational in 1999, augmenting the RIM-67Cs already deployed. (See Appendix 4 for an overview of the Standard family.)

Important improvements in the RIM-156 system are a new booster and the fact that it is compatible with the modular Mk.41 Vertical launching System (VLS),which is standard equipment aboard Aegis missile ships. The VLS is easy to use, has a faster reaction time than turret or rail launchers, and has long since become the world's standard shipboard launch platform for many missile types, including the Tomahawk cruise missile.

A RIM-156B SM-2ER Block IVA variant with an anti-ballistic missile capability was developed and tested, but cancelled in 2001 in favor of the next-generation RIM-161A Standard Missile 3 (SM-3), which is based on the RIM-156A (see RIM-161). Meanwhile, a land attack variant (SM-4) was developed under the designation RGM-165A. The designated successor to the RIM-156A is the RIM-174 (SM-6) Standard ERAM.

Manufacturer: Raytheon

Length: 21 feet 6 inches (6.55 meters)

Diameter: 21 inches (0.53 meters)

Span (fins): 5 feet 2 inches (1.58 meters)

Weight: 3,200 pounds (1,450 kilograms)

Range: 150 miles (240 kilometers)

Speed: Mach 3.5

Ceiling: 110,000 feet (33,000 kilometers)

Guidance system: inertial guidance with semi-active radar homing in terminal phase

Propulsion system: two-stage solid-rocket

Warhead: blast fragmentation

First tested: 1992

First deployed: 1999

(Specifications for RIM-156A)

The Arleigh Burke-class guided-missile destroyer USS Stout *launches a RIM-156 Standard SM-2ER Block IV Standard Missile from its aft missile bay against the target ship USS* O'Bannon *during a sinking exercise on October 6, 2008 in the Pacific Ocean.* (US Navy photo by Mass Communication Specialist 3rd class Zachary Martin)

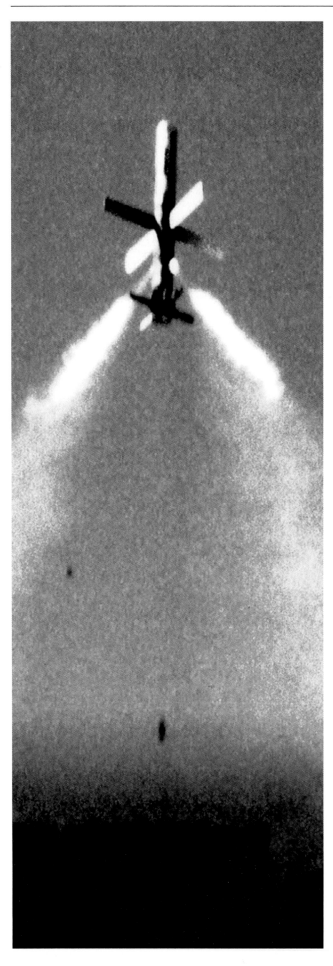

MGM-157 EFOGM

The Enhanced Fiber Optic Guided Missile (EFOGM) program grew out of the Fiber Optic Guided Missile (FOG-M) research program of 1984-1990, which studied the use of fibers rather than wires for guiding small tactical missiles similar to the wire-guided BGM-71 TOW. The concept reemerged in 1992 and became EFOGM in 1994. The YMGM-157A was aimed by the operator using images from an electro-optical/infrared camera system in the missile, with communication being via an unspooling optical fiber. It was designed to be deployed in an eight-tube launch system aboard a Hum-Vee.

An extensive program testing YMGM-157A and YMGM-157B missiles that took place between 1998 and 2002 was deemed successful, but the US Army chose not to acquire and deploy an operational EFOGM.

Manufacturer: Raytheon

Length: 6 feet 4 inches (1.93 meters)

Diameter: 6.6 inches (0.17 meters)

Span (fins): 3 feet 9 inches (1.14 meters)

Weight: 118 pounds (53 kilograms)

Range: 9 miles (15 kilometers)

Speed: 160 mph (360 km/h)

Guidance system: fiber optic cable with electro-optical and infrared seeker

Propulsion system: dual thrust solid-fuel rocket

Warhead: shaped charge

First tested: 1998

First deployed: never

(Specifications for YMGM-157B)

The US Army successfully completed the third test flight of its MGM-157 Enhanced Fiber Optic Guided Missile (EFOGM) on May 7, 1998. (Raytheon)

Staff Sergeant Jason Murphy, Senior Airman Eric Noblin, and Senior Airman Andrew Littleton of the 34th Aircraft Maintenance Unit, work to secure an AGM-158 Joint Air-to-Surface Standoff Missile (JASSM) and loading platform to the mechanical ram assembly prior to loading it into a B-1 Lancer aircraft at Ellsworth AFB in August 2006. (US Air Force photo by Airman 1st Class Angela Ruiz)

AGM-158 JASSM

The US Air Force Joint Air-to-Surface Standoff Missile (JASSM) program was undertaken one year after the termination of the AGM-137 Tri-Service Standoff Attack Missile (TSSAM) in 1994. Like its predecessor, JASSM was expected to make use of low-observable (stealth) technology. Both Lockheed Martin and McDonnell Douglas were selected in 1996 to submit competitive design proposals under the designations AGM-158 and AGM-159.

In 1998, the Lockheed Martin proposal was selected for production. Flight and operational testing of the AGM-158A, which began in 1999, was marred by a disturbing number of problems which were addressed at the customer's expense. In 2004, work began on developing an extended range AGM-158B JASSM-ER.

Initially, the JASSMs equipped B-52s, but they are compatible with all Air Force strike aircraft. Australia, the Netherlands and South Korea are also considering or acquiring the JASSM. The US Navy, a partner in the TSSM program, briefly considered the JASSM as an alternative to the AGM-84 SLAM-ER.

Manufacturer: Lockheed Martin
Length: 14 feet (4.27 meters)
Wingspan: 7 feet 11 inches (2.41 meters)
Weight: 2,250 pounds (1,020 kilograms)
Range: more than 230 miles (370 kilometers)
Speed: circa Mach 0.8
Guidance system: inertial navigation with GPS support, and an imaging infrared seeker
Propulsion system: Teledyne turbojet
Warhead: hard-target penetrating munitions
First tested: 1999
First deployed: 2009
(Specifications for AGM-158A)

Above: *An AGM-158 Joint Air-to-Surface Standoff Missile (JASSM) flying in formation with an F-16.* (Lockheed Martin)

Left: *A dramatic studio image of the AGM-158 Joint Air-to-Surface Standoff Missile* (JASSM). (Lockheed Martin)

Left: *A dramatic studio image of the AGM-158 Joint Air-to-Surface Standoff Missile* (JASSM). (Lockheed Martin)

AGM-159 JASSM

The US Air Force Joint Air-to-Surface Standoff Missile (JASSM) program was undertaken one year after the termination of the AGM-137 Tri-Service Standoff Attack Missile (TSSAM) in 1994. Like its predecessor, JASSM was expected to make use of low-observable (stealth) technology. Both Lockheed Martin and McDonnell Douglas were selected in 1996 to submit competitive design proposals under the designations AGM-158 and AGM-159. In 1998, the Lockheed Martin proposal was selected for production and work on the AGM-159 stopped.

The ADM-160 Miniature Air-Launched Decoy (MALD) was evaluated against 169th Fighter Wing F-16s in a July 1999 Suppression of Enemy Air Defenses (SEAD) exercise at Nellis AFB, Nevada. (Northrop Grumman)

ADM-160 MALD

The Miniature Air Launched Decoy (MALD) program originated with DARPA in 1995 with the objective of developing a low-cost decoy vehicle. It was initially built by Teledyne Ryan (Northrop Grumman after 1999), but Raytheon took over production after 2003. Raytheon developed the larger ADM-160B, which first flew under its own power in 2007.

Operationally, the ADM-160A can simulate every US Air Force aircraft using a radar-based Signature Augmentation System (SAS). It can also be carried by all Air Force strike aircraft. Air Force interest in acquiring the MALD has fluctuated. Initially strong, it later waned, only to bounce back with a 2010 order for what Raytheon called a "significant quantity."

Manufacturer: Teledyne Ryan (Northrop Grumman after 1999), and later Raytheon

Length: 7 feet 10 inches (2.41 meters)

Diameter: 6 inches (0.15 meters)

Wingspan: 2 feet 2 inches (0.65 meters)

Weight: 100 pounds (45 kilograms)

Range: 285 miles 460 (kilometers)

Speed: Mach 0.8

Ceiling: 30,000 feet (9,000 meters)

Guidance system: inertial navigation with GPS support and manual override

Propulsion system: Hamilton Sunstrand turbojet

Warhead: none

First tested: 1999

First deployed: 2001

(Specifications for ADM-160A)

RIM-161 SM-3

The RIM-161 Standard Missile 3 (SM-3) is a direct derivative of the RIM-156 Standard Missile 2, Extended Range (SM-2ER) ship-launched anti-aircraft and anti-ship missile deployed in 1999. It came about as part of a project to develop a Standard Missile derivative with an anti-ballistic missile capability as part of the Navy Theater Wide Theater Ballistic Missile Defense (NTW-TBMD) program. Developed for the US Navy, the SM-3 is also in service with the Japanese navy.

Originally, there was a plan for a missile designated as RIM-156B SM-2ER Block IVA, but it was cancelled in favor of the RIM-161A. (See Appendix 4 for an overview of the Standard family.)

The RIM-161A has the same airframe and engine as the RIM-156A, but includes a third stage that constitutes the payload, the Lightweight Exo-Atmospheric Projectile (LEAP). It is a kinetic energy ("hit-to-kill") weapon, containing no explosive warhead, because hitting a ballistic missile at high speed (like hitting a bottle with a rifle bullet) is sufficient to destroy it — or at least to knock it off course.

Dating back to studies conducted by the Strategic Defense Initiative Office (SDIO) in the 1980s, the LEAP weapon preceded the RIM-161A. It was developed and then tested during the 1990s using RIM-2 and RIM-156A missiles.

Operationally, the RIM-161A third stage rocket motor carries the LEAP outside the atmosphere, taking it to within 30 seconds of hitting the target. At this point, the LEAP's forward-looking infrared (FLIR) guidance and solid-fuel divert and attitude control system (SDACS) maneuver it to a high-speed impact.

The first test of the RIM-161A came in 1999, and in January 2002, a fully configured RIM-161A with a LEAP payload, launched from a US Navy Aegis warship, succeeded in hitting a target missile. In 2007, a RIM-161A fired by a Japanese Aegis ship destroyed a ballistic missile for the first time. While the near-perfect test program success rate claimed by the Defense Department has been called into question by independent analysts, it seems apparent that this rate is at least much higher than with the early stages of many previous missile programs.

Meanwhile, the US Navy also undertook to develop an anti-satellite capability for the RIM-161A. In February 2008 the guided-missile cruiser USS *Lake Erie* successfully downed the National Reconnaissance Office USA-193 reconnaissance satellite 150 miles above the North Pacific.

Left: *A RIM-161 Standard Missile-3 (SM-3) is launched from the guided-missile cruiser USS* Lake Erie *while under way in the Pacific Ocean in November 2007 against a ballistic missile target launched from the Pacific Missile Range Test Facility in Kauai.* (US Navy)

A RIM-161B Standard Missile-3 (SM-3) Block 1A is launched from the Japan Maritime Self-Defense Force destroyer JS Myoko *in a joint missile defense intercept test with the US Missile Defense Agency in the Pacific Ocean in October 2009. The SM-3 successfully intercepted a medium-range target that had been launched minutes earlier from the Pacific Missile Range Facility at Barking Sands, Kauai.* (DoD)

The payload of the RIM-161 is the Raytheon Lightweight Exo-Atmospheric Projectile (LEAP), a hit-to-kill kinetic warhead. (Raytheon)

Like the RIM-156, the RIM-161 is compatible with the modular Mk.41 Vertical launching System (VLS) which is standard equipment aboard Aegis missile ships.

Upgrades to the basic operational missile include the SM-3 Block IA with streamlined maintenance, and the Block IB with an improved infrared seeker and a ten-thruster SDACS for better accuracy.

In addition to Japan, the Netherlands has expressed interest in the shipboard SM-3 system, while Poland, and possibly Israel, will acquire a land-based variant of the missile.

Manufacturer: Raytheon

Length: 21 feet 6 inches (6.55 meters)

Diameter: 21 inches (0.53 meters)

Span (fins): 5 feet 2 inches (1.58 meters)

Range: 150 miles (240 kilometers)

Speed: Mach 3.5

Ceiling: 150 miles (240 kilometers)

Guidance system: inertial guidance with semi-active radar homing in terminal phase and midcourse guidance from the launching vessel using GPS

Propulsion system: two-stage solid-rocket

Warhead: kinetic energy ("hit-to-kill") LEAP upper stage

First tested: 1999

First deployed: 2009

(Specifications for RIM-161A)

RIM-162 ESSM

In 1988, the US Navy began considering a new missile to supersede its RIM-7 Sea Sparrow. The idea was for a weapon capable of engaging a variety of threats, especially low flying cruise missiles. In 1995, Hughes received the contract to begin work on the RIM-162 Evolved Sea Sparrow Missile (ESSM), which first flew in 1998. Production included the RIM-162A, deployed aboard warships equipped with the Aegis Combat System (ACS), and the RIM-162B, which arms ships without Aegis.

Both variants are launched from the Mk.41 Vertical Launching System (VLS). Meanwhile, the RIM-162C is designed for the Mk.48 VLS, and the RIM-162D for the Mk.29 box launcher.

Though the ESSM became operational with the fleet in 2004, the first kill achieved against a flying target during a training exercise came in October 2008.

In addition to the US Navy, the ESSM has been acquired by the navies of Australia, Canada, Denmark, Germany, Greece, the Netherlands, New Zealand, Norway, Spain, Turkey and the United Arab Emirates. Raytheon reached the 1,000-unit mark for deliveries of ESSMs in August 2009.

Manufacturer: Hughes Aircraft (Raytheon after 1997)

Length: 12 feet (3.66 meters)

Diameter: 10 inches (0.25 meters)

Weight: 620 pounds (280 kilograms)

Range: 32 miles (50 kilometers)

Speed: Mach 4

Guidance system: midcourse data link, with infrared terminal homing

Propulsion system: solid-fuel rocket

Warhead: blast fragmentation

First tested: 1998

First deployed: 2004

(Specifications for RIM-162A)

A Link-Belt crane loads a "quad-pack" canister containing a RIM-162 Evolved Sea Sparrow Missile (ESSM) into a Mk.41 vertical launch system (VLS), aboard the guided missile destroyer USS McCampbell. The ship's namesake, Captain David McCampbell, would have been pleased with the symbolism. A World War II fighter pilot, he shot down more enemy aircraft (34) than any other American naval aviator. (US Navy photo by LTJG Joel Jackson)

A RIM-162D ESSM launches from the aircraft carrier USS John C. Stennis during combat system ships qualification trials in October 2008. (US Navy photo by Mass Communication Specialist 3rd Class Kyle Steckler)

A GQM-163A Coyote flies over the bow of a US Navy observation ship during a routine test. (Orbital Sciences Corporation)

GQM-163 Coyote

Through the 1970s and 1980s, the US Navy entertained a number of concepts for a target drone that could simulate a supersonic, low-altitude cruise missile. These included the BQM-90, BQM-111, and the AQM-127 SLAT, none of which entered service. Until the arrival of the Coyote, the Navy had to make do with a stock of MQM-8 Vandals, as well as some Russian-built Zvezda Kh-31s that were modified by McDonnell Douglas. Ironically, these were the exact cruise missiles that target missiles had been intended to simulate!

The GQM-163 Coyote Supersonic Sea-Skimming Target (SSST) was created by Orbital Sciences, the company responsible for the unique Pegasus air-launched space launch vehicles, and the X-43 spaceplane. The company's proposal beat out a competing Boeing proposal which would have been based on the Kh-31.

Manufacturer: Orbital Sciences
Length: 31 feet 3 inches (9.52 meters) with booster
Diameter: 18 inches (0.46 meters)
Range: 70 miles (110 kilometers)
Speed: Mach 2.8
Propulsion system: Aerojet solid-fuel rocket with Hercules solid-fuel booster
First tested: 2004
First deployed: 2007
(Specifications for GQM-163A)

An artist's rendering of the GQM-163A Coyote Supersonic Sea Skimming Target. (Orbital Sciences Corporation)

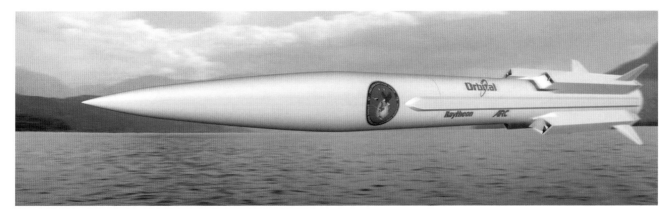

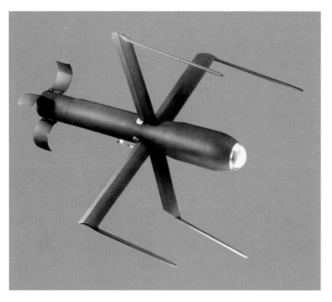

The MGM-164 Block II was derived from the MGM-140 Army Tactical Missile System (ATACMS). The Block II variants were designed to deliver the Brilliant Anti-Tank (BAT) guided submunition seen here. (Lockheed Martin)

MGM-164 ATACMS II

The MGM-164A was the Block II variant of the MGM-140, the missile component of the M39 US Army Tactical Missile System (Army TACMS or ATACMS), which earned the nickname "Steel Rain" from Iraqi field commanders in the 1991 Gulf War.

Originally designated as MGM-140C, the Block II ATACMS was similar to the MGM-140A, but it is GPS-guided and is armed with the Northrop Brilliant Anti-Tank (BAT) guided submunition. The MGM-164A was developed as part of the TACMS 2000 or T2K program, an effort to lower unit costs. However, after successful initial test flights, the ATACMS II was cancelled in 2003. (See also MGM-140 and MGM-168.)

Manufacturer: Loral Vought Systems
(Lockheed Martin after 1996)

Length: 13 feet (3.96 meters)

Diameter: 2 feet (0.61 meters)

Span (fins): 4 feet 7 inches (1.40 meters)

Weight: 3,270 pounds (1,480 kilograms)

Range: 90 miles (140 kilometers)

Guidance system: inertial guidance aided by GPS

Propulsion system: solid-fuel rocket

Warhead: BAT submunitions

First tested: 2004

First deployed: never

(Specifications for MGM-164A)

RGM-165 (SM-4) LASM

Dating back to the 1960s, the US Navy's family of "Standard" missiles were conceived as anti-aircraft weapons, with a built-in secondary anti-ship mission. In the late 1990s, the Land Attack Standard Missile (LASM) concept evolved as a means of adapting the Standard's secondary capability to attack long-range targets ashore in support of US Marine Corps operations.

The RGM-165A, also mentioned in the literature as Standard Missile 4, was adapted from the RIM-66 SM-2MR and plans were laid for converting several hundred of these to RGM-156A configuration.. However, the program was cancelled in 2002 before the LASM became operational. (See Appendix 4 for an overview of the Standard family.)

Manufacturer: Raytheon

Length: 15 feet 6 inches (4.72 meters)

Diameter: 13.5 inches (0.34 meters)

Span (fins): 42.3 inches (1.07 meters)

Weight: 1,370 pounds (620 kilograms)

Range: 175 miles (280 kilometers)

Speed: Mach 3.5

Guidance system: inertial guidance with GPS

Propulsion system: solid-fuel rocket

Warhead: blast fragmentation

First tested: 1997

First deployed: never

(Specifications for RGM-165A)

A Line-of-Sight Anti-Tank (LOSAT) weapon in flight. In 2002, LOSAT evolved into the Lockheed Martin MGM-166 Kinetic Energy Missile (KEM). (Lockheed Martin)

MGM-166 KEM

Simply put, the MGM-166 is a rocket-propelled kinetic energy "bullet" fired from a launcher on a vehicle such as a Hum-Vee. Kinetic, or "hit-to-kill," projectiles have been created for use against missiles, where even a small impact can neutralize them off course. The Kinetic Energy Missile (KEM) was designed for use against tanks, using extremely high speed impacts to harness destructive power.

After a number of early experimental kinetic anti-tank projects such as its Hyper-Velocity Missile (HVM), Vought proposed the KEM for the US Army's Line-of-Sight Anti-Tank (LOSAT) program. After having received the designation MGM-166A, indicating that it was on track to be an operational weapon, it was downgraded to a demonstration program. Scheduled for cancellation in 1996, the program was revived, only to be finally terminated in 2004.

As a follow-on, Lockheed Martin continues to develop the hypersonic Compact Kinetic Energy Missile (CKEM), which is just over half the size of the KEM, and which was first tested in 2003.

Manufacturer: Loral Vought Systems (Lockheed Martin after 1996)
Length: 9 feet 3 inches (2.82 meters)
Diameter: 6.4 inches (0.16 meters)
Weight: 175 pounds (80 kilograms)
Range: 2.5 miles (4 kilometers)
Speed: 3,400 mph (5,500 km/h)
Guidance system: line-of-sight Forward-Looking Infrared (FLIR)
Propulsion system: solid-fuel rocket
Warhead: kinetic energy
First tested: 1990
First deployed: never
(Specifications for MGM-166A)

This artist's conception depicts a Compact Kinetic Energy Missile (CKEM) being launched from a US Army Future Combat Vehicle (FCV). The Lockheed Martin CKEM evolved from the MGM-166 LOSAT/KEM. (Lockheed Martin)

BQM-167 Skeeter

As with any expendable munition, as target drones are used, they are used up. The Skeeter was developed under the Air Force Subscale Aerial Target (AFSAT) program to address the US Air Force need to replace declining stocks of drones such as the BQM-107E Streaker, which remained in production until 2003.

Created by Sacramento-based Composite Engineering, Inc., the Skeeter is similar in size and appearance to the Streaker, and like the Streaker it can be launched from either air or ground. However, being constructed of composites, it is lighter than either the Streaker or the venerable Firebee. A recoverable, multi-mission Skeeter variant has been suggested.

Manufacturer: Composite Engineering (with Boeing)

Length: 20 feet (6.10 meters)

Diameter: 2 feet (0.61 meters)

Wingspan: 11 feet (3.52 meters)

Range: circa 1,800 miles (2,900 kilometers)

Speed: Mach 0.9

Ceiling: 50,000 feet (15,000 meters)

Guidance system: preprogrammed, or radio control override

Propulsion system: turbojet

First tested: 2001

First deployed: 2004

(Specifications for BQM-167A)

The MGM-168 Army Tactical Missile System (ATACMS) Block IVA "Unitary" single-warhead missile is a variant of the MGM-140B ATACMS Block IA. (Lockheed Martin)

MGM-168 ATACMS IA Unitary

The MGM-168A is a derivative of the MGM-140, the missile component of the M39 US Army Tactical Missile System (Army TACMS or ATACMS), which earned the nickname "Steel Rain" from Iraqi field commanders in the 1991 Gulf War. Like the MGM-164A ATACMS II, the MGM-168A was a spin-off of the MGM-140 program (they were originally designated as MGM-140B and MGM-140E, respectively). Unlike the MGM-140A, which was armed with multiple submunitions, the MGM-168A ATACMS IA Unitary (some sources call it ATACMS IVA) carries a single 500-pound warhead.

ATACMS variants have basically the same airframe, but vary by guidance and armament. The two later variants are GPS-guided and were developed as part of the TACMS 2000 or T2K program, an effort to lower unit costs.

ATACMS is also compatible with the US Army's High Mobility Artillery Rocket System (HIMARS) a light, truck-mounted multiple rocket launch system. HIMARS carries six rockets or one ATACMS, and can use all MLRS munitions. HIMARS was first operationally deployed with the 14th Marine Regiment in 2007 in Iraq's Al Anbar province.

Manufacturer: Lockheed Martin

Length: 13 feet (3.96 meters)

Diameter: 2 feet (0.61 meters)

Span (fins): 4 feet 7 inches (1.40 meters)

Weight: circa 2,900 pounds (1,320 kilograms)

Range: 186 miles (300 kilometers)

Guidance system: inertial guidance aided by GPS

Propulsion system: solid-fuel rocket

Warhead: unitary high explosive

First tested: 2001

First deployed: 2008

(Specifications for MGM-168A)

AGM-169 JCM

The idea behind the 2002 Joint Common Missile (JCM) program was to develop a replacement for the air-to-ground AGM-65 Maverick and AGM-114 Hellfire which would satisfy the requirements of the US Army, Navy and Marine Corps. Two years later, the industry team of Lockheed Martin and Raytheon beat out Boeing and Northrop Grumman at the proposal phase, and moved forward with a prototype missile designated as YAGM-169A. The same size as the Hellfire, it was designed to be adapted to Hellfire launch systems.

Beginning at the end of 2004, the program proceeded in a series of fits and starts, being suspended for budget reasons, resumed, paused, restarted, and so on. Final cancellation came in 2007, as the services involved transferred their attention to the JCM successor program, known as the Joint Air-to-Ground Missile (JAGM). This missile is seen is a potential replacement for the Hellfire and Maverick, as well as the BGM-71 TOW.

Above right: The AGM-169 Joint Common Missile (JCM) was originally conceived as a successor to a variety of missiles, including the AGM-114 Hellfire (which it resembles) and the AGM-65 Maverick. (Lockheed Martin)

Manufacturer: Lockheed Martin

Length: 5 feet 10 inches (1.80 meters)

Diameter: 7 inches (0.18 meters)

Span (fins): 12 inches (0.33 meters)

Weight: 108 pounds (49 kilograms)

Range: 15 miles (25 kilometers)

Guidance system: multi-mode imaging infrared, laser homing and millimeter-wave radar seekers

Propulsion system: solid-fuel rocket

Warhead: blast fragmentation or shaped charge

First tested: 2005

First deployed: never

(Specifications for YAGM-169A)

The MQM-170 Outlaw UAV was developed as an aerial target, but it is capable of a variety of missions befitting the capabilities of a light aircraft of its type. (Griffon Aerospace)

MQM-170 Outlaw

The MQM-170 and MQM-171 are both light-weight, low-radar-observable UAVs created for the US Army by Alabama-based Griffon Aerospace. Because they can serve as aerial targets as well as in other UAV roles, they were given "M For Missile" rather than "Q for Drone" designations. In each, internal payload bays can be configured to accommodate fuel or sensors. Both are catapult-launched and recoverable with landing skids or landing gear.

Manufacturer: Griffon Aerospace

Length: 8 feet 5 inches (2.56 meters)

Wingspan: 13 feet 7 inches (4.15 meters)

Weight: 120 pounds (55 kilograms)

Range: circa 480 miles (800 kilometers)

Speed: 120 mph (200 km/h)

Ceiling: 16,000 feet (4,900 meters)

Guidance system: manual visual line of sight or autopilot using GPS waypoint navigation

Propulsion system: piston engine

First tested: 2003

First deployed: 2004

(Specifications for MQM-170A)

The MQM-171 Broadsword UAV is a scaled up variation on its sister ship, the MQM-170A Outlaw. The Broadsword is deployed with the US Army in a variety of roles. (Griffon Aerospace)

MQM-171 Broadsword

The MQM-170 and MQM-171 are both light-weight, low-radar-observable UAVs created for the US Army by Alabama-based Griffon Aerospace. Because they can serve as aerial targets as well as in other UAV roles, they were given "M For Missile" rather than "Q for Drone" designations. In each, internal payload bays can be configured to accommodate fuel or sensors. Both are catapult-launched and recoverable with landing skids or landing gear.

The Broadsword is a much larger derivative of the MQM-170A. Griffon describes it as an "inexpensive airframe for use as an observation platform or a test/development vehicle for sensors and new propulsion systems."

Manufacturer: Griffon Aerospace

Length: 14 feet 10 inches (4.52 meters)

Wingspan: 22 feet 6 inches (6.86 meters)

Weight: 550 pounds (250 kilograms)

Range: circa 750 miles (1,200 kilometers)

Speed: 125 mph (200 km/h)

Ceiling: 14,000 feet (4,300 meters)

Guidance system: manual visual line of sight or autopilot using GPS waypoint navigation

Propulsion system: piston engine

First tested: 2010

First deployed: pending

(Specifications for MQM-171A)

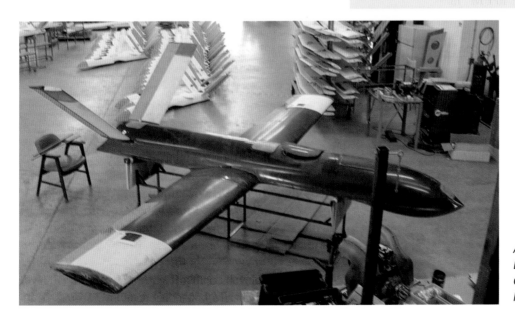

A completed MQM-171 Broadsword UAV on the Griffon Aerospace production line. (Griffon Aerospace)

The lengthy development program leading to the Short-Range Assault Weapon (SRAW) was initiated in the 1980s, and was aimed at developing a guided missile successor to the shoulder-fired, unguided Light Anti-armor Weapon (LAW). The resulting SRAW missile was eventually designated as FGM-172. (Lockheed Martin)

FGM-172 SRAW

The light-weight, man-portable Short-Range Assault Weapon (SRAW) program was aimed at creating a fire-and-forget successor to the likes of the unguided M72 Light Anti-armor Weapon (LAW). The long-running project stretched out over two decades, starting in 1987. Though tests of competing designs took place in 1991, low-rate production did not begin until 2004, and the FGM-172 designation was not assigned until 2006 (hence the high number). The SRAW is a US Marine Corps weapon, with the US Army and the United Kingdom having considered, but rejected, acquisition of it.

Two variants were developed, an FGM-172A for attacking the tops of tanks from above, and an FGM-172B Multi-Purpose Variant (MPV) used as an assault weapon for other targets. Beginning in 2005, all FGM-172As were retrofitted as FGM-172Bs. Operationally they are used in conjunction with the FGM-148 Javelin.

Manufacturer: Loral Systems (Lockheed Martin after 1996)

Length: 28 inches (0.7 meter)

Diameter: 5.5 inches (0.14 meter)

Weight: 14 pounds (6.4 kilograms)

Range: 2,000 (600 kilometers)

Speed: 560 mph (900 km/h)

Guidance system: inertial guidance

Propulsion system: dual solid-fuel rocket

Warhead: shaped charge (FGM-172A), blast fragmentation (FGM-172B)

First tested: 1991

First deployed: 2002

(Specifications for FGM-172A)

An artist's rendition of the US Navy's proposed GQM-173 Multi-Stage Supersonic Target (MSST). (PRNewsFoto/ Alliant Techsystems)

GQM-173 MSST

In August 2008, the US Navy awarded a contract to Minnesota-based Alliant Techsystems for the design, development, integration, and testing of the Multi-Stage Supersonic Target (MSST). Designated as GQM-173, the vehicle is designed to simulate a two-stage anti-ship cruise missile threat, complementing the capabilities of the GQM-163 Coyote SSST.

The two MSST stages are a subsonic winged vehicle and the supersonic vehicle which makes the final dash to the target. This stage is built by Composites Engineering, Inc. who makes the forward section of the GQM-163.

As the company explains, the MSST will be used "to evaluate the operational effectiveness of weapons/combat systems against next-generation surface-to-surface anti-ship missiles that cruise at subsonic speeds, initiate a separation event, and then make a supersonic dash to the intended target."

Manufacturer: Alliant Techsystems
Speed: supersonic
Propulsion system: solid-fuel rocket
First tested: circa 2011
First deployed: pending
(Specifications unreleased at press time)

RIM-174 (SM-6) ERAM

The RIM-174 Standard Missile 6 (SM-6) was developed early in the twenty-first century under the Extended Range Anti-Air Warfare Missile (ERAM) as the next generation successor to the RIM-156 Standard Missile 2 (SM-3) ship-launched anti-aircraft and anti-ship missile. Another RIM-156 derivative, the RIM-161, is an anti-ballistic missile system, but the RIM-174 is a long-range anti-aircraft weapon. It is being produced for the Royal Australian Navy as well as the US Navy. (See Appendix 4 for an overview of the Standard family.)

The standardized airframe is essentially the same as the RIM-156, but the RIM-174 trades semi-active radar homing for an active radar seeker such as that used in the AIM-120C AMRAAM, specifically to track and kill highly maneuverable foes.

Manufacturer: Raytheon

Length: 21 feet 6 inches (6.55 meters)

Diameter: 21 inches (0.53 meters)

Span (fins): 5 feet 2 inches (1.57 meters)

Weight: 3,300 pounds (1,500 kilograms)

Range: 150 miles (240 kilometers)

Speed: Mach 3.5

Ceiling: 110,000 feet (33,000 kilometers)

Guidance system: inertial guidance with active radar homing

Propulsion system: two-stage solid-rocket

Warhead: blast fragmentation

First tested: 2008 (first successful live intercept)

First deployed: circa 2010

(Specifications for RIM-174A)

A fully configured EADS Do-DT45 (MQM-175B). (Bastlmichi photo, released for publication)

MQM-175

The MQM-175 designation was reportedly assigned by the Defense Department to a family of low-cost aerial target vehicles developed by the European Aeronautic Defence and Space Company (EADS), with the EADS Do-DT35 (DT-35) becoming the MQM-175A and the Do-DT40 (DT-40) designated as MQM-175B. EADS reports that on June 27, 2006, the US Army conducted two demonstration flights of the twin-jet drones within a 90-minute period at the McGregor Range in New Mexico, "accurately performing flight profiles that were pre-determined by the Army. Both jet-powered targets met the full requirements of the demonstration, including their tracking by Army sensors."

According to John Young, the Chief Executive Officer of EADS North America Defense, these drones offer the US Army "a truly capable and effective solution for its subsonic, subscale aerial target requirements."

The MQM-175 drones are powered launched by means of a Robonic MC2555LLR portable pneumatic catapult launcher. In turn, they are radar or infrared guided, and are equipped with a radar altimeter allowing them to fly at altitudes as low as 17 feet to simulate a sea-skimming anti-ship missile.

An EADS Do-DT45 (MQM-175B) on its portable catapult launcher during testing. (Bastlmichi photo, released for publication)

Manufacturer: European Aeronautic Defence and Space Company N.V. (EADS)

Length: 7 feet (2.15 meters)

Wingspan: 5 feet (1.52 meters)

Weight: 165 pounds (75 kilograms)

Endurance: 60 minutes

Speed: 475 mph (770 km/h)

Ceiling: 27,000 feet (8,300 meters)

Guidance system: radar or infrared and/or heat-seeking

Propulsion system: 2 jet engines

First tested: 2006 (first US Army demonstration flights)

First deployed: pending

(Specifications for MQM-175B)

Addendum 1:

Selected Classic Guided Missiles

SINCE WORLD WAR II, most major postwar missile programs have received "M for Missile" designation in the nomenclature system of 1963. These designators were assigned retroactively to programs begun before 1963 that were still active in 1963 (and, inexplicably, to some terminated before 1963), and they have been assigned to programs initiated since 1963. These are the 174 missiles described in the main body of this book.

This addendum describes a subjectively selected group of historically important guided missiles that never wore an "M For Missile" designator. The Snark, Rascal and Navaho were significant programs that would have worn such a designation had they not been terminated before 1963.

A Northrop SM-62 (formerly B-62) Snark intercontinental cruise missile during flight testing in the late 1950s. (National Archives)

A Northrop SM-62 (formerly B-62) Snark intercontinental cruise missile in Strategic Air Command markings in December 1960. (National Archives)

B-62 (later SM-62) Snark

The Snark (Northrop Model N-69) was the first ballistic missile capable of intercontinental range, as well as being the first very long range cruise missile. It was designed to fly under remote control for up to 6,300 miles, then fire a detachable nose cone containing a warhead.

The MX-775 research project was undertaken in 1946 by the USAAF (US Air Force after September 1947), with Northrop awarded a contract calling for development of the subsonic MX-775A Snark and the supersonic MX-775B Boojum. The latter was cancelled, but the Snark moved to the hardware stage under the initial designation XSSM-A-3. Progress was slow because of difficulties with cutting edge technology and budget constraints. Scheduled for 1949, the first successful flight finally occurred in August 1953. Given a "B for Bomber" designation as B-62 in 1951, the Snark was redesignated again as the SM-62 strategic missile in 1955.

Through the years, test flights were conducted by the Air Research & Development Command over the Atlantic, launching from Cape Canaveral, Florida. In September 1955, the slow-moving test and evaluation program for the Snark picked up momentum as President Eisenhower established a high priority for ICBMs. The range of the Snark is illustrated by one embarrassing moment in 1956 when one drifted off course and crashed in the Brazilian rain forest. Such problems with guidance would dog the Snark throughout its test program.

From about 1957, the program was gradually transferred to the Strategic Air Command, with testing handled by the 556th Strategic Missile Squadron at Patrick AFB, Florida. The first test-range flight with a dummy warhead delivery came in October.

SAC's first operational unit was 702nd Strategic Missile Wing, activated in 1959 at Presque Isle AFB, Maine, and the first Snark went on alert on its mobile launcher in March 1960. It took a year before the 702nd was fully operational, but in June 1961, the incoming Kennedy Administration ordered the phase-out of the Snark, officially describing it as "obsolete and of marginal military value."

The role of the ICBM was seen as better served by the likes of the Atlas, Titan and upcoming Minuteman.

Manufacturer: Northrop

Length: 67 feet 2 inches (20.47 meters) (without sensor probe)

Height: 14 feet 10 inches (4.52 meters)

Wingspan: 42 feet 3 inches (12.88 meters)

Weight without booster: 49,600 pounds (22,500 kilograms)

Weight with booster: 60,965 pounds (27,650 kilograms)

Range: 6,300 miles (10,180 kilometers)

Speed: Mach 0.9

Ceiling: 50,250 feet (15,320 meters)

Guidance system: star-tracking celestial navigation

Propulsion system: Pratt & Whitney turbojet, with two Aerojet solid-fuel rocket boosters

Warhead: nuclear

First tested: 1949

First deployed: 1960

(Specifications for SM-62A)

A Bell GAM-63 (formerly B-63) Rascal supersonic nuclear-armed standoff missile. (US Air Force)

B-63 (later GAM-63) Rascal

The specific mission of the Rascal was based on the experiences of bomber crews in World War II. It was conceived as a supersonic, air-launched, stand-off land attack missile, designed to extend the reach of B-29 and B-50 strategic bombers by allowing them to strike heavily defended targets without endangering aircrews. As such, it was a precursor to later and current stand-off cruise missiles from the AGM-28 Hound Dog to the AGM-86 ALCM.

The program originated with Project Mastiff, one of many varied missile design studies begun in 1946 by the USAAF (US Air Force after September 1947). After proposals were evaluated, Bell received a contract for the MX-776 project, which involved the MX-776A flight test vehicle and the follow-on MX-776B, the prototype of the full-scale missile that would take shape as the Rascal.

The finished MX-776A was redesignated as Rocket Test Vehicle RTV-A-4, but redesignated again as an "X-Plane," X-9, before its first powered flight tests in 1950. Named Shrike (not to be confused with the AGM-45 Shrike), the X-9 made a number of flights through 1953 which provided important guidance and control system data for the Rascal program.

Like the MX-776A, the missile which evolved under the MX-776B leg of the program went through a series of nomenclature changes. Named Rascal and initially designated as ASM-A-2, it became the B-63 bomber in 1951 and the GAM-63 ground attack missile in 1955. Leading the development work was Walter Dornberger, an important figure in the German wartime V-2 program, who had been hired by Bell.

The first test flight of the Rascal occurred at White Sands Missile Range in 1951, while the Air Force considered which type of aircraft should be modified as a carrier aircraft. With the impending phase-out of the B-29 and B-50, the B-36 and B-47 were considered, and both were test flown with the missile.

Finally, the DB-47E variant of the latter was earmarked to be armed with the Rascal, with all operational Rascals and their carriers assigned to the 321st Bomb Wing at McCoy AFB, Florida. However, the fast progress of missile technology overtook the obsolescent Rascal, and the Air Force cancelled the whole program in November 1958 before any Rascals became operational.

They were superseded by the longer range Hound Dogs, carried by B-52s.

Manufacturer: Bell Aircraft

Length: 32 feet (9.75 meters)

Diameter: 4 feet (1.22 meters)

Wingspan: 16 feet 8 inches (5.08 meters)

Weight: 13,500 pounds (6,120 kilograms)

Range: 100 miles (160 kilometers)

Speed: Mach 1.6

Guidance system: remote-control from launching aircraft

Propulsion system: liquid-fuel rocket

Warhead: thermonuclear

First tested: 1951

First deployed: never

(Specifications for GAM-63A)

Above: *The North American SM-64 Navaho was preceded by the smaller, but similar X-10 vehicle, which was first flown in 1953 at Edwards Air Force Base.* (Author's collection)

Left: *A North American SM-64 (formerly B-64) Navaho supersonic intercontinental cruise missile on its launch pad, circa 1957.* (Author's collection)

B-64 (later SM-64) Navaho

Like the Snark, the Navaho was created as a cruise missile with intercontinental range, a precursor both to ICBMs and to later generation cruise missiles. Like the Rascal, the full-scale Navaho was preceded by an "X-Plane," the X-10, which explored and validated certain design parameters. Like both Snark and Rascal, Navaho was born in the flurry of guided missile design studies initiated by the USAAF and the US Air Force in the years after World War II.

The Navaho began with the MX-770 project, as a short-range, ground-launched cruise missile, but evolved into a much more ambitious program. The initial step was the turbojet-powered RTV-A-5 Navaho, which was redesignated as X-10 and first flown in 1955. The second step was the XSSM-A-4 Navaho II, which became the XB-64, and later the XSM-64. The final step was the XSSM-A-6 Navaho III, which became the XB-64A, and later the XSM-64A.

Navahos II and III were dual ramjet-powered and boosted by liquid-fuel rockets. Navahos I and II were roughly the same size, while the XB-64A Navaho III was roughly 25 percent larger. It was seen as a production prototype and had intercontinental range.

The XSM-64 Navaho II made its first flight in late 1956, but the program was cancelled the following summer before the XSM-64A flew. The reason was that among cruise missiles, the Snark was already operationally ready. Of course, the US Air Force was already viewing ICBMs as superior technology.

Manufacturer: North American Aviation
Length with booster: 92 feet 1 inch (28.07 meters)
Diameter: 7 feet 10 inches (2.39 meters)
Wingspan: 42 feet 8 inches (13.00 meters)
Weight with booster: 300,500 pounds (136,000 kilograms)
Range: 6,300 miles (10,000 kilometers)
Speed: Mach 3.25
Ceiling: 80,000 feet (24,000 meters)
Guidance system: inertial navigation
Propulsion system: 2 ramjets augmented by a liquid-fuel rocket booster
Warhead: thermonuclear
First tested: 1956 (XSM-64)
First deployed:
(Specifications for XSM-64A)

Addendum 2:

Operational Guided Anti-Missile Missiles

IN THIS ADDENDUM, we include three missile defense missiles that were or are operational, but which were not assigned an "M For Missile" designation.

All were contemporaries of anti-missile missiles that were so designated, but these were not. In 1975, the Sprint was a complement of the LIM-49 Spartan within the Safeguard system. In the twenty-first century, the Ground Based Interceptor and THAAD are part of the National Missile Defense program's Ballistic Missile Defense System (BMDS), along with the RIM-161 SM-3 (Aegis) and the PAC-3 variant of the MIM-104 Patriot.

A doctored image of a Defense Department photo release from November 1964, the first time that the Sprint interceptor missile was officially unveiled to the public. (DoD via Author's collection)

Sprint

The undesignated Sprint anti-ballistic missile was designed to work in coordination with the LIM-49A Spartan as part of Projects Sentinel and Safeguard, the first missile systems conceived to protect the United States from a ballistic missile attack.

While the Spartan was an exoatmospheric weapon, the smaller Sprint was designed to operate within the atmosphere. Spartan was intended to knock down high flying ICBMs at the mid point of their trajectory and before the reentry vehicle carrying their nuclear weapons had reentered the Earth's atmosphere. Sprint was described as a quick-shot, fast reaction anti-ballistic missile. It was a last-minute weapon, to be used to intercept submarine-launched missiles traveling in a shallow trajectory or ICBMs that Spartan missed. Both were nuclear-armed missiles.

The first Sprint test launch occurred in 1965 at the US Army facility at White Sands in New Mexico. In contrast to the silo launched Spartan, the Sprint was designed for immediate surface launching and fast acceleration. It is said to have been capable of reaching speeds of ten times that of sound in a few seconds. After a test series at White Sands, the program moved to Kwajalein at the end of

1970. Here, the first test against a Minuteman fired from Vandenberg AFB was successful. In May 1971, it successfully intercepted a Polaris SLBM that was launched from the USS *Observation Island*. More than 40 tests were conducted from Kwajalein with only a handful being written off as failures.

Later in 1971, Martin Marietta received a contract to develop a more maneuverable Sprint II anti-ballistic missile. This project is still classified, but it is not believed to have reached the flight test stage.

Like Spartan, Sprint became operational in 1975, but both were withdrawn from service before the end of the year for political reasons.

There were originally to be three Safeguard sites, two protecting Minuteman ICBM sites, and the third to defend Washington, DC. The Anti-Ballistic Missile Treaty between the United States and the Soviet Union, signed in 1972, permitted each side to keep a single anti-ballistic missile site. The Soviet Union chose to keep one protecting Moscow. The United States kept the one near Grand Forks AFB, the site nearest to completion. It achieved IOC in April 1975, with 28 Sprint and eight Spartan missiles in place. The full compliment of 100 missiles was on alert by October. However, the United States Congress abruptly took the unexpected step of ordering the Ford Administration to deactivate the site almost as soon as it became fully operational.

Despite their demonstrated speed and accuracy, neither Sprint nor Spartan were revived among the projects undertaken during the Strategic Defense Initiative (SDI) in the 1980s. The reason cited was that both systems used nuclear weapons to destroy incoming ICBMs. Under SDI, non-nuclear weapons would be used to destroy ICBMs. Nevertheless, elements of the technology developed for Safeguard was found valuable in various SDI programs.

Manufacturer: Martin Marietta

Length: 26 feet 11 inches (8.20 meters)

Diameter: 4 feet 5 inches (1.35 meters)

Weight: 7,700 pounds (3,500 kilograms)

Range: 25 miles (40 kilometers)

Speed: Mach 10

Ceiling: 100,000 feet (30,000 meters)

Guidance system: radio command remote control

Propulsion system: two solid-fuel rocket stages

Warhead: thermonuclear

First tested: 1965

First deployed: 1975

Ground Based Interceptor

The Ground Based Interceptor is the missile segment of the Ground-based Midcourse Defense (GMD) System, which went active in 2004 as the first land-based, operationally deployed missile defense program to defend the United States against long-range ballistic missile attacks since Safeguard was scrapped in 1975.

The overall system is designed to provide early detection and tracking of enemy ICBMs during their boost phase, as well as midcourse target discrimination, precision intercept and destruction. The latter is accomplished by the kinetic energy ("hit-to-kill") Exoatmospheric Kill Vehicle (EKV) payload, which is capable of maneuvering to catch the incoming warhead.

Initiated in 1998, the GMD was developed through the experience of a number of experimental programs dating back to the Strategic Defense Initiative (SDI) of the 1980s. These include the Homing Overlay Experiment (HOE) and the Exoatmospheric Reentry Interceptor Subsystem (ERIS).

The Raytheon EKV was first successfully tested using a surrogate booster in 1999, and the Ground Based Interceptor was first test flown in 2001.

The first operational GMD site opened at Fort Greely Alaska in July 2004, and by the end of the year, the first interceptor was loaded into its launch silo at the second GMD site at Vandenberg AFB in California. A proposal for a third site at Redzikowo in Poland was cancelled in 2009. Meanwhile, Ground Based Interceptors succeeded in achieving eight successful intercepts of ballistic missile target vehicles in 15 intercept tests conducted between October 1999 and January 2010.

Manufacturer: Boeing (lead systems integrator), with Lockheed Martin, Orbital Sciences Corporation and Raytheon (for the EKV)

Height: 55 feet (16.76 meters)

Diameter: 50 inches (1.27 meters)

Weight: 28,000 pounds (12,700 kilograms)

Range/Ceiling: 1,250 miles (3,000 kilometers)

Guidance system: radar ground control with infrared terminal seeker

Propulsion system: three stages of Alliant Tech Systems Orion solid-fuel rockets

Warhead: Exoatmospheric Kill Vehicle (EKV)

First tested: 2001

First deployed: 2004

In this photo, a prototype Exoatmospheric Kill Vehicle (EKV) is launched from Meck Island at the Kwajalein Missile Range on December 3, 2001. It successfully intercepted a modified Minuteman ICBM launched from Vandenberg AFB in California. (DoD)

Opposite: A Ground-Based Interceptor payload launch vehicle of the type used to carry a prototype Exoatmospheric Kill Vehicle (EKV) in test launches from the Kwajalein Missile Range. (DoD)

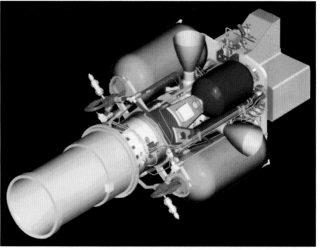

Above: *A detailed cutaway illustration of the Ground-Based Interceptor's Exoatmospheric Kill Vehicle (EKV) interceptor. Note that a sizable proportion of the interior volume consists of the fuel and oxidizer tanks. The goblet-shaped retro-rockets provide the EKV with maneuverability in space.* (Raytheon)

Left: *A Ground-Based Interceptor lifts off from Vandenberg AFB in December 2008 to successfully intercept a long-range target launched from Kodiak, Alaska.* (DoD photo by Joe Davila, US Air Force)

On November 22, 2005 a successful launch was achieved of a THAAD interceptor missile. THAAD was touted by the Missile Defense Agency as "the first missile defense system that is capable of intercepting a target missile both inside and outside the atmosphere." (Missile Defense Agency)

THAAD

One of many projects to flow from the technology developed by the SDIO in the 1980s, the Theater High Altitude Area Defense (THAAD) program was initiated in 1987.

Lockheed Martin was selected by the US Army as the lead systems integrator in 1992. Flight tests began in April 1995, but the first successful intercepts occurred in June and August 1999 after six misses in earlier attempts during the program's validation phase. The success rate of launches during the engineering phase, which began in 2005 was considerably improved. Within this phase, flight tests moved from the White Sands Missile Range to the Pacific Missile range Facility at Barking Sands on the Hawaiian Island of Kauai.

In 2004, the program was renamed as the Terminal High Altitude Area Defense (THAAD), reflecting the mission, which is to intercept enemy ICBMs during the terminal or final phase of their trajectory. In this sense the relationship of the THAAD to the Ground-Based Interceptor is roughly analogous to that of the Sprint to the Spartan within the 1970s Safeguard system. THAAD is capable of intercepts both within and outside the Earth's atmosphere.

While the program itself has been transferred from the US Army to the Missile Defense Agency, operational missiles are managed and deployed by US Army personnel.

In 2008 and 2009, the US Army activated its first operational THAAD units, two batteries within the 4th and 6th Air Defense Artillery Regiments of the 11th Air Defense Artillery Brigade. Each battery was assigned 24 of more than 1,400 THAAD interceptor missiles that the Army intends to deploy.

Since 2009, US Army THAAD units on Kauai are routinely placed on alert during North Korean missile tests.

Manufacturer: Lockheed Martin

Length: 20 feet 3 inches (6.17 meters)

Diameter: 14.5 inches (0.37 meters)

Weight: 2,000 pounds (900 kilograms)

Range: 125 miles (200 kilometers)

Speed: 6,275 mph (10,000 km/h)

Ceiling: 93 miles (150 kilometers)

Guidance system: radio ground control with infrared terminal seeker

Propulsion system: Pratt & Whitney solid-fuel rocket

Warhead: "hit-to-kill" kinetic vehicle

First tested: 1995

First deployed: 2008

Addendum 3:

The "R for Rocket" Designation Lineage

At the same time that the "M for Missile" designation system was introduced for guided weapons, a parallel system was created for unguided weapons, designating them "R for Rocket."

	Name or Program	Manufacturer	Customer
MGR-1	Honest John	Douglas	US Army
AIR-2	Genie	Douglas	USAF
MGR-3	Little John	Emerson Electric	US Army
RUR-4	Weapon Alpha	Naval Ordnance Test Station	US Navy
RUR-5	ASROC*	Honeywell	US Navy
MER-6	Blue Scout ERCS**	Ford	USAF
ADR-7	None	Raytheon	USAF
ADR-8	None	Tracor	USAF
ADR-9	None	Tracor	USAF
ADR-10	None	Raytheon	USAF
ADR-11	None	(never built)	USAF
ADR-12	None	(never built)	USAF
MQR-13	BMTS***	US Army Missile Command	US Army
AGR-14	ZAP****	Martin Marietta	US Navy
MTR-15	BATS*****	US Army Missile Command	US Army
MQR-16	Gunrunner	Atlantic Research	US Army
FGR-17	Viper	General Dynamics	US Army
GTR-18	Smokey Sam	Naval Weapons Center	US Navy

* Anti-Submarine Rocket
** Emergency Rocket Communications System
*** Ballistic Missile Target System
**** Zero Anti-Aircraft Potential
***** Ballistic Aerial Target System

As with missiles designated since 1963, the basic designations of the rockets consist of three letters preceding the consecutive numbers. Occasionally, an "X" or "Y" preceded the three letters. As in aircraft, these stand for "experimental" or "service test."

Among the three basic letters, the third is always "R." The other two letters are keyed out as follows:

First letter: Launch or Deployment Environment:

A: Air launched
F: Individual launched
M: Mobile (ground) launched
R: Surface Ship launched

Middle Letter: Mission Type:

D: Decoy
E: Electronics
G: Surface (Ground) Attack
Q: Target Drone
T: Training*
U: Underwater Attack

* Some rockets had training variants in which the "T" was inserted as a middle letter and all other digits remained the same.

Note: In addition to the designated rockets, there were a number of undesignated sounding rockets. These were designed simply to carry a specific scientific payload to a high, but suborbital altitude. In the early years after World War II, captured V-2s were used for this purpose. Other sounding rockets included Nike derivatives, as well as such named rockets as Aerobee, Arcon, Argo, Aries, Astrobee, Black Brant, Hasp, Iris, Jaguar, Loki Dart, Loki-Wasp, Phoenix, Raven, and Strongarm. Variants of some of these were designated, and appear in Appendix 1.

Appendix 1:

Missiles Designated Under the Joint Designation System of 1947

Under this system, two letters preceded the "M for Missile" letter in designations of combat missiles. These defined the launch location and target location, with "A" denoting air and "S" denoting surface. An air-to-air missile was an "AAM," a surface-to-air missile was a "SAM," and so on. The US Navy later used "U" to denote underwater.

Non-combat test missiles received the designation "TV" for "Test Vehicle" instead of "M for Missile" with a prefix denoting the purpose of the test. These were "C for Control," "L for Launch," "P for Propulsion," and an "R" indicated "Research."

The usual aircraft prefixes "X for Experimental," and "Y for Service Test" were applied when relevant to missiles that were ultimately intended to be combat weapons.

In the center of the designation bracketed by hyphens was a single letter denoting the originating service. These were "A" for Air Force and "N" for Navy, with "G" for the Army, a reference to the fact that the Army had only ground-launched missiles.

The following list contains Army missiles from 1947 through 1955, and Air Force missiles from 1947 through 1951, the latter dates being the dates that the services withdrew from the system.

AAM-A-1 Firebird	RTV-A-4 Shrike	SAM-A-19 Plato	SAM-A-27 Sergeant
AAM-A-2 Falcon	RTV-A-5	SAM-A-25 Nike Hercules	SAM-G-8 Hermes A-3A
ASM-A-1 TARZON	RTV-G-1 WAC Corporal	SAM-G-7 Nike Ajax	SAM-G-9 Hermes B-2
ASM-A-2 Rascal	RTV-G-10 Hermes A-2	SAM-A-1 Matador	SAM-G-12 Martin Lacrosse
CTV-G-5 Hermes A-1	RTV-G-2 Corporal E	SAM-A-2 Navaho	SAM-G-13 Hermes A-2
LTV-A-1 Doodle Bug	RTV-G-3 Hermes II	SAM-A-3 Snark	SAM-G-14 Redstone
PTV-A-1	RTV-G-4 Bumper	SAM-A-4 Navaho II	SAM-G-15 Hermes A-1
RTV-A-1	RTV-G-6 Hermes B-1	SAM-A-5 Boojum	SAM-G-16 Hermes A-3B
RTV-A-2 HIROC	SAM-A-1 GAPA	SAM-A-6 Navaho III	SAM-G-17 Corporal
RTV-A-3 NATIV	SAM-A-18 Hawk	SAM-A-23 Dart	

The following list contains Navy missiles from 1947 through 1963, when the current "M for Missile" designation system was adopted.

AAM-N-2 Sparrow I*	ASM-N-8 Corvus*	SAM-N-4 Taurus	PTV-N-2 Gorgon IV
AAM-N-3 Sparrow II*	ASM-N-10 Shrike	SSM-N-6 Rigel	PTV-N-4 Bumblebee BTV
AAM-N-4 Oriole	ASM-N-11 Condor	SSM-N-8 Regulus*	RTV-N-2 Gargoyle
AAM-N-5 Meteor	AUM-N-2 Petrel	SAM-N-9 Lacrosse*	RTV-N-4 Gorgon IIIC
AAM-N-6 Sparrow III*	AUM-N-4 Diver	SSM-N-9 Regulus II*	RTV-N-6 Bumblebee XPM
AAM-N-7 Sidewinder*	AUM-N-6 Puffin	SUM-N-2 Grebe	RTV-N-8 Aerobee
AAM-N-9 Sparrow X*	SAM-N-2 Lark	CTV-N-2 Gorgon IIC	RTV-N-10 Aerobee
AAM-N-10 Eagle	SAM-N-4 Lark	CTV-N-4 Gorgon IIA	RTV-N-12 Viking
AAM-N-11 Phoenix	SAM-N-6 Talos*	CTV-N-6 Gorgon IIIA	RTV-N-13 Aerobee 150
ASM-N-2 Bat	SAM-N-7 Terrier*	CTV-N-8 Bumblebee STV	RTV-N-15 Pollux
ASM-N-4 Dove	SAM-N-8 Zeus*	CTV-N-9 Lark	RTV-N-16 Oriole
ASM-N-5 Gorgon V	SAM-N-8 Typhon LR	CTV-N-10 Lark	
ASM-N-6 Omar	SAM-N-9 Typhon MR	LTV-N-2 Loon	
ASM-N-7 Bullpup*	SSM-N-2 Triton	LTV-N-4 NOTS	

* These missiles were later redesignated with an "M for Missile" designation and are therefore profiled in the main body of this book.

Appendix 2:

US Air Force Missiles Designated Under the 1951 and 1955 Designation Systems

Under the 1951 system, the Air Force redesignated all of its missiles under the "B for Bomber," "F for Fighter" or "X for Experimental" designations that it used for aircraft.

Under the 1955 system, the Air Force changed to the following prefixes:

GAM: Guided Air-Launched Missile

GAR: Guided Air-Launched Rocket

IM: Intercept Missile

RM: Research Missile

SM: Strategic Missile

TM: Tactical Missile

The following list begins with the proper name and follows with the designations for each pre-1963 missile under the 1951, 1955 and 1963 designation systems.

Missiles numbered in the "B for Bomber" (B-61 to B-92) lineage (1951-1963):

Name	1951	1955	1963
Matador	B-61	TM-61	MGM-1
Snark	B-62	SM-62	
Rascal	B-63	GAM-63	
Navaho	B-64	SM-64	
Atlas	B-65	SM-65	CGM-16/HGM-16
Crossbow	B-67	GAM-67	
Titan	B-68	SM-68	HGM-25/LGM-25
Bomarc	F-99	IM-69*	CIM-10
Talos	IM-70	RIM-8	
Buck Duck	GAM-71		
Quail	GAM-72	ADM-20	
Bull Goose	SM-73		
	XSM-74**		
Thor	SM-75	PGM-17	
Mace	TM-76	MGM-13	
Hound Dog	GAM-77	AGM-28	
Jupiter	SM-78	PGM-19	
White Lance	GAM-79		
Minuteman	SM-80	AGM-28	
Agena	RM-81		
Loki Dart	RM-82		
Bullpup	GAM-83	AGM-12	
Aerobee-Hi	RM-84		
Nike-Cajun	RM-85		
Exos	RM-86		
Skybolt	GAM-87	AGM-48	
Rocksonde	SRM-88		
Blue Scout I	RM-89		
Blue Scout II	RM-90		
Blue Scout Junior	RM-91		
Blue Scout Junior	RM-92		

* The Bomarc was only briefly designated as IM-69. It was quickly redesignated as IM-99 to correspond to its earlier F-99 designation.

** The Convair SM-74 was unnamed and had no "M for Missile" equivalent.

Other US Air Force missiles (1951-1963):

Name	1951	1955	1963
Genie	GAR-1		
Falcon	F-98*	**	AIM-4**
Falcon	GAR-9	AIM-47***	
Falcon	GAR-11	AIM-26***	
Bomarc	F-99	IM-99	CIM-10****
	X-7		
Aerobee	X-8		
Shrike	X-9		
	X-10		
	X-11		
	(Former MX-774, B-65 Atlas Precursor)		
	X-12		
	(B-65 Atlas Precursor)		
	X-17		
Sidewinder	GAR-8	AIM-9	

* The Falcon was briefly designated as F-104, but this designation was reassigned to the Lockheed Starfighter manned aircraft.

** In 1955, variants of the conventional Falcon were designated as GAR-1 through GAR-6. These all became variants of the AIM-4 after 1963.

*** The GAR-9 (AIM-47) was a long-range version developed for the North American XF-108 Rapier and Lockheed YF-12 interceptors. The GAR-11 (AIM-26) was a Falcon armed with a quarter-kiloton nuclear warhead.

**** The Bomarc was briefly designated as IM-69 and quickly redesignated as IM-99 to correspond to its earlier F-99 designation.

Appendix 3:

US Army Missiles Designated Under the 1947, 1955 and 1963 Designation Systems

In 1955, the US Army superseded the 1947 designation system with one that corresponded to its designations for its other weapons and vehicles. In the 1955 system, numerals were preceded with an "M," an "ordnance designator" that stood, not for "Missile," but a "Model" of guided artillery missiles.

The following list begins with the proper name and follows with the designations for each pre-1963 missile under the 1947, 1955 and 1963 designation systems.

Until 1963, the US Army designated its unguided rockets as it did its missiles, that is with an "M" ordnance designator implying "Model," not "Missile." In 1963, the joint-service rocket designation system was introduced. The following rockets were redesignated under that system.

Name	1947	1955	1963
Nike-Ajax	SAM-G-7	M1	MIM-3
Corporal	RTV-G-17	M2	MGM-5
Hawk	SAM-A-18	M3	MIM-23
Lacrosse	SAM-G-12	M4	MGM-18
Nike-Hercules	SAM-G-25	M6	MIM-14
Redstone	SAM-G-14	M8	PGM-11
Redstone		M9*	PTM-11
Shillelagh		M13	MGM-51
Pershing		M14	MGM-31
Sergeant	SAM-A-27	M15	MGM-29
Hawk		M16**	MTM-29
Hawk		M18**	MTM-29
Pershing		M19***	MTM-29
HEAT "Super Bazooka"		M28	none
Redeye		M41	FIM-43
Dragon		M47	FGM-77****
Chemical Rocket		M55	remained as M55
Light Anti-tank Weapon (LAW)		M72	remained as M72
Incendiary Rocket		M74	remained as M74

Name	Pre-1963	Post-1963
Honest John	M31	MGR-1
Little John	M47	MGR-3

* The M9 was a non-flying training dummy for the M8.

** The M16 and M18 were training variants of the M3.

*** The M19 was an inert training variant of the M14.

**** The M47 Dragon was redesignated as FGM-77, but was retrodesignated back to M47.

Appendix 4:

Standard Missile Checklist

The US Navy's family of "Standard" Missiles each have their "M For Missile" equivalents. This checklist is to cross reference them from their "SM" designations to their sequential "M" designations. They are included in this book by thier "M" designations

Standard Missile SM-1MR	= RIM-66
Standard Missile SM-1ER	= RIM-67
Standard Missile SM-2MR	= RIM-66
Standard Missile SM-2ER	= RIM-67 and RIM-156
Standard Anti-radiation Missile (ARM)	= AGM-78 (Based on RIM-66)
Standard Missile SM-3	= RIM-161
Standard Missile SM-4	= RIM-165 LASM
Standard Missile SM-6	= RIM-174 Standard ERAM

Appendix 5:

Selected Acronyms (including Designation Prefixes)

AAAM Advanced Air-to-Air Missile

AAM Air-to-Air Missile

AARGM Advanced Anti Radiation Guided Missile

ABM Anti-Ballistic Missile

ACS Aegis Combat System

AGM Air-to-Ground Missile

AIM Air Intercept Missile

AIMVAL Air Intercept Missile Evaluation

AIR Air Intercept Rocket

ALCM Air-Launched Cruise Missile

AMRAAM Advanced Medium Range Air-to-Air Missile

APL Applied Physics Laboratory at Johns Hopkins University

ARM Anti-Radiation (Anti-Radar) Missile

ASM Air-to-Surface Missile

ASRAAM Advanced Short-Range Air-to-Air Missile

ASROC Anti-Submarine ROCket

ATACMS Army Tactical Missile System

ATD Advanced Technology Demonstration

AUM Air-to-Underwater Missile

BAe British Aerospace

BGM Multiple launch platform surface attack missile

BLU Bomb, Live Unit

BMD Ballistic Missile Defense

BMDS Ballistic Missile Defense System

BQM Subsonic Target (recoverable)

BTV Ballistic Test Vehicle

CALCM Conventional Air-Launched Cruise Missile

CIM Coffin Based Interceptor Missile

CKEM Compact Kinetic Energy Missile

CLAWS Complementary Low-Altitude Weapon System

CMM Common Modular Missile

DARPA Defense Advanced Research Projects Agency

EFOGM Enhanced Fiber Optic Guided Missile

EKV Exoatmospheric Kill Vehicle

ERAM Extended Range Anti-Air Warfare Missile

ERCS Emergency Rocket Communications System

ERDL Extended Range Data Link

ERIS Exoatmospheric Reentry Interceptor Subsystem

FAAD Forward Area Air Defense

FBM Fleet Ballistic Missile

FFAR Folding-Fin Aircraft Rocket

FIM Shoulder-fired [Air] Intercept Missile

FLIR Forward-Looking Infrared

FOG Fiber Optic Gyro, or Guided

FOG-M Fiber Optic Guided Missile

GAM Guided Aircraft Missile

GAR Guided Aircraft Rocket

GBI Ground-Based Interceptor

GBU Guided Bomb Unit

GLCM Ground-Launched Cruise Missile

GMD Ground-based Midcourse Defense

GPS Global Positioning System

HARM High Speed Anti-Radiation (Anti-Radar) Missile

HATM Hypervelocity Anti-Tank Missile

HE High Explosive

HEAT High Explosive-AntiTank

HEI High Explosive-Incendiary

HEL High Energy Laser

HIMARS High Mobility Artillery Rocket System

HOE Homing Overlay Experiment

HVM HyperVelocity Missile (anti-armor)

ICBM Intercontinental Ballistic Missile

INS Inertial Navigation System

IOC Initial Operational Capability

IRBM Intermediate Range Ballistic Missile

JAGM Joint Air-to-Ground Missile

JASSM Joint Air-to-Surface Standoff Missile

JCM Joint Common Missile

JDAM Joint Direct-Attack Munition

JSAM Joint Standoff Attack Missile

JSASM Joint Standoff Air-to-Surface Missile

JSOW Joint Stand-Off Weapon

KEM Kinetic Energy Missile

LASM Land Attack Standard Missile

LAW Light Anti-tank Weapon

LEAP Lightweight Exo-Atmospheric Projectile

LEM Silo-Launched Electronics Missile

LGB Laser Guided Bomb

LGM Silo-launched Strategic Ballistic Missile

LLTV Low-Light Television

LOCAAS Low-Cost Autonomous Attack System

LOSAT Line-of-Sight Anti-Tank (missile)

MBDA Matra-BAe Dynamics-Alenia

MDA Missile Defense Agency

MDS Mission Design Series

MEADS Medium Extended Air Defense System

MGM Mobile Guided Missile

MIM Mobile Intercept Missile (SAM)

MIRV Multiple Independently-targetable Reentry Vehicle

MLRS Multiple Launch Rocket System

MQM Ground-launched target drone

MRBM Medium Range Ballistic Missile

MSST Multi-Stage Supersonic Target

NMB National Missile Defense

PAC Patriot Advanced Capability
PGM Soft Pad Launched Missile
RAM Rolling Airframe Missile (SAM)
RGM Ship-launched SAM
RIM Ship-launched Radar Intercept Missile
RPV Remotely Piloted Vehicle
RTV Rocket Test Vehicle
SAM Surface-to-Air Missile
SAM Surface-to-Surface Missile
SDACS Solid-fuel Divert and Attitude Control System
SDD System Development and Demonstration
SDI Strategic Defense Initiative
SDIO Strategic Defense Initiative Office
SLAM Standoff Land Attack Missile
SLAM-ER Standoff Land Attack Missile Expanded Response
SLAMRAAM Surface-Launched AMRAAM
SLAT Supersonic Low Altitude Target
SLBM Submarine-Launched (or Sea-Launched) Ballistic Missile
SLCM Submarine-Launched (or Sea-Launched) Cruise Missile
SRAM Short-Range Attack Missile
SSST Supersonic Sea-Skimming Target
STAM Submarine Tactical Missile
STAWS Submarine Anti-ship Weapon System
SUBROC SUBmarine ROCket
TALD Tactical Air-Launched Decoy
TEDS Tactical Expendable Drone System
THAAD Terminal High Altitude Area Defense (1987-2004)
THAAD Theater High Altitude Area Defense (since 2004)
TLAM Tomahawk Land Attack Missile (BGM-109)
TOW Tube-launched, Optically-tracked, Wire data link
TSSAM Tri-Service Standoff Attack Missile
UAS Unmanned Aerial System
UAV Unmanned Aerial Vehicle
UGM Submarine-launched surface-to-air missile
USAAF US Army Air Forces
VLS Vertical Launching System

Bibliography

Anderson, Fred: *Northrop. An Aeronautical History*, Northrop, 1976

Bowman, Norman: *The Handbook of Rockets and Guided Missiles*, Perastadion Press, 1963

Chant, Christopher: *World Encyclopedia of Modern Air Weapons*, Patrick Stephens Ltd., 1988

Fahey, James: *The Ships and Aircraft of the U.S. Fleet*, various editions, US Naval Institute, 1965

Francillon, Rene: *Lockheed Aircraft since 1913*, Putnam, 1987

Friedman, Norman: *US Naval Weapons*, Conway Maritime Press, 1983

Friedman, Norman: *World Naval Weapons Systems*, Naval Institute Press, 1997

Gunston, Bill: *The Illustrated Encyclopedia of Rockets and Missiles*, Salamander Books Ltd, 1979

Jenkins, Dennis and Tony M. Landis: *Experimental & Prototype U.S. Air Force Jet Fighters*, Specialty Press, 2008

Miller, Jay: *The X-Planes X-1 to X-45*, Midland Publishing, 2001

Munson, Kenneth: *World Unmanned Aircraft*, Jane's, 1988

Neufeld, Jacob: *Ballistic Missiles in the United States Air Force, 1945-1960*, Office of Air Force History, 1990

Pelletier, A.J.: *Beech Aircraft and their Predecessors*, Putnam, 1995

Polmar, Norman: Ships and Aircraft of the US Fleet, Naval Institute Press, 1993

US Navy Department: *Model Designation of Naval Aircraft, KD Targets, and BuAer Guided Missiles*, US Navy, 1958

Wakeford, Ronald and Frederick Ordway: *International Missile and Spacecraft Guide*, McGraw-Hill, 1960

Werrell, Kenneth: *The Evolution of the Cruise Missile*, Air University Press, 1985

Yenne, Bill: *Attack of the Drones, A History of Unmanned Aerial Combat*; Zenith (USA); 2004

Yenne, Bill: *Birds of Prey: Predators, Reapers and America's Newest UAVs in Combat*; Specialty Press (US) 2010

Yenne, Bill: *Encyclopedia of US Spacecraft*; Simon & Schuster (USA), Bison/Hamlyn (UK); 1985

Yenne, Bill: *History of the US Air Force*; Simon & Schuster (USA), Bison/Hamlyn (UK); 1984 and 1992

Yenne, Bill: *Into the Sunset: The Convair Story*; General Dynamics Corporation/Greenwich Publishing (USA); 1995

Yenne, Bill: *Lockheed*; Random House (USA), Photobook Information Service (UK); 1987

Yenne, Bill: *McDonnell Douglas: A Tale of Two Giants*; Random House (USA), Arms & Armor (UK); 1985

Yenne, Bill: *Rockwell: The Heritage of North American*; Random House/Crescent (USA); 1989

Yenne, Bill: *SAC: A Primer of Modern Strategic Air Power*; Presidio (USA), Arms & Armor (UK); 1985

Yenne, Bill: *Secret Weapons of the Cold War*; Penguin Putnam Berkley, (USA); 2005

Yenne, Bill: *Secret Weapons of World War II*; Penguin Putnam, Berkley, (USA); 2003

Yenne, Bill: *The Story of the Boeing Company*; AGS BookWorks and Zenith Press (USA); 2003, 2005, 2010

Periodicals

Air Force Magazine

Aviation Week

Jane's Defence Industry

Jane's Intelligence Review

Jane's International Defence Review

Jane's Missiles & Rockets

Jane's Navy International

Jane's Defence Weekly

Websites

AMI International: http://www.amiinter.com/

Army Technology: http://www.army-technology.com/

Aviation Week: http://www.aviationweek.com/

Boeing Military Aircraft: http://www.boeing.com/bds/military_aircraft/index.html

Boeing Missiles: http://www.boeing.com/defense-space/missiles/

Boeing: Defense, Space and Security: http://www.boeing.com/bds/index.html

Center for Defense Information: http://www.cdi.org/

Composites Engineering: http://www.compositesengineering.com/

Deagel: http://www.deagel.com/MissilesMunitions.htm

Defense Advanced Research Projects Agency: http://www.darpa.mil/

Defense Industry Daily: http://www.defenseindustrydaily.com/

Defense Update: http://www.defense-update.com/

Federation of American Scientists: http://www.fas.org/man/dod-101/sys/land/mgm-157.htm

Forecast International: http://www.forecastinternational.com/

Global Security: http://www.globalsecurity.org/

Griffon Aerospace: http://www.griffon-aerospace.com/

MBDA: http://www.mbda.co.uk/

Missile Defense Agency Media Library: http://www.mda.mil/news/media_library.html

Missile Defense Agency: http://www.mda.mil/system/system.html

Northrop Grumman: http://www.northropgrumman.com/

Orbital Sciences Corporation: http://www.orbital.com/

Parsch, Andreas: Designation Systems: http://www.designation-systems.net/

Raytheon Media Center: http://raytheon.mediaroom.com/index

Redstone Arsenal Historical Information, Office of the Command Historian: http://www.redstone.army.mil/history/

Vought Heritage: http://www.voughtaircraft.com/heritage/

Wade, Mark: Encyclopedia Astronautica: http://www.astronautix.com/

Index

Other books from Crécy Publishing

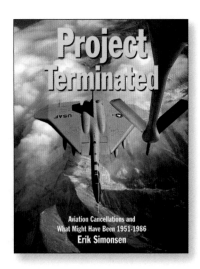

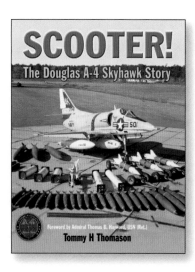

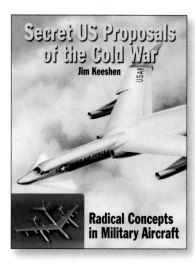

Project Terminated

Aviation Cancellations and What Might Have Been 1951-1986

Erik Simonsen

Throughout aerospace history, production contracts for military aircraft programs have been awarded and then cancelled as changing times and politics dictated. For the very first time we see what might have happened had such designs as, amongst others, the Northrop YB-49 Flying Wing, the Canadian CF-105 Arrow, and the Mach 3 Lockheed YF-12 Interceptor entered production.

ISBN: 9 780859 791731
Binding: Hardback
Dimensions: 290mm x 216mm
Pages: 160
Photos/Illustrations: Over 200 colour and 25 b+w photographs
Price: £23.95 $39.95

Scooter!

The Douglas A-4 Skyhawk Story

Tommy H Thomason

A fascinating chronicle of the A-4s early years, its subsequent development and its service with at least nine different air arms outside its US service. In their own words, the engineers and pilots who designed and flew the Skyhawk provide exciting new insights into not just the A-4, but also the workings of naval aviation and aircraft carrier operations during the Cold War heyday of the 1950s and 1960s.

ISBN: 9 780859 791601
Binding: Hardback
Dimensions: 290mm x 216mm
Pages: 272
Photos/Illustrations: Over 250 b+w and 100 colour photographs
Price: £27.95 $44.95

Secret US Proposals of the Cold War

Radical concepts in Military Aircraft

Jim Keeshen

At the peak of the Cold War, countless proposals for radical US military aircraft were developed. Rare and historic models of these proposals bear witness to that bygone era and are given new recognition with an explanation of their mission requirements and the use of original archival photography.

ISBN: 9 780859 791618
Binding: Hardback
Dimensions: 290mm x 216mm
Pages: 160
Photos/Illustrations: Over 200 b+w and 100 colour photographs
Price: £19.95 $34.95

All titles from
Crécy Publishing Ltd
1a Ringway Trading Est
Shadowmoss Rd
Manchester M22 5LH
www.crecy.co.uk

Distributed in the USA by
Specialty Press
39966 Grand Ave
North Branch, MN 55056 USA
(651) 277-1400/(800) 895-4585
www.specialtypress.com